THE ULTIMATE GUIDE
TO BLACKPOWDER HUNTING

Previous books by Al Raychard

Flyfishing in Maine

Flying In for Trout

Trout and Salmon: Fishing in Northern New England

Remote Trout Ponds in Maine

Salar

Tarpon, Bonefish and Permit: A Flyfishing Guide

Flyfishing the Salt

THE ULTIMATE GUIDE TO BLACKPOWDER HUNTING

How to get in on one of the fastest
growing outdoor sports

AL RAYCHARD

The Lyons Press
Guilford, Connecticut
An imprint of The Globe Pequot Press

DEDICATION

To Diane, my friend, my favorite hunting partner, my wife, who under-stands my need to travel afield to challenge things wild. When I am there, I often think of you.

The Lyons Press is an imprint of The Globe Pequot Press.

Printed in the United States of America

Designed by Compset, Inc.

10 9 8 7 6 5 4 3 2 1

Library of Congress Cataloging-in-Publication Data

Raychard, Al
    The ultimate guide to black powder hunting: how to get in on one of the fastest-growing outdoor sports/Al Raychard.
      p. cm.
    ISBN 1-58574-220-1
    1. Muzzleloader hunting.   I. Title.
SK39.2.R39 2001
799.2'028'3—dc21

2001041313

CONTENTS

INTRODUCTION

The tree stand was positioned high on the side of a hardwood ridge in northwestern Maine. It was early September, the first week of bear hunting season, and I was on my first-ever bear hunt. From my vantage point 15 feet above the forest floor I had a clear view of a small pond in the valley far below. Surrounded by rolling hills, it glistened in the late afternoon sun like a piece of broken glass.

Sitting there, I remember being somewhat apprehensive. This was my first bear hunt after all, and I really didn't know what to expect. I had read a great deal about the animal, had viewed some videos, and had seen them in the wild. But sitting alone in a tree stand miles from nowhere, knowing there was a good chance a bear, or several bears, were in the area and might show up at any time was a whole lot different than reading about it or watching videos in the comfort and security of my living room. It is not that I was frightened. It was just the not-knowing part which kept the adrenalin flowing and my heart pumping faster than normal.

But something else had me on edge, too. I was sitting there with a muzzleloader. Blackpowder rifles had been part of my hunting style for a few years and I was familiar with them. I had taken several deer in Maine and caribou in northern Quebec and I had little doubt concerning the capabilities of a .54-caliber against antlered and horned game. But I had some concerns about its ability to dispatch an animal with so much fat, dense muscle, and heavy bone mass. Sitting in the tree stand that early autumn day, those doubts rolled around and around in the back of my mind, and I questioned whether I should have brought my 30/06.

But it was a .54-caliber Lyman Great Plains Rifle that kept me company that day. It was my first muzzleloader, carrying a 32-inch browned barrel and hardware. Rifled with a 1-in-66 twist specifically for patched roundball and carrying open sights, it was nothing fancy but it shot straight and true and I felt—up to that point—comfortable with it. It rested across my knees, pointed in the direction of the bait area some 20 yards away.

Minutes that seemed like hours ticked by. My rear-end started to lose all sense of feeling and every bone and muscle in my body started reminding me they were not pleased with the accommodations, a single board about eight inches wide wedged and nailed in a crotch in the tree. After an hour discomfort got the best of me. I scanned the area to make sure I was alone and decided to shift slightly to ease some growing aches. Just as I came to this decision, however, a sudden twig snap to my left and farther up the ridge broke the silence.

Almost as if someone had slammed a door, the world around me went silent. The chickadees stopped singing. The Canadian jays disappeared like phantoms, and the chipmunks that had been busy in the area since my arrival headed for cover. Even the wind seemed to die, and the leaves and branches about me hung motionless. It was eerie. I had never experienced anything like it and my instincts told me something was definitely out there. I didn't know exactly what, although I had a good idea, and the more I thought about it the faster my heart beat in my chest.

Several minutes passed, then another snap. Softer than before but obvious, it was followed by a slow, almost muffled shuffling of leaves and undergrowth, as if something was trying to sneak through the woods but was having difficulty doing so. Struggling to contain my growing excitement I gazed up the ridge. More minutes passed and then from behind a stand of trees I had not even noticed before I spotted the head and shoulders of a bear!

Not more than 30 yards away, the black form was one of the most impressive creatures I had ever seen in the wild. Instead of moving toward the bait, to my surprise, the bear just stood there providing me ample opportunity to look it over. As I watched I grew so mesmerized at its presence, its size and blackness, I nearly forgot why I was there. I suddenly found myself totally calm. The bear slowly stepped into full view and moved toward the bait. My inexperience could not tell me whether the animal was large or small, but at the time it looked like the biggest thing I had ever seen. The bear worked to the bait, lifted itself off the ground on its hind legs and stuck its head into the bait barrel with its back in my direction. Taking advantage of the opportunity I slowly raised the Lyman, cocking the hammer in the process.

The Great Plains Rifle shattered the late afternoon silence like a cannon. It seemed so loud the first thing that came to mind was that if the patched roundball didn't dispatch the bear the sound of the blast surely would. But as the cloud of blue haze faded I could see the bear lying next to the bait. I quickly reloaded, keeping a watchful eye on the bear. After several minutes, I was convinced that the Lyman and I had done our job and descended from the stand to approach my prize.

On closer inspection it quickly became apparent the bear was not that big, perhaps 150 to 160 pounds. It had a fine coat of thick black hair, and though not a monster or trophy, it was my first bear. And I had taken it with a muzzleloader!

More than two decades have passed since that day in the Maine hills, and muzzleloaders have played a big part in my hunting life ever since. In fact, whenever I hunt these days I carry nothing else. Muzzleloaders, with that distinct odor of blackpowder and Pyrodex, have become as much a part of my hunting style as hunting itself. It has come to the point that I cannot imagine using anything else. Without question I have fallen under the spell of this historic and challenging method of taking game, and the longer that kinship continues the deeper I get.

But I am not alone in the arena. Presently, muzzleloader shooting and hunting is one of the fastest growing shooting sports in the United States and Canada. Nearly all fifty states now offer some kind of "primitive" or muzzleloader hunting season. Most are on deer, but some states in the west offer muzzleloading seasons on other game species as well, particularly elk and antelope. According to available figures the number of muzzleloader hunting licenses being sold is on the rise in every state and more and more muzzleloaders are being seen afield these days during regular shotgun and firearms seasons, as well. The sale of blackpowder rifles and related items has also mushroomed.

There are also more hunting and shooting publications dealing with the sport than ever before. I could name a half-dozen or more annuals, bi-annuals, quarterlies, and monthly publications dedicated to the sport, and each year new offerings seem to be on the newsstands and in bookstores. Enthusiasts now have three organizations specifically catering to the blackpowder shooter, history buff, hunter, and trophy hunter. They include the National Muzzleloading Rifle Association (NMLRA) of Friendship, Indiana; The Longhunter Society, a big game record-keeping association specifically for blackpowder hunters much like the Boone & Crockett Club, established and administered by the NMLRA; and the International Blackpowder Hunting Association of Glen Rock, Wyoming.

The modern muzzleloader shooters and hunters also have more types of firearms, powders, loads, and other products available to choose from than our ancestors ever thought possible. There are flintlocks and percussion models like early hunters used, but there are also modern in-lines, all in popular hunting calibers from .45 to .54. When it comes to loads, there are patched roundballs and various conicals and sabot-jacketed non-lead expandable projectiles. There are also several different grades of blackpowder and Pyrodex (a blackpowder substitute). To help the hunter and shooter afield, an impressive number of innovative gadgets have been made available that make the sport easier and more user-friendly. All these products are built of better materials, are more accurate, burn hotter, and are more reliable than anything preceding them. And if that is not enough, several new cleaning and maintenance products have appeared that make it easier for novices to enjoy the sport.

To say the least it is an exciting time to be a blackpowder enthusiast and hunter. I am personally more excited about the sport than I was 20 years ago when I took my first black bear, and I think every hunter in North America should give muzzleloading a try. It is not only challenging, but puts a whole new perspective on the art, craft, and sport of shooting and taking game, big or small.

But with so many options available these days, muzzleloading has also become more confusing for the novice hunter or first-timer thinking about getting into the sport. It is no longer as simple as it was at Lexington and Concord when blackpowder ignited the "shot heard 'round the world." What type of ignition system is best or most reliable? How do you safely load these firearms and find the optimum load? What about projectiles? What exactly is a roundball, conical, or sabot, anyway? What are the different calibers and projectiles available, and which is best for hunting big game? How do you maintain and clean these firearms?

Despite what is often heard, this is not a complicated way to hunt. Like any endeavor, its mysteries must be unraveled, but once a basic knowledge is obtained the rest seems to fall into place. The following pages will hopefully provide a better understanding and appreciation for these rifles, not only as shooting arms but as a more challenging way of taking big game. I have little doubt that after taking the first step, the "one-shot challenge" will play a major roll in your shooting and hunting life.

Al Raychard
Lyman, Maine
June 2001

1

WHY HUNT WITH A MUZZLELOADER?

My brother Dave is a bowhunting nut. The man is as enthusiastic about compound bows, aluminum-alloy arrows, and broadheads as I am over rifles that load from the muzzle, blackpowder, Pyrodex, conicals, and patched roundballs. We grew up in rural southern Maine, and when deer hunting as boys we carried .410 and 20-gauge shotguns loaded with slugs, graduating to .30/.30s and other modern centerfire rifles in our late teens. That was the way things were done then, and such were the hunting arms of choice. As time went on, like many hunters young and old, Dave and I desired new challenges. By the time we entered our early twenties my older sibling took one road and I took the other. So it continues today. The love of shooting and hunting still burns within us, we just do it different ways.

What it was about muzzleloaders that interested me in the beginning is difficult to say. I never gave it much thought. All I know is that when I first put my hands on a muzzleloader it just felt right. Its balance seemed perfect, and its styling, wood-to-metal fit, long browned barrel, and sidelock ignition seemed just right. The grain of the walnut stock was one of the most aesthetically pleasing combinations in a firearm I had ever seen. I fell madly in love. I was hooked and have been ever since. Even now, a quarter-century later, no other type of firearm feels as comfortable to carry or as pleasing to the eye. None are nearly as much fun to shoot, and each time I travel afield in search of big game a muzzleloader fills my hands. In fact, I don't even own a modern centerfire.

With so many options available these days it might be difficult for fans of .308s, .30/06s, 7mms, and the like to understand the interest in taking afield a rifle generally limited to one shot; a rifle that, compared to more high-powered, flatter, and longer-shooting modern counterparts, brings with it a host of limitations. Bowhunters, like my brother understand, for those who hunt with bow and arrow share many of the same passions and ideals as blackpowder enthusiasts and welcome many of the same challenges those limitations present.

For one thing, we feel one shot is enough, or should be enough, to humanely dispatch an animal. If more than one shot is required due to extreme range or because the target is moving or the situation presents less than a clean shot, then the shot should not be taken. Getting to know the game we hunt, its habits, travel routes, feeding, bedding, and watering areas, allows us to get close enough for a clean kill. Most muzzleloader shots at big game are at less than 100 yards, with any shot over 150 yards or so considered by many enthusiasts to be shooting not hunting. This is simply a more personal and challenging way to hunt, not a test of long-range marksmanship.

The truth is that hunters who use muzzleloaders love to hunt more than shoot. How we take game matters more, not whether we do. Not every big game hunter will agree with this philosophy, but combined with the unique challenges a muzzleloader presents afield, such as shorter range and the availability of just one shot, it is a philosophy shared by a growing number of enthusiasts of all ages and both sexes who have made hunting with muzzleloaders one of the fastest growing shooting sports today.

But other reasons are also responsible for the current popularity of hunting with muzzleloaders. For many, they represent a link with our past. It was blackpowder that won the freedom of a new country. Muzzleloaders were at Bunker Hill, Lexington, and Concord. Blackpowder propelled the first volley on Fort Sumter, made a stand at the Alamo, accompanied Lewis and Clark, and for decades fed a growing population as America achieved its manifest destiny. Blackpowder and muzzleloaders are part of the heritage of each American who hunts, and most modern enthusiasts seem to sense this connection to some degree whether they use one of the more traditional sidelocks or in-lines or substitute Pyrodex for blackpowder.

On a personal note, I have often thought that if I lived during the early days of America I would have been a woodsman like Daniel Boone or a mountain man like Jim Bridger, an explorer of wild, untamed lands. I would have traveled through the Cumberland Gap and been one of the first to explore the Rockies and the splendor of the west. In reality, however, I question whether I would have taken that road, whether I would have had the mettle. I am a product of the twentieth century, with all its conveniences and comforts. I cherish wild places and hunting game with muzzleloaders, but I like my Monday Night Football, Mr. Coffee machine, and jumping in my four-wheel drive to return to a warm house at the end of a day afield. And I like sleeping at night without fear of getting my hair lifted. I have little doubt things would have been different from what fantasy has so often envisioned. But it is that sliver of wonder and "what if" that intrigued me when I purchased my first muzzleloader and that intrigues me still. It seems to be one of the factors attracting others as well.

There is also something aesthetically pleasing about muzzleloaders, particularly the traditional sidelock models that makes it difficult to look upon any other firearm in quite the same light. Nothing else seems to have the same graceful lines and styling. Simple yet rugged, they were designed to do a job and they did it dependably. They still do. Each is a piece of art, easy to look upon and a pleasure to hold. Those frontloaders equipped with brass accessories and either blued or browned barrels are particularly appealing. Even the new in-lines have a certain appeal. In no way do they resemble the traditional sidelock muzzleloader with their conventional styling, particularly those with laminated or synthetic stocks and stainless steel barrels. Though they lack the historic connection to the past important to many blackpowder enthusiasts, they shoot extremely well, are easy to clean, and offer other attributes that have not only revolutionized the sport of muzzleloading but taken it to unparalleled heights.

Other factors, however, are probably more responsible for the current popularity of hunting with muzzleloaders. In all fifty states and those provinces of Canada currently offering big game hunting opportunities, muzzleloaders are legal arms during regular firearms hunting seasons on deer and other species. The last state not allowing muzzleloaders to be used during its regular gun season on deer was Delaware, and it changed the law in 1992. This means that even in those states, or areas of some states and provinces, which restrict the hunting of deer or other game to the use of shotguns during the regular firearms season, muzzleloaders can be used. Not all hunters are comfortable with the ability of shotguns loaded with buckshot, or even slugs, to dispatch deer-sized game humanely at a range greater than 50 yards. This is an average shot for a muzzleloader, even those loaded with patched roundball. Muzzleloaders are more accurate, deliver more power at greater range, and in the case of buckshot, are safer as only one projectile is fired each time the trigger is pulled rather than several.

All but one or two states now offer special muzzleloader hunting seasons on deer in addition to the regular firearms season. Indications are that those final states will establish muzzleloader seasons in the near future. Some western states also offer muzzleloader hunts on other big game species as well, particularly elk and pronghorn, and in some provinces in Canada on moose.

What this all boils down to is the fact that blackpowder enthusiasts now have more time in which to hunt than at any time since hunting seasons were first established before the turn of the century. In many states, special muzzleloader seasons have extended the opportunity to hunt by more than a month, in some states longer. In most cases the special seasons are just an extra week, perhaps two, but all provide additional time to hunt. It is now often legal to harvest a deer during the regular firearms season and a second during the special muzzleloader season.

For these reasons, more and more enthusiasts are joining the fold. There is also a good chance that even more muzzleloader seasons on big game species other than deer will be established in the future as interest in blackpowder hunting increases and game populations grow. Think of it! A muzzleloader season on black bear in Maine or Idaho, on caribou in Alaska, or mule deer in Wyoming, perhaps on elk or antelope. Considering what is available, and what might be made available in the future, it is an exciting time to be a blackpowder hunter.

My love affair with muzzleloaders started early, and my transition from conventional arms was immediate and complete. One reason for such a drastic change is the idea of going afield with a firearm offering limited range and one shot, a firearm often susceptible to inclement weather conditions and other limitations. This truly challenged me as a hunter, marksman, and woodsman.

I discovered that hunting with a muzzleloader adds a new perspective to the sport of hunting and establishes a whole different set of ground rules when it comes to taking game. Because only one shot is available and there are range limitations for traditional sidelock models, and rapid loss of power of some projectiles, a good hunter is made a better hunter due to the need to get relatively close and make that one shot count. There are no second chances once the trigger is pulled, and that fact is always present in the back of your mind. Hunting with a muzzleloader can also help develop patience, forcing the hunter to learn habits of the animal being hunted and to take advantage of them. These aspects are something not all hunters carrying more conventional rifles equipped with high-powered scopes and capable of delivering five or six shots at great range prefer, but I revel in them.

Even when I hunted with centerfire rifles as a young man, little thrill or satisfaction was obtained by taking game at long distances. Somehow it showed little respect to pull the trigger on an animal which had clearly out-smarted me at close range in a given situation only to suddenly show itself 250 or 300 yards away. There is no doubt modern hunting rifles equipped with scopes and the right bullet will reach out that far, even farther, and cleanly dispatch big game, but such guns give the hunter an unfair advantage and seem rather unsporting. While fans of such guns will argue differently, there is little real hunting here. It is more shooting, an ego trip to see how far your gun will reach, to test marksmanship rather than woodsmanship. There are places and times for that sort of thing, but not when an animal is in your sights.

The farther away the target the greater the chance of missing that target. Worse yet, of wounding an animal, not finding it, and having it die a wasted death. Missing can be dangerous, particularly in areas growing more urban or frequented by other hunters. Leaving wounded game in the field is unthinkable. The muzzleloader hunter must be certain of hitting his target and dispatching it quickly and humanely before pulling the trigger. If not, he or she, like all hunters, should be willing to go home empty handed.

Indeed, one of the things about hunting with muzzleloaders many enthusiasts seem to enjoy most and find personally challenging is that it requires getting relatively close to the target. There are blackpowder in-line rifles out there consistently able to take game at 200 yards or longer, particularly those loaded with saboted pistol bullets and equipped with scopes, but the average muzzleloader shot is much less. In the thickly-wooded East where the whitetail is king the average shot is 50 or 60 yards. The same is true on the vast majority of baited black bear hunts, in some cases when hunting caribou on the barrens, even some elk in the tall timber. In the West, when hunting pronghorn, mule and whitetail deer, sheep, and goat, longer shots are generally required. But even in these situations, for most blackpowder hunters it is knowing your target, where it feeds, beds, waters, its travel and escape routes to and from these areas, using the wind and terrain to your advantage, getting within a clean shooting range on belly and knees if need be that makes this mode of hunting such a fun challenge.

On one of my first hunting trips to Wyoming years ago I booked a mule deer hunt with an outfitter who operated at the base of the Wind River Range east of Jackson Hole. When I booked the hunt the outfitter was honest about my prospects. "We don't have a lot of mulies in this part of the Winds, Al," the outfitter said, "but what we do have are big. And we'll do our best to get you into one."

To make a long story short I did not fill my tag. But I did see game, including a respectable buck I would have loved to claim, but at more than 300 yards it was beyond the accepted range of my .50-caliber sidelock. I could have taken a shot and hoped for the best, but I don't hunt that way. And I could have tried a stalk to cut the range, but the terrain and wind were not in my favor. Instead, I just sat there and watched the buck against the towering backdrop of the mighty Winds until it disappeared over a sage-covered saddle. But the hunt was far from a failure. I got to explore the Wind River Range by horse, places where Jim Bridger and other mountain men of that rich era explored. I saw elk, heard the cry of a mountain lion, and even had a black bear raid the kitchen tent one night. No hunting trip should be measured solely in terms of whether game is taken. Muzzleloader enthusiasts, for the most part, understand this and accept it. They understand the limitations of their chosen method of taking game and consider animals beyond their means not as an opportunity lost but part of the experienced gained, part of the challenge to overcome.

And there is that one shot. It is always in the back of the mind regardless of the amount of experience. Even after more than thirty years of hunting with these guns my body temperature seems to rise and my heart shifts into high gear when it comes time to pull the trigger. It is this one-shot challenge that dedicated enthusiasts find interesting.

When you think about it, with such high-powered, flat-shooting, and far-reaching conventional rifles available today, using a muzzleloader does seem a bit odd. It is understandable how stalking moose, elk, bear, pronghorn, even whitetail deer with a single shot might seem unthinkable, perhaps even bordering on the irrational and extreme. It may even make some ask why anyone would want to. Personally, however, even in the beginning I found something profoundly wrong with hunting with a rifle that could rattle off a half-dozen shots as fast as I could pull the trigger. It fell in that same category as taking game 250 or 300 yards away. It didn't seem sporting, showed little respect for the animal, and I derived little satisfaction from it. Since getting into blackpowder hunting, especially as the sole means of taking game, I have discovered several things. One of the most fundamental is that hunting with a muzzleloader either fits your philosophy or it doesn't.

The safety factor also comes into play. I don't know how many times I have been deer hunting in November, or on some other hunt, and heard a rifle sing out several shots in just a few seconds. In some cases, one series of reports followed another, perhaps the result of one hunter jumping a deer, shooting at it and missing, only to have that animal cross the path of another hunter down the ridge and run into another gauntlet of flying lead. Whether singularly or in quick succession it sounds like a war zone, and on each occurrence I can't help but wonder where all that lead is going.

Considering how fast each shot is being rattled off and the fact that the animal is no doubt moving after the first shot is fired, it is safe to assume the hunter can't keep track of them all. Nor is it easy to accept the idea that a hunter with so much adrenalin pumping through his veins can react quick enough to pull away or not shoot should his target cross the path of another hunter.

Hunting accidents can and do happen with muzzleloaders, but I am convinced that the chances are far less than during regular rifle season or with conventional rifles that can hold a half-dozen shells. This belief is based on the simple premise that blackpowder hunters, in a majority of cases, must get close to their target to make sure that their one shot counts. For this reason, hunting with muzzleloaders is one of the safest ways to hunt big game in today's world.

Despite these varied reasons for hunting with a muzzleloader—the extended and special seasons, the history and lore, the different perspective and special challenges afield, and the safety factor—perhaps the biggest reason for the increasing popularity is that muzzleloaders are simply fun. I have hunted with conventional rifles and bow and arrow, and none have elevated the joy and excitement of the hunt to such heights of pleasure and satisfaction. The bow hunting fraternity likes to brag that there is no more challenging way to take game than with a modern compound or recurve. They can think what they want, but when it comes to hunting big game, a muzzleloader is no less exciting, or demanding. If a hunter happens to be in the market for a new challenge there is little doubt a muzzleloader will provide it.

2

ANATOMY OF A MUZZLELOADER

If you pick up a muzzleloader and look at it, really look at it, it quickly becomes apparent how simple it is. Years ago, the expression "lock, stock, and barrel" was rather common, and basically this is what a muzzleloader is. A barrel, stock and trigger, and lock assembly. That's it. The new in-lines are a little more involved of course, with their sliding bolts and modern safety mechanisms. Granted, loading a muzzleloader is more complicated than a modern centerfire, but when push comes to shove a muzzleloader remains one of the most simple yet functional firearms man has ever devised.

As muzzleloaders must be cleaned after a hunt and sometimes repaired in remote places, it is helpful to understand their basic anatomy. The key word here is basic. Following normal use afield it is generally the barrel, lock, trigger assembly, and stock exterior which draw the most attention, but despite their general appearance a typical sidelock percussion or flintlock muzzleloading rifle has over a hundred parts counting all the various screws, pins, springs, and other components we don't see or tend to during normal cleaning. All are important and serve a purpose, but to understand the anatomy of a muzzleloader and how it works, many are not important. The barrel, stock, trigger assembly, lock, and a few other parts, however, are a different story.

THE STOCK

Let's look at the stock first, the most simple of the three major components of a muzzleloader. The primary function of the stock is to provide a base on which to attach the barrel, trigger assembly, lock, and other components. It is the foundation of the entire firearm. As simple as that sounds, the stock plays several important rolls other than the most obvious that might affect a muzzleloader's accuracy.

Two things come to mind. The first is how it "fits." Muzzleloaders are like any hunting rifle. Depending upon individual body build they all fit differently when brought to shoulder. Before purchasing any muzzleloader, while at the gun shop, bring it to an aiming position. Does it settle comfortably against the shoulder or around the armpit? If not, perhaps the deep curving buttplate is the reason. Traditional buttplates common on many replica sidelock percussion and flintlock muzzleloaders were designed to hook into the armpit, not against the shoulder. If the muzzleloader carries this type of buttplate and feels uncomfortable several options are available: adapt a different shooting style, have a gunsmith install a flat, padded buttplate, or select a muzzleloader with a more conventional padded buttplate. At the same time make sure your cheek comes naturally and comfortably to rest against the stock and that your eyes align with the sights. When you snap that muzzleloader into position everything should fall into place.

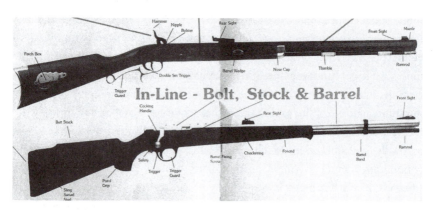

The traditional sidelock ignition system and the modern in-line. Both styles are popular among blackpowder enthusiasts.

Also, check the barrel channel, or mortice, for imperfections that may put pressure on the barrel. Regardless of how small, these imperfections can actually press against the barrel as it flexes when fired and affect accuracy. Many percussion and flintlock barrels, such as those on the popular Hawken-style rifles and Plains rifles are held to the stock with single or double flat wedges or keys. After checking the wood-to-metal fit for uniformity and tightness, ask the dealer to remove the barrel and run your fingers down the channel. It should be well-formed, smooth, and with straight edges. Notice how easy or difficult the barrel slips out and back into the channel. The barrel should lay back in place as easily as it came out and the barrel keys should hold the barrel solidly in position.

Stocks come in different lengths and styles depending on the rifle design. The most popular models are considered half or three-quarter stock, meaning they extend halfway or slightly more down the length of the barrel. The popular Hawken-types, carbines, and other similar replicas as well as in-lines fall into this category. The barrels on these muzzleloaders are rather short, anywhere from 24 inches to 32 inches and a long stock simply isn't required to hold the barrel in position.

Other muzzleloaders have full stocks, meaning the wood flows beneath the whole length of the barrel. The famous Pennsylvania Long Rifle, Hatfield Squirrel Rifle, and many smoothbore muskets are prime examples. The barrels on these muzzleloaders are long, from 39 inches to 42 inches. These barrels are also heavy and the longer stock helps absorb shock, keep the longer barrel seated, and balance the firearm. Some stocks have a straight neck, a pistol grip (a neck that curves downward), or a Monte Carlo design. The best choice is the one that fits and feels comfortable, it is entirely a personal choice.

Traditionally, stocks were made of wood. Wood was readily available and therefore practical. It was inexpensive, and back in the days when muzzleloaders were the standard craftsman routinely took a piece of rough stock and fashioned it into a functional tool. Walnut, maple, and other native hardwoods were generally preferred primarily because of their availability, strength, and durability. Back then, beauty had little to do with it. Craftsmen still exist who create handcrafted pieces of art, but custom-built muzzleloaders with select hardwood stocks are expensive these days, and most hunters feel less than comfortable taking them afield. Still, solid or laminated wood remains the standard within the industry. Most stocks are mass-produced and shaped by machine these days, perhaps fine-tuned and final-finished by hand. Most carry an oil finish for protection against the elements and to enhance the grain and beauty. Overall, wood makes a good stock, is a thing of beauty when well crafted, and remains the first choice among many enthusiasts.

But that may change. Synthetic, or composite, stocks have become quite popular in recent years. They lack any historical significance, but that seems to matter little to a growing number of hunters more interested in the advantages synthetic stocks offer. The most attractive aspect is that they are impervious to the weather and therefore require less maintenance. Composite stocks are more resistant to scratches and dents and can take more abuse. Muzzleloaders with composite stocks are also slightly lighter and less expensive than comparable models with wood stocks. Here again, it is a personal choice. For pure aesthetics nothing compares to a fine piece of walnut or maple with some distinctive grain and a tight metal-to-wood fit. But for the serious hunter, the enthusiast who beats the brush in tough weather, who travels into mountain

This flintlock Hawken-style rifle is typical of many non-replica muzzleloaders. It is durable, reliable and offers some historical styling. Most include brass hardware.

country on horseback and carries his rifle in a scabbard, or the hunter who cares little for cleaning and maintenance, composite stocks are difficult to beat.

Besides the barrel several other components are attached to the stock, particularly on more traditional replicas. These other pieces are often made of brass. The original designers and builders understood these firearms would be in the elements much of the time, not just a few weeks a year as most are today. Guns were used constantly to protect life and liberty and to put meat on the table. These rifles had to be rugged, strong, and reliable, and they had to last. Brass provided all this, and it did not rust. On some original and replica muzzleloaders German silver was also used.

On the foremost end of the stock many percussion and flintlock muzzleloaders have an end cap, or nose cap. This has no functional use except to protect the nose of the stocks. Traveling down the stock, the barrel is held in place by one or a pair of keys or wedges that slip through a lug or lugs on the barrel called a tenon. On the exterior of the stock these keys rest against metal escutcheons that are inlet in place. Most escutcheons are oval, although some may be star-shaped. On modern in-line muzzleloaders the barrel is held in place by a barrel fixing screw that attaches beneath the stock.

Beneath the forearm, the trigger guard is also inlet into the stock in its own mortice. Trigger guards vary in design but all serve one basic function, to protect the trigger assembly and to prevent accidental contact and firing. On modern in-lines the trigger guard is of conventional design and on synthetic stocks is often made of the same material. The same design is use on some sidelock percussion carbines. The trigger guard on Hawken-style muzzleloaders, however, is rather different. It extends down the underside of the neck and offers finger supports to help stabilize the rifle. It is not a pistol grip exactly, but it does help support the hand. Inside the trigger guard the trigger assembly is set in its own mortice, called a trigger mortice, and directly above, on the side of the stock, is the lock plate which is also inlet in a lock mortice. The lock mortice and trigger mortice are more than mere cutouts. They must allow sufficient room for free movement of lock and trigger parts and must accommodate lock bolts, yet offer good wood-to-metal fit. For this reason they must be precisely cut.

On the butt of the stock is a buttplate, either made of metal, plastic, or rubber, depending upon the type and style of muzzleloader. Metal buttplates, such as those on Hawken-style muzzleloaders are inlet in a mortice for tight metal-to-wood fit. Hawken-style muzzleloaders also have a metal patch box. Today the patch box is primarily ornamental, but originally they provided storage for patches or patch material used when firing roundballs. This, too, is inlet into the stock in a mortice. The patch box and all other parts are attached to the stock with screws, bolts, or pins.

THE BARREL

The barrel of a muzzleloader is where all the action takes place. It is in the breech end of the barrel where the initial spark is delivered, where the primary ignition takes place and sends the projectile down the bore and out the muzzle. It sounds rather simple, but there are several components of a muzzleloader barrel which play important rolls in how the gun works.

Barrels are made of steel with the bore drilled the entire length. The bore is then rifled, or given a twist, which puts a spin on the projectile that allows the roundball, conical, or saboted-pistol bullet to maintain accuracy downrange. Regardless of rifle style, the plugging of the breech end is accomplished using a breech plug. Considering the pressure during primary ignition in the breech end of the barrel, breech plug fit and seating are crucial to proper function and safety. So much so that some companies, such as Thomp-

The major components of a flintlock system, including the lock, barrel and tang, stock and mortice, trigger assembly and trigger guard.

son/Center, fit each breech plug to each individual barrel at the factory. If a breech plug becomes damaged, which is rare, the entire barrel is typically returned and a new plug is made and fitted at the factory.

Depending on the type of muzzleloader and ignition system, breech plug designs may vary. On traditional muzzleloaders and in-lines the breech plug is tightly fitted or screwed into the breech end of the barrel, but on percussion and in-line models the breech plug also holds the nipple. On flintlock muzzleloaders there is a touch-hole drilled through the side of the breech plug which provides a channel allowing a spark from the flash pan to travel into the breech to ignite the main charge. Whatever the case, on some percussion and flintlock models the breech plug is formed with a tang, or extension, on its back or rear-end to help fasten the barrel in place. On others the breech plug actually has a hook, called a hooked breech, which fits into a female receptacle in the front of the tang. When joined and locked with the barrel wedges the barrel is solidly fixed to the stock. In-

The percussion system, including lock, barrel and tang, fiberglass stock with mortice, and trigger assembly. The flintlock and percussion systems are quite similar.

line breech plugs also screw into the end of the barrel and offer an advantage over traditional percussion and flintlock counterparts in that they can be easily removed, thus opening both ends of the barrel for easy cleaning.

Two other components are also attached to the barrel, depending on the design: the front and rear sight system. Many barrels can accommodate scopes these days and come pre-drilled from the factory.

On certain designs, primarily percussion and flintlock muzzleloaders, a rib extends along the entire underside of the barrel. One or two thimbles designed to hold the ramrod are attached to the rib, depending on the length of the barrel and ramrod. The rib helps align the ramrod, which enters the forward-most part of the stock through a hole in the nose cap. The majority of in-line muzzleloaders typically have no rib, and because the barrels are short, just one thimble. Ramrods used to seat the projectile are made of wood or fiberglass. On one end they carry a metal bullet seater and on the other a jag adapter making it possible to accept different tools for cleaning and maintenance.

THE LOCK AND TRIGGER ASSEMBLIES

Locks and ignition systems will be covered in greater detail in Chapter 4, but it is important here to obtain at least a basic idea of the lock's function and mechanical parts. This is also true of the trigger assembly. Both components are relatively trouble-free on quality-built muzzleloaders, but all experience normal wear and should be kept clean for proper function. They may even have to be repaired. If the barrel is the heart of a muzzleloader, where all the hot action takes place, the lock and trigger assemblies are the brains.

On the outside, the percussion and flintlock lock system looks rather simple and basically it is. There is the lock plate and the hammer. That's it. It is on the inside where the real mechanics are found.

Historically, the flintlock and percussion systems were the only means of igniting a muzzleloader. These systems are still available and remain popular, but modern enthusiasts also have the in-line system. The flintlock used a piece of flint affixed to a hammer, and when the trigger was pulled the hammer propelled the flint against a metal frizzen. The action creates sparks which in turn ignited powder in a pan, which ignited powder in the breech.

The percussion system works basically the same way but instead of using flint and steal to create ignition the hammer strikes a cap filled with fulminates situated on a nipple attached in the breech of the barrel. Fulminates are pressure-sensitive, and when struck explode. When contained in a cap and controlled through a nipple the fulminates provide the spark which ignites the main charge in the breech. As we will discover later the percussion design is faster and generally more reliable, which is what made it popular with early explorers of the west and keeps them popular with today's blackpowder hunting enthusiasts. The in-line design is basically the same, except the nipple is situated at the base of the breech, rather than off to the side. When the cap ignites spark is forced straight into the beech, hence the name "in-line."

The hammer is attached to a tumbler which is notched both front and rear. The tumbler rotates back as the hammer is cocked to half-cock or full-cock and forward when the trigger is pulled. The rear notches are engaged by the sear, which operates in conjunction with a sear spring. When the hammer is cocked the sear spring is depressed, putting downward pressure on the nose of the sear notches. There is also a mainspring. This puts pressure on a forward notch in the sear which powers the hammer forward when the trigger is pulled. The lock may also have a bridle, basically a piece of metal spanning both tumbler and sear which provides pivot points for both components. In double-set triggers, which are common on Hawken-style percussion and flintlock muzzleloaders, there may also be a fly, or detent, that prevents the sear from falling into half-cock position when the trigger is pulled. Basically, it is an override mechanism which ensures full activation of the hammer from the full-cock position. Some lock systems may also have a stirrup. It rests between the tumbler and mainspring and helps reduce friction at this point. Whether of single or double-set trigger design, the half-cock position on the hammer serves as the safety.

As noted, the inner workings of such a lock system are reliable and generally easy to clean and maintain, but maintained and cleaned they must be for proper function. Most locks can be easily removed by loosening two bolts on the side of the lock plate. Inside dirt and moisture should be wiped away with a rag dampened with oil, and several drops of gun oil should then be applied to springs, tumbler, and pivot points. The lock can then be replaced, making sure the trigger and lock assemblies are properly aligned.

In-line lock systems are different. In fact, the in-line system is best described as a plunger system, or sliding bolt system. In most designs a plunger or sliding bolt is cocked backward and locked into position by a release-type mechanism mounted on top of the trigger assembly. When the trigger is pulled a powerful spring mounted directly in back of the plunger forces it forward, striking a percussion cap seated on the nipple located at the rear of the

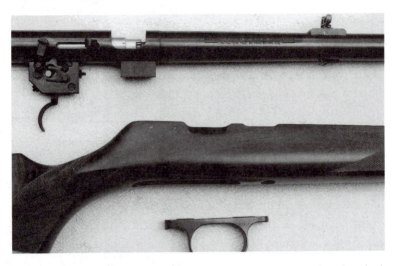

The modern in-line looks much like the modern centerfire rifle. The barrel and trigger assembly, stock, and trigger guard are shown here.

barrel. Because in-line mainsprings are much more powerful than those in sidelock muzzleloaders, and the spark from the cap goes directly into the breech and travels a shorter distance—rather than through the nipple and then ninety-degrees into the breech as on sidelock systems—the in-line offers a nearly instantaneous and more reliable ignition of the main charge.

Trigger systems can be complex or somewhat simple and there are several different types. The most common in use today include the single trigger, the double-set trigger, and modern trigger assembly. The modern in-line system resembles those used on contemporary cartridge rifles, with the same basic safety features, and therefore is more involved. Both the single and double-set designs have fewer parts, no intricate safety, and are less complicated.

Other than keeping them clean and lubricated there is little of concern regarding any of these designs, except sidelock designs with double-set triggers that can be fired either in the set or unset position. The rear trigger serves as the set trigger while the front is the hair trigger. An adjustment screw, generally located between the two triggers, but sometimes in front, alters the amount of desired let-off. Normally the deeper the set-screw is screwed in, the lighter the pull. If the rear trigger is not set, the muzzleloader can still be fired by pulling just the front trigger. The danger here is that the set trigger can be set too light, allowing the front trigger to discharge at a mere touch. Hunters who use this system generally prefer a slightly stiff pull to prevent discharge prematurely, which is not only dangerous but can result in missed game.

3

MUZZLELOADER TYPES AND DESIGNS

Back in the early 1970s when blackpowder first got in my blood selecting a muzzleloader was relatively easy. In-lines had yet to come on the scene, only a handful of companies were making muzzleloaders, and the selection was rather limited. With the exception of blackpowder cartridge rifles such as the .45–70 Government and others, those that were available were of traditional flintlock or percussion design and were classified as replicas or non-replicas. Little has changed. The in-line generally comes under the heading of modern muzzleloader, but when it comes to sidelocks it is a replica or non-replica muzzleloader most hunters carry afield these days. The only difference is that more companies are building muzzleloaders now than ever before in modern times, and these companies are offering wider selections. An example is the blackpowder carbine. They were rarely heard of two decades ago but now are quite common.

NON-REPLICA AND REPLICA MUZZLELOADERS

While in Wyoming several years ago on an elk hunt I happened to be traveling through the small town of Pinedale, about a two-hour drive south of Jackson Hole. The area is rich in history from the mountain-man era. It was not far from Pinedale, on the Green River, where trappers, traders, and native Americans often gathered between 1820 and 1840 for their famous yearly rendezvous. Nearby Fremont Lake is named for John Charles Fremont, U.S. Army officer and eventual politician, who explored the area. My hunt was to take me by pack train into the Bridger Wilderness of Bridger-Teton National Forest, an area covering more than three million acres, much of it prime big game territory and little changed since the arrival of the first mountain men.

Just outside Pinedale I passed The Museum of the Mountain Man. Being somewhat of a history buff of that adventurous time I made a pit stop and went inside. Among the captivating exhibits on the fur trade, western exploration, Indians who inhabited the area, and early settlement of western Wyoming, I came across a Hawken-style muzzleloader hanging on a wall. I don't recall who owned it or other historical particulars, but I do remember that it had a percussion lock and that the stock was quite dark and had obviously been well used in its day. The barrel was browned. I also recall its .58-caliber bore and weight, which was somewhere in the neighborhood of twelve pounds. The piece seemed rather large, even cumbersome compared to the muzzleloaders I was used to, but the fact is this true Hawken was typical for its day, heavy, large-calibered, with a lengthy barrel and, indeed, is nothing like the percussion or flintlock "Hawken" rifles hunters carry and use today.

Indeed, the name "Hawken" has become rather generic when talking about sidelock ignition muzzleloaders. There are numerous replicas on the market and in use these days that carry the name, but the originals were built during a short time span and more than any other firearm contributed to the opening of the west during the era of the mountain man, fur trapper and westward expansion.

History tells us the Hawken name in the craft of building guns extends back to about 1724 when Henry Hawken was building rifles in Lancaster, Pennsylvania. Although the elder Hawken had a respectable reputation as a rifle maker during his time, it was his grandsons, Jacob and Sam Hawken who would securely establish the family name in the trade. Jacob, or "Jake" moved to St. Louis in 1807 and opened his first gun shop in 1815. Hearty souls had been venturing west of the Mississippi before the Lewis and Clark expedition, but by the time Jacob Hawken opened his shop the fur trade was getting under way. Those early trappers and explorers carried light caliber, flintlock rifles common at the time but by the time Sam Hawken moved from Ohio following the death of his wife and joined his brother in 1822, the fur trade was in full swing and the need for a ruggedly built, heavy caliber firearm suitable for large western game was evident.

The Hawken brothers provided what was needed. Calibers were wide ranging but .58 to .64 were common. Barrels were fixed to a half-stock, held in position by two keys. Although it is not well known early versions carried a flintlock ignition but starting around 1830 the Hawken brothers introduced their Rocky Mountain Rifle. What made this rifle unique was the ignition system. Starting as early as 1816 Joshua Shaw of Philadelphia was producing a "detonation" cap. It proved unreliable as well as highly corrosive, however, until 1824 when the oxymuriate of potash used to ignite the cap was replaced with fulminate of mercury. The new material was not as corrosive and just as important could be made rather waterproof, a highly important factor to the rugged individuals who live their life outdoors. Starting around 1830 this new cap was readily available and it became standard on the Hawken as the west and world came to know them. The rest, as they say, is history and the Hawken, like no other frontloading blackpowder rifle before or since has remained an American classic and lives on in replica and non-replica muzzleloaders that carry the name.

Jacob Hawken departed for the next world of cholera in May of 1849 having never traveled west. Sam continued to build rifles in St. Louis until 1859 when he eventually crossed the Mississippi traveling to the land he helped tame. He visited Pikes Peak but eventually settled in Denver and once again started building rifles. He remained their until 1861 when he returned to St. Louis and continued his trade. He died on May 9, 1884 at the age of 92.

Of course, the Hawken-style muzzleloader is not the only design to be copied and altered in recent years. The Pennsylvania Long Rifle and other full-stock muzzleloaders have been reproduced extensively by several companies, and with some offerings it can be a test of historical knowledge to discern a non-replica from an original. Many manufacturers do seem to follow more historical lines with these American classics, but they remain non-replicas nonethe-

The Thompson/Center Hawken is the best selling non-replica muzzleloader in the world. Since its introduction in 1970 over one-half million have been sold. This popular muzzle-loader is available in .50- and .54-caliber with percussion or flintlock ignition and right or left hand models.

less. And then there are the carbines and compacts. Historically, short, light-weight muzzleloaders are nothing new, but they were not as common as you might think and were never as popular or widespread as the Hawken. It was not until the mid-to-late 1980s when manufacturers, in an effort to offer a wider se-lection to a growing number of enthusiasts and knowing some hunters simply prefer compact rifles, reinvented the design. These models are lightweight and short-barrelled but are capable of taking big game at reasonable yardage.

Without question, not including the modern in-line, it is the non-replica muzzleloader which rekindled America's love affair with blackpowder. With-out it, there is little doubt the interest in blackpowder shooting and hunting would be far less than it is, and good or bad depending upon your personal view, perhaps the in-line never would have come along. The muzzleloading industry, like every other industry, survives by supplying what the buyer de-mands. As true originals faded away and became difficult to find and hand-crafted replicas grew increasingly expensive, folks like Warren Center and Ken

The Renegade from Thompson/Center is a rugged hunting rifle. With a 1:48 rifle twist and 26-inch barrel, it shoots roundballs and conicals well. It is available in .50-, .54-, and .58-caliber.

Thompson of Thompson/Center Arms, Turner Kirkland of Dixie Gun Works and Val Forgett of Navy Arms, to name but a few of the early pioneers, saw the demand and delivered. The interest in muzzleloading continues to grow to new heights, and though the in-line has been greatly responsible, it all started with the non-replica.

The question becomes what made the Hawken and other non-replica muzzleloaders so popular? It would be possible to discuss the various reasons for weeks, but there are some simple answers. One is cost. Antique muzzleloaders are expensive, if you can find them, and even if an original is purchased one would have to question the sense of taking it afield. These guns represent a special link to an exciting era during the exploration and settlement of America and so few remain in sound workable condition it borders on sacrilege to use them for big game hunting.

The same is almost true of replicas, muzzleloaders built from scratch by custom gunsmiths. These muzzleloaders typically exhibit few differences from originals, take weeks or sometimes months to build, and here again can set the purchaser back more than a few bucks, perhaps two or three times the most expensive non-replica or in-line depending on the builder and style. There exists a contingent of traditionalists and buckskinners within the blackpowder arena who believe muzzleloading in any form, whether it be shooting or hunting, should be based on historical perspective. These folks shun anything not original, or close to it, even non-replicas. And in-lines? Don't even mention them. They may load from the front and use blackpowder or Pyrodex, but to the purist they are an abomination. But this contingent is small compared to the overall muzzleloading ranks who have overwhelmingly accepted close imitations and modern in-lines.

Fortunately, a handful of companies, big and small, offer replicas or close reproductions for those who prefer them at much more affordable prices.

The author and his favorite roundball muzzleloader, the Lyman Great Plains Rifle in .54-caliber. This classic is also available in .50-caliber. The larger caliber is a good choice for elk, moose, and caribou, while the smaller .50-caliber makes an excellent deer rifle.

Many are no more costly than mid-range non-replicas or the better in-lines. They are handsomely-crafted specimens generally designed to shoot patch and roundball. Most are available in .50- or .54-caliber and because they don't require a second morgage to purchase are well suited for every day big game hunting. Navy Arms of Ridgefield, New Jersey probably offers more replica than non-replica muzzleloaders, such as their Ithaca Hawken, which was first offered by the Ithaca Gun Company. Lyman of Middletown, Connecticut has their Great Plains Rifle. With its 32-inch barrel and 1:60 twist for patch and roundball in either .50- or .54-caliber, double-set triggers, and other amenities of an earlier era, the Great Plains Rifle is perhaps the closest factory built or kit form example of authentic Plains rifle style and design available on the market. Lyman also offers a similiar version called Great Plains Hunter. This is a special version for the hunter who wants traditional styling but prefers hunting with conicals and sabots rather than roundball. The fast 1:32 twist, shallow-grooved barrel is ideal for modern projectiles and offers the best of both worlds. Mountain State Muzzleloading, Dixie Gun Works, and Mowray Gun Works of Waldron, Indiana all offer replica muzzleloaders or examples close enough to the originals to keep all but the strict purist satisfied.

Non-replica muzzleloaders are also popular because of their affordabilty. This was true back in the early 1970s when they were first introduced and it remains true today. Most cost only a fraction of an original or replica built by a custom builder. The reason for this is that non-replicas are made with modern gun manufacturing methods and materials and can be made faster and at less cost. Dollar for dollar, for the enthusiast who puts little importance in historical connection and replication but who wants at least the spirit of an original, the non-replica is the best thing going.

Affordable cost is certainly one attractive aspect non-replica muzzleloaders offer, but so are quality and dependabilty. A good number of original muzzleloaders have stood the test of time and are a true testament to the craftsmanship of their era. Custom-built originals are also of the same high quality and no doubt an example hand-built in a small one or two-man shop somewhere will be around for years to come. But most non-replicas built in a factory have nothing to be ashamed of. I own a Thompson/Center Hawken with a low serial number built in the early 1970s, and though it has its share of scratches and nicks from years of use it continues to perform well. The whole idea behind the non-replica concept was affordable cost but also ruggedness and reliability. With proper care non-replicas will literally last a lifetime and perform well for the duration. Unlike many original and replica muzzleloaders which are quite heavy, the non-replica is lighter in weight, most under eight or nine pounds due in part to their shorter barrel. They remain more than accurate enough to take game within their recommended range.

Non-replicas are also extremely versatile these days, again for the hunter wanting the look and feel of the past but the advantages of modern firearms. Some are rifled exclusively for patch and roundball, but to accommodate the

The Black Mountain Express from Thompson/Center offers the look of a traditional side-lock with state of the art performance. Available in .50- and .54-caliber, synthetic stock, and 1:28 twist, it fires both conicals and sabots very well. The internal breech is designed to accommodate Pyrodex Pellets as well as granular propellents.

Thompson/Center's Big Bore is available in .58-caliber. It is excellent for big game such as bear, moose, and elk when loaded with 100 grains of powder. With a 1:48 twist, it shoots heavy conicals with power and good muzzle velocity.

growing interest in conicals and sabots for big game hunting many are built with fast rifle twists of 1:48, 1:32, even 1:28. They come with synthetic stocks, stainless barrels, in caplock and flintlock ignition, in right-hand as well as left-hand models, with traditional brass or browned-steel hardware and in the three most popular hunting calibers: .45, .50, and .54. You name it and chances are it is available in a non-replica.

COMPACT MUZZLELOADERS

For years many non-replica muzzleloaders were of a standard size, depending on the design. Most versions carrying the Hawken name, for example, were roughly 44 to 45 inches in length, weighed around 7 or 8 pounds, and carried a 28-inch octagon barrel. In general, the typical non-replica muzzleloader was designed and built shorter and lighter than the originals, but starting in the late 1980s hunters were looking for something compact and lighter still, yet wanted to maintain accuracy. It was about this time that the muzzleloading carbine came on the scene. They have been with us ever since and judging by their popularity will continue to be with us for years to come.

The important thing to keep in mind about the muzzleloading carbines now available is that they are designed for the modern hunter. Unfortunately, many enthusiasts care very little about the historical aspects of the muzzleloader they carry, so things like traditional styling, brass hardware, patchbox, fancy trigger guard, double-set triggers, even octagon barrels and wood ramrods, are of little consequence. On carbines this hardware has been eliminated. Double-set triggers have been replaced by single trigger assemblies, on some models wood stocks are available but so are synthetic stocks. Ramrods may be wood, PVC, or other synthetic material. In appearance, carbines have little style, but today's hunter seems to care less.

In fact, a large number who hunt with muzzleloaders these days, and those just getting into muzzleloading, are not dedicated muzzleloader users at all. They purchase frontloaders primarily to take advantage of special black-powder hunting seasons or to hunt areas where conventional hunting arms are prohibited. Whatever the case, like other traditional components, the flintlock ignition system has also gone by the wayside for the most part with nearly all compacts fired by a caplock system. The Buckskinner Flintlock Carbine offered by Traditions and the Pennsylvania Hunter Carbine by Thompson/Center are two exceptions. There are others, but flintlock carbines are not nearly as prevalent as caplock carbines.

The reason for this is that the caplock has a reputation for providing faster ignition and being more reliable, particularly under hunting conditions in rain, sleet, snow, and damp weather. This is not necessarily true, but modern hunters are convinced it is, and, among other things, they simply wanted dependability. Along with the elimination of traditional hardware, barrels were also shortened to cut weight. The typical carbine carries a 20- to 22-inch barrel rather than the 24-, 26-, or 28-inch barrel of most muzzleloading rifles. Most carbine barrels are also round rather than octagonal, which cuts weight even more. In the end, the average carbine runs from 6 to slightly more than 7 pounds, a full 2 to 3 pounds less than many muzzleloading rifles of similiar design. Just a couple of pounds may not seem like a lot of weight, but for the hunter who covers a lot of ground and hunts rugged mountain and hill country, it is certainly appreciated.

Because of reduced barrel length, overall carbine length is also less than full-sized muzzleloading rifles. Thompson/Center's Pennsylvania Hunter Rifle is a full 45 inches, but its carbine counterpart is 38 inches overall. Tradition's Deerhunter Rifle is 40 inches overall, but its Buckskinner Carbine, while not actually the same muzzleloader but close enough for a comparison, is just 37 1/2 inches. The shorter overall length makes the carbine easy to lift, achieves swift target alignment, and also provides easy swing with less chance of hitting an obstruction in thick cover. For specific hunting conditions and in cases where age and physical condition necessitate a lighter firearm, carbines definitely have their advantages.

But carbines do have their disadvantages, although they are certainly manageable. Because of their short barrel and light weight, recoil from a carbine is much greater than from heavier, longer muzzleloaders. The short barrel also cuts down on the sighting plane, which can be a factor governing proper shot placement, or even consistent accuracy for hunters with poor eyesight. If this is the case, a scope may prove a great benefit.

Muzzle velocity and range are also lost with short barrels. About 10 fps (feet per second) is lost for every 1 inch of barrel loss. In other words, a projectile from a 22-inch barrel will exit 40 fps slower than a comparable projectile from a 26-inch barrel. This is not a major decrease, but it can make a difference when hunting deer and other fast game on the move. A whitetail can move upwards of 40 mph, more than 58 feet per second. Pronghorn are even faster. While I have to question even pulling the trigger on an animal running full speed in most cases, game often bolts or hunches down slightly when the trigger is pulled and the time it takes a projectile to reach 100 yards can be crucial. The slower the bullet and the greater the range, the greater the possibility of hitting behind the target. Even if a hit is made, it may not be in the heart or lungs, resulting in a long blood trail or even the loss of a wounded animal. For this reason carbines are considered excellent close-range brush guns but are not recommended for over 100 yards, even when rifled for long-shooting conicals and sabots.

THE MODERN IN-LINE

No other muzzleloader design in recent history, perhaps in all of history, has created as much controversy within the ranks as the in-line, also referred to as the modern muzzleloader. Among purists the in-line is simply disdained. There are the middle-of-the-roaders who can take them or leave them, who use them on occasion but also revert back to more traditional styles (this writer included). And there are those who use nothing else, who like the in-line's configuration, handling, sights, and operational features. Despite the controversy, one thing is certain: the in-line muzzleloader is here to stay and its popularity is rapidly growing.

It may be interesting to briefly note here the in-line ignition concept is not new. History tells us the concept was in use before the turn of the century. Doc Carlson, a muzzleloading firearm writer of note mentions the Paczelt flintlock in-line in the 1966 *Gun Digest* under the title of *"The In-Line Muzzleloader"* for those inclined to research it, but even the plunger-type in-line common today has been know for years.

It was not until 1985 when Tony Knight of Knight Muzzleloading brought the idea up to date. Using modern techniques and materials, that year Knight introduced the first modern in-line using the plunger concept and the muzzleloading world has not been the same since. Although other companies quickly jumped on the bandwagon, in large part, the Knight in-line is responsible for the current high popularity of muzzleloading not only for target shooting but hunting. In the years that followed, Knight pioneered the removable breech plug which helps in easy, more efficient cleaning, and most recently gave muzzleloading the revolutionary disc rifle. The design is based on the system Mauser patented back in the 1880's. There is no nipple, and no capping or decapping tools are required to load or unload. Instead, the user simply cocks the firing hammer opening the breech, inserts a plastic disc holding either a No. 11 or 209 shotgun primer, closes the bolt and it is ready to fire. The design is extremely user friendly, fast, reliable in all kinds of weather and increases safety.

As noted, numerous in-lines are available today from a lengthy list of manufacturers. They include some of America's oldest and most reputable gun makers, as well as some who are historically known for more traditional muzzleloader designs. Most are worth taking a close look at, but it was Knight that got the ball rolling and continues to set the standard.

Non-replica muzzleloaders remain a top choice among hunters and shooters, but modern muzzleloaders comprise about 80 percent of all frontloaders sold. So hot is the in-line that muzzleloader makers like Thompson/Center, Connecticut Valley Arms, Lyman, and Navy Arms—folks who have been making sidelock non-replicas and near replics for years—had to jump on the bandwagon or get lost in the dust. For others in the business, like Traditions, the in-line is their best-selling muzzleloader by far, a fact most others

The Black Diamond from Thompson/Center is a good example of the modern in-line. It come standard with three ignition options: No. 11 caps, 209 shotgun primers and Musket Caps. The Black Diamond comes with a 22-inch barrel rifled with a 1:28 twist, ideal for conicals and sabots.

would have to agree with. For some companies, such as Knight, Gonic, and Muzzleloading Technologies, makers of the White line of muzzleloaders, the in-line is the primary muzzleloader offered. Even some of the industry's oldest gunmakers are getting in on the act. Remington offers a blackpowder version of their famous Model 700 bolt-action rifle with their Model 700ML, and Ruger has their All-Weather 77/50.

Besides the purists, it should be noted that some game managers and state wildlife departments are not entirely pleased with the in-line concept, especially now that some manufacturers are offering "magnum" versions capable of taking a 150-grain charge, compressed powder pellets, different size ignition caps, and projectiles more than twice as long as their diameter. Colorado outlawed the use of in-lines for its muzzleloader hunts in 1998. Whether the ban will stick is unknown, but other states such as New Mexico, Idaho, Utah, and New Jersey have recently questioned in-line use during their special muzzleloading seasons.

In-lines are legal in most states and Canadian provinces that offer special muzzleloader hunting seasons, with restrictions, but as the design progresses and continues to push the envelope, things could change. Hopefully, this will not happen. There is enough anti-hunting pressure and sufficient regulation as it is. Whatever the end result may be, would-be in-line buyers should make a point to check local regulations where they hunt before putting their money down.

But the question remains, what makes the in-line muzzleloader such a hot ticket? The White Model 97 Whitetail Hunter manufactured by Muzzleloading Technologies of Roosevelt, Utah is a prime example of the modern in-line. First introduced in 1993, the Whitetail Hunter represents the typical in-line except that it lacks the bolt-style cocking mechanism which has become so popular. Instead, it has a lever cocking system that is pulled directly back to engage. In all other aspects it is of the same high quality of others in the class.

The HunterBolt MusketMag from Connecticut Valley Arms is available in .50-caliber and comes with CVA's 3-way ignition system for No. 11 caps, 209 shotgun primers or Musket caps, fiber optic sights, synthetic stock, and 24-inch, 1:32 rifled barrel.

What is most striking about the Whitetail Hunter (and other modern muzzleloaders) is its appearance, its lines or styling if you will. It truly looks modern, like a conventional high-powered hunting rifle. Everything about it is familiar, and that is the intent: to provide hunters purchasing their first muzzleloader with something that looks and feels familiar.

So contemporary in configuration is the Whitetail Hunter and other in-lines that it is often necessary to take a second, closer look to make certain they really are muzzleloaders. More than once a newcomer has picked up one in my office or living room gun cabinet, perhaps my Knight MK-85 Stalker, the Gonic Model 93 Deluxe, Thompson/Center Black Diamond, or Connecticut Valley Arms FireBolt MusketMag, looked at me and asked rather surprised, "This is a muzzleloader?" It never fails.

The modern in-line's even feel like current rifles. They are extremely well balanced, and depending upon the model and manufacturer, the stock may be straight with a slight drop at comb or offer a more pronounced pistol grip. Stocks are made of solid wood or laminate, although reinforced composite stocks are quickly taking over. They are easy to maintain, nearly impervious to harsh weather, and tolerate hard hunting conditions. The in-line barrel is typically round and short, generally from 20 to 22 inches, which helps balance and limit weight. Most models weigh under 7 pounds and because of their excellent balance make for easy carrying. Again, depending on the model, barrels can be blued or made of 416 stainless steel. The latter are becoming popular, especially on models with composite stocks.

On nearly all in-lines the butt carries a rubber recoil paid to help offset heavy loads. Several "magnum" models can now accommodate 150 grains of granular or compressed propellent and heavy projectiles, but even on more

CVA's Elkmaster is an excellent in-line complete with pistol grip.

35

standard loads the rubber recoil pad is often appreciated due to the short barrel and light weight.

The typical in-line includes a modern safety system. Most are of the sliding type but some models have double safeties. My White Whitetail Hunter is one example. It has a sliding thumb safety on the right side of the breech which locks the trigger plus a "hook" in the breech that locks the plunger.

As for trigger assemblies, most are of modern design, right off contemporary drawing boards. Nearly every in-line I have ever seen comes pre-tapped for scope mounting. Scopes are not legal in every state during special muzzleloader season, however, so check local regulations. The standard sight system is adjustable for windage and elevation and may include click adjustable or steel-ramp-type on the rear and sliding-ramp-type with bead on front. Fiber optic sights, marketed under various trademarks such as Tru-Glo and Illuminator II have become standard on many models. Fiber optic sights are covered in greater detail in Chapter 7, but are basically designed to help illuminate open sights in low light conditions. Keeping in mind the in-line was designed for the modern hunter, the stocks come equipped with sling swivel studs for easy carrying and stability when shooting and a lightweight composite ramrod.

Several other aspects set the in-line apart. One is the ignition system, which will be covered in more detail in the next chapter. Another is the removeable breech plug. In replica and non-replica muzzleloaders the breech plug can't be removed, at least for general maintenance, and cleaning must be done from the muzzle end. Nearly all in-lines, however, have a removeable breech plug that allows cleaning to be done from the rear or breech end. This makes maintenance much easier as both ends of the barrel are open to a complete through-the-barrel cleaning, a real advantage in maintaining a muzzleloader.

Finally, there is barrel twist and the projectiles that in-lines shoot. Projectiles and barrel twist, or rifling, will be discussed in following chapters, but

The White Super 91 is one of the finest in-line muzzleloaders available.

it is important to note here that unlike non-replicas which, depending upon barrel twist, can shoot patched roundball or conical bullets and sabot/bullet combinations, the modern in-line is designed specifically to shoot conical and sabot loads. Very few in-line or modern muzzleloaders exist with a slow rifle twist, which is intended for patched roundball. It is vital to keep this in mind because it relates directly to projectile stabilization and accuracy, both important factors when hunting big game.

SELECTING A MUZZLELOADER DESIGN FOR BIG GAME

Deciding which muzzleloader design to purchase can be difficult. So many variations are available these days, such as replicas, customs, and an array of non-replicas and in-lines, that the newcomer is often overwhelmed. Keep in mind here that I am not talking about features like the best caliber for big game hunting or the best bullet weight or shape, but basic muzzleloader design. While still important, compared to these other aspects, selecting a muzzleloader design is not a difficult task.

I say this with a high degree of certainty based on my long-held belief that choosing a muzzleloader is a personal thing. Friends, "experts," and those with more experience under their belt are often quick to provide opinions, but those opinions are often based upon what *they* like. You are a different person, a different hunter. What counts the most is what you like, and especially how and where you hunt. It is important to keep in mind, however, the two often conflict so one may prove more important than the other. That is what sometimes makes selecting a muzzleloader design difficult, because what is often most appealing is not always the best selection from a hunting perspective.

For example, the Pennsylvania-style long rifle in full flintlock dress and brass regalia has always been appealing. The shorter but still long Kentucky flintlock runs a close second. I suppose it goes back to childhood when I was an avid watcher of Davy Crockett and Daniel Boone on televison. Back then, I often envisioned exploring wilderness places and living off the land but despite the aesthetic appeal of these muzzleloaders, in all my years of hunting I have yet to take one afield. I came to the conclusion years ago that I am not a flintlock enthusiast. I have nothing against them. Within their limits I understand they provide the same accuracy and downrange killing power as sidelock percussion counterparts loaded with comparable charge and projectile. And I realize they have taken their share of game, and still do. For hunting, however, I feel more comfortable with, and have more confidence in, the sidelock percussion or in-line systems. This preference may derive from a lack of experience with the flintlock design, but it is simply the way I developed as a muzzleloader hunter. I also find flintlocks overly long and somewhat heavy, yet I have one hanging over my fireplace.

The point is, what first appeals to the eye may not be the best choice. Examine your hunting style and the type of terrain you hunt. If you hunt rugged mountain and hill country where the going is tough the last thing you want is a heavy muzzleloader to weigh you down. By the same token, if the country is thick with cover a long muzzleloader might prove a hindrance. In both scenarios, or wherever the average shot is 50 to 70 yards, a carbine might be the way to go. If history has little or no relevence for you and you want light weight and dependability, or if you really want to reach out and touch something in the open country of the West, an in-line might be the answer. If you desire some spirit of the past, want to shoot conicals and sabots, and shoot out to only 100 yards or so, perhaps a Hawken-style non-replica muzzleloader might be in order.

There is a muzzleloader design out there for every type of hunting and accepted range for taking big game. Just give it some thought beforehand. Don't worry about caliber or projectile type. That will come later. With the exception of the flintlock, the three most popular big game calibers are provided in nearly all muzzleloader designs, and those designs come with an assortment of barrels rifled to shoot just about any projectile available. Don't let the "experts" or hunting buddies tell you what is best. Base the decision on your own needs and preferences. But keep in mind that basic muzzleloader design, except for those designed exclusively for roundball and carbines or compacts with short barrels, have little to do with how far you can reach out and tag something or how much power a projectile will deliver.

CVA's Youth Hunter is a short, light muzzleloader ideal for youngsters just getting into muzzleloading. At just 5½ pounds, with its 24-inch, 1:48 rifled barrel, it is easy to carry and shoots both patched roundballs and conicals. It is a good deer rifle at short range.

4

IGNITION SYSTEMS

Through the centuries several ingenious methods have been developed to ignite the main charge in a muzzleloader. History tells us of matchlocks, wheellocks, snaphances, and pill locks, and though each played a roll in the evolution of the firearm, when it comes to big game hunting these days the flintlock, percussion, and modern in-line are most common. In fact, it is impossible to find one of the other ignition systems on a factory-made non-replica, and it is safe to say that the vast majority of blackpowder hunters have never even heard of them unless they are history buffs and have done a great deal of reading.

For obvious reasons a muzzleloader's ignition system is very important. In simple form it is responsible for setting off a chain of events that ignites the main charge in the breech which in turn propels the projectile to the target. In his fine book, *Blackpowder Whitetails*, fellow scribe Dave Ehrig of Pennsylvania says "all ignition systems are not created equal." Dave knows his stuff and this is especially true from a big game hunting perspective. Some systems are slower than others and since lock speed affects the ignition speed of the main charge and accuracy, the type of ignition can determine how close a hunter actually hits to where he or she is aiming, particularly on moving game or game that bolts or jumps once the trigger is pulled.

Some ignition systems are also more reliable than others. I don't know a big game hunter who hasn't hunted in falling snow, rain, sleet, or in damp weather conditions. Many of us actually enjoy it. During such conditions it is common to stalk and pursue game or follow fresh tracks in thick cover where accumulated snow and rain on overhead branches often soaks head, shoulders, and firearm when disturbed.

By the same token, it is not uncommon to sit for hours in these same conditions waiting for that whitetail, elk or black bear to come along, and invariably the ignition system gets wet. Just taking a muzzleloader from a warm hunting camp into cold temperatures, especially if done so several times during the course of a day or week-long hunt, can affect ignition reliability. In these cases extreme change in temperature creates condensation inside the barrel which affects powder potency. This is more a propellent problem than ignition system problem, but it goes to show how everything has to be just right to obtain reliable ignition under less than perfect hunting conditions. Because in most states and provinces a muzzleloader is considered legally unloaded if it has not been primed or does not have a cap (check local regulations), many hunters at the end of the day stow their muzzleloader carrying main charge and projectile in a secure location outside where consistent temperatures has little effect on the main charge.

THE FLINTLOCK IGNITION SYSTEM

When the early settlers of this continent went out to put meat on the table they carried a flintlock muzzleloader. Davy Crockett shot one, so did Daniel Boone, and the flintlock was with the first mountain men as they explored the Rocky Mountains. Until the arrival of the percussion ignition system in the 1800s the flintlock was it. For more than 250 years in this country and across the northern border in Canada the flintlock has proved itself in time of war and peace. And though not as popular as it once was, this system has probably taken more game than any other simply because it has been around longer.

There are two main reasons why the flintlock is not as popular with today's hunters as it once was. In fact, had the percussion system and modern in-line been available the flintlock would have lost its place as the primary igni-

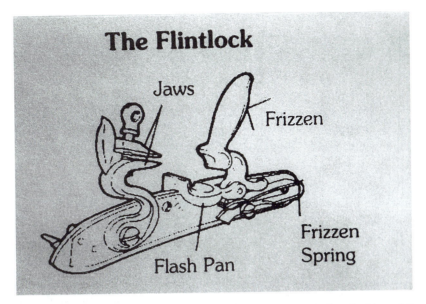

The Flintlock

Jaws

Frizzen

Frizzen Spring

Flash Pan

The flintlock ignition system is the oldest ignition system used today. Ignition of the main powder charge is slower than the percussion and in-line designs and the flintlock has a reputation for being susceptible to foul weather conditions.

tion system long before it did. One reason is time. A great deal in the hunting world is based on proper timing and of the three types of ignition systems just mentioned the flintlock is the slowest. Once the trigger is pulled a delay from five-hundreds to as much as eleven-hundreds of a second occurs before the main charge ignites. The variation depends a great deal on the quality of the lock and flint, but when the hammer falls on a flintlock a delay is inevitable.

The delay comes from the way a flintlock operates. When the trigger is pulled the hammer falls forward, forcing the flint to strike the frizzen, which is pulled forward over the priming charge in the pan. The frizzen is made of steal. Frizzen size varies slightly depending upon the maker but they all are de-signed to flow backwards upon impact from the hammer and flint. The pur-pose of the frizzen upon contact with the flint is to create a shower of sparks which flow downward into the flash pan. This in turn ignites the priming charge which journeys through a touch-hole in the breech and ignites the main charge. This is the reason for the delay, and from a hunting perspective this is very important.

With today's modern centerfire rifles, hunters are accustomed to instantaneous ignition. At normal hunting range the bullet from a .30/30 or .30/06 has already hit the target by the time the hunter hears the explosion from the rifle. This is not true with the flintlock ignition system. The ignition of powder in the flash pan is quite obvious and often causes game within 100 yards, the best range for most flintlock guns rifled for patch and roundball, to flinch or bolt. Because of this the flintlock hunter must learn to maintain his or her aiming point, even following or leading the target until the main charge ignites, not easy to do. The same is true on running game. Knowing the time of delay and learning to properly lead the target are critical to cleanly dispatching game. For hunters using a flintlock for the first time, hitting where they aim is one of the biggest problems. Until they get used to the delay they often hit over or behind the point of aim, or miss completely because the animal either flinched or jumped, or because they failed to allow a proper lead.

Another problem with the flintlock system is reliability. Die-hards will argue the point, but flintlocks are simply more susceptible to misfire than the percussion system. The reason for this is that the priming charge is exposed. It sits in an external flash pan on the side of the lock, and though partially covered it is far from totally protected from the elements. During extreme weather conditions and even fog and drizzle, water or dampness can find its way to the priming charge, caking the powder and making it useless. It is vital to keep the priming charge dry and the lock clean and in good operating condition.

Cleaning and maintaining a muzzleloader will be covered in greater detail in a future chapter but for flintlocks it is particularly important. To begin with, make sure the lock is properly tuned. This is also essential with percussion sidelock systems. To obtain optimum spark from a flintlock the edge of the flint should hit squarely in the middle of the frizzen when the trigger is pulled. This can be easily tested (making sure the muzzleloader is not loaded with a projectile, of course). Pull the frizzen forward and then place the hammer on half-cock. The edge of the flint should be square with, and slightly back from, the frizzen surface. By the same token, the hammer on a percussion system should hit the primer cap squarely.

It should be noted that the most important part of the flintlock ignition system is the flint. Most production models are equipped with a stone called agate that is very hard and creates considerable spark when it strikes steel. The problem is that it dulls rather quickly and must be either sharpened or turned

The flintlock ignition system is generally considered the slowest and least reliable of the three most popular ignition types. But even when shooting the roundball they pack enough power to dispatch game within their range limits and will always have a following.

to ensure optimum ignition. Agate is so hard it can only be sharpened on a grinding wheel. True flints, those used by our ancestors, are a combination of silica and historically came from England, France, and Germany. They are more expensive and not as readily available as their agate counterparts, but their advantage is that they can easily be resharpened or "knapped." It is also believed by a good number of enthusiasts that true flints shower a larger amount of spark, thus increasing ignition of the main charge. For hunting purposes, or simply target shooting, these better quality flints are the way to go.

The flint must also be sharp. As the hammer comes forward and the flint strikes the frizzen the knife-edge of the flint is actually cutting modules of metal off the frizzen. These modules are super-heated to about 2000 degrees Fahrenheit. As noted earlier, these sparks drop into the flash pan and ignite the priming charge. The sharper the flint the more sparks or modules it cuts and the faster the main charge ignites. It is equally important that the flint is secure in the jaws. If the flint is loose it simply will not function properly.

True flints are a compound of silica found in the chalk beds of England, France and Germany, and they are costly. Today, agate such as this is more common. It is extremely hard and creates good spark but becomes increasingly dulled when fired. It can only be resharpened on a grinding wheel.

Also, make sure the edge of the flint, flash pan, and especially the frizzen, are free of grease and oil, even oil from your hands. Clean them with isopropyl alcohol. Alcohol easily cleans away grease and oil, evaporates quickly even in cold temperatures, and has no effect on black powder.

Make sure the hammer falls freely. In other words make sure it is clean and well lubricated with a light touch of oil. This quickens hammer time, which increases ignition speed. Make a point to clean, again with alcohol, and lube the cam beneath the frizzen, where it bears on the frizzen spring. To obtain an optimum amount of spark, some hunters also "preheat" their frizzen. They claim heating the frizzen for about ten seconds with a butane lighter at the beginning of a day's hunt sweats away any moisture in the steel. If you do this make sure not to apply too much heat, doing so may retemper the steal. Wipe away any carbon using an alcohol patch.

Finally, give some attention to the touch-hole. Using a pipe cleaner soaked in alcohol, run it through the vent between the pan and bore. This will help loosen any residue. A second dry pipe cleaner will soak up or remove any oil or grease which turns into a thick goo when it comes into contact with blackpowder.

While actually hunting, try to protect the lock from the elements. This can be done by carrying the muzzleloader with the lock underneath your arm. This not only helps keep it dry but, to a certain degree, warm as well. This is not always possible or convenient, however, so try a "cow's knee" over the lock. In old times this was a piece of oiled leather cut and shaped to fit over the lock and held in place by a leather thong tied to the trigger guard. When the time came to fire it was simply slid off the lock. These devices are available at many gun shops, or through the mail from places like Dixie Guns Works, The Log Cabin Shop, Mountain State Muzzleloading, and other mail-order outlets. Similar covers are also available for the frizzen, although one can easily be made at home by cutting the finger off an old leather glove and attaching it to the trigger guard with a thong.

About the only other thing the flintlocker can do to help ensure ignition in foul weather is to change the priming charge every half-hour to hour or so, depending on the conditions. You can also try experimenting with FFFg instead of FFFFg for priming. It does not absorb moisture as readily nor does it seem to cake as fast.

THE PERCUSSION IGNITION SYSTEM

The ignition time of a percussion system is about 50 percent faster than that of a flintlock. At approximately two-hundredths of a second once the trigger is pulled, it is almost instantaneous and not much slower than the modern in-line. The reason for this is that many percussion locks have a shorter stroke than flintlock's, which means the primer is hit in less time. Also, because the distance from cap to main charge is shorter, ignition time is greatly increased.

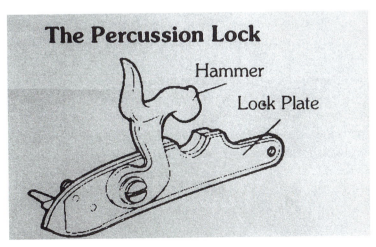

A cap fits over a nipple and when the trigger is pulled the hammer sends a spark into the main charge. The percussion system is faster and generally considered more reliable than the flintlock system.

In most cases, once the hunter hears the rifle explosion the projectile is well on its way or has already hit the target, depending on the range.

The percussion system is also considered more reliable. The only powder involved is inside the barrel, relatively protected from moisture. The main charge comes from a cap that fits snugly over a nipple screwed into a thimble, or bolster, on the side of the breech. Although all percussion caps do lose potency over time, the top brands such as Dynamit Nobel, CVA, Remington, CCI, and RWS are relatively moisture resistant, even waterproof. Further weather protection to the cap can be provided by using cap guards such as those available from Traditions, and CVA's Cap Grippers. These are basically small plastic "O" rings that slip over the cap to help retard moisture. Even the nipple/bolster connection on the percussion system is rather watertight. Because everything is enclosed the percussion system can literally be used in a downpour with a high degree of reliability. For this reason, and because of increased ignition speed, this is by far the top choice among hunters who prefer sidelock ignition.

But the percussion system is not infallible. Although it has fewer moving parts, to work properly and provide consistent ignition, proper maintenance and tuning are no less important. Lubrication with light gun oil should be given to the spring and tumbler on the inside of the lock plate. This allows free movement of the hammer and helps ensure fast ignition. On the lock itself this is basically it, but there are other items to tend to.

For one, it is vital that the vent hole through the nipple is clean and free of residue. This is the channel through which spark from the cap travels to ignite the main charge. If clogged, a hangfire, actually a delay in main ignition, or total misfire could occur. In either situation continue to aim downrange or in a safe direction and *never* point the firearm at another person or yourself. The muzzleloader could still go off, even after more than a minute! Special tools with small clean-out picks, some of which fit inside a nipple wrench for easy and convenient storage, are available specifically for cleaning the nipple vent. I carry mine in a small waist pack while hunting just in case it is needed. The blow-hole through the bolster leading to the breech should be clean and dry, as well. This can easily be done with a pipe cleaner, just like on a flintlock. Finally, when the hammer falls it should hit squarely against the nipple. If the hammer falls at an angle, striking the corner of a cap, the chance of a hangfire or misfire is greatly increased. You want the hammer striking the nipple full-force, sending its entire charge into the breech.

Just like flint is the key to ignition with a flintlock system, the cap is the key to the percussion system. Most percussion muzzleloaders these days take a standard No. 11 cap, but not all caps are created equal. There is considerable variation in cap size from brand to brand even though all may state they are No. 11. It may take some experimentation with different brands, but the best cap is one that fits snugly, not tightly, over the nipple on your particular muzzleloader. Too loose and it may dislodge while hunting, too tight, it may be difficult to seat or even become damaged while trying to seat it on the nipple. If a particular brand fits loosely, try a different brand, change nipples, or try one of the cap grippers mentioned earlier.

Caps also vary in construction. Some cap bodies are ribbed, others are smooth. Both work equally well and the choice personal. By the same token, some caps are rather brittle and actually fragment upon firing. Others have a tendency to smash or flatten against the nipple and either fall away following impact or can be physically removed. Both seem to work well, but considering the relatively close distance between the aiming eye and the cap on ignition and the possibility of flying fragments, I prefer the latter type. Experimentation will let you find your favorite.

Besides varying in size, caps also vary in intensity between brands. Most deliver around 3000 degrees Fahrenheit into the breech area, but economy caps generally deliver less, still enough to ignite the main charge but not with the same zip as the better quality brands. Stick with the better brands. They are more consistent, provide plenty of controlled yet sustained spark and have proven themselves time and time again. In the majority of hunting situations they are all that is needed. Some caps, however, are advertised as being "hot." In other words they deliver more spark. Years ago when they first came on the scene these hot caps delivered more spark than necessary and actually caused pieces of shrapnel to fly upon impact. At times, this flying debris clogged the nipple which often caused a misfire or hangfire. Today hot caps have been greatly improved, and though they are a bit more forceful they provide great reliability and consistency. Here again, the shooter must experiment to determine if they are actually needed. Over the years, the standard caps offered by Dynamite Noble have served me well in all types of hunting situations and weather conditions, provided my muzzleloader was properly maintained, clean, and dry. Even with an in-line I seldom use anything else.

It should be kept in mind that percussion caps are small explosive devices. Originally, fulminating mercury was used for ignition but instability and deterioration were problematic. The invention of the Sinoxid priming compound in 1926 completely revolutionized the ignition process by replacing the old fulminate of mercury with organic substances trycinate and tetranzene. The oxidizing agents borium nitrate and lead dioxide together with sulfer antimony and calcium silicide were later added to provide a highly combustible, smooth-burning mixture with anticorrosive properties. This is the basis for all standard percussion caps and primers used in muzzleloading today, but they remain sensitive to blows and heat so some common sense is called for during use and storage. Keep them away from children and away from heat. They are best stored in their original tins in a locked area such as a gun cabinet or out of reach. When hunting, they are more conveniently carried in "cappers." Several types are available. Modern in-lines require an in-line capper, while side-lock percussion muzzleloaders take the magazine type. I own several of each. The sidelock cappers are made of plastic which reduces the chance of a mishap, and are basically a round tin that holds extra caps. Five fingers extend outward, each of which holds a cap. To reload, one of these fingers is simply placed over the nipple, and when removed the cap remains in place on the nipple. It is a fast way to reload, especially when excited or during cold temperatures. I carry mine around my neck on a thong for easy access. The plastic is light, resistant to weather, and quiet, a key factor when hunting game.

The nipple on a percussion system is also important. There are several designs and the hunter will have to do some testing to see which is preferred. Some nipples have a large channel or orifice from base to cone, others have a smaller pinhole, while some, often called "hot" nipples, have an orifice that tapers to help provide a more concentrated and consistent flow of pressurized gases to the breech. Some also have a small port near the cone to help vent excess gas, which prevents hammer blow back. Hot nipples such as Thompson/Center's Hot Shot Nipple and CVA's Perfect Nipple are designed for most sidelock ignition systems but not recommended for under-hammer rifles nor all sidelock systems. The T/C Hot Shot Nipple, for example, should not be used on their Scout, Cherokee, and Seneca muzzleloaders. Check your owner's manual. If it fails to state whether a hot nipple can be used, contact a reputable dealer or the manufacturer. Most hot nipples are made of stainless steel which makes them somewhat more resistant to harsh weather. They also seem to wear longer.

Several of my muzzleloaders are equipped with hot nipples, and I generally like them, particularly for hunting in cold, wet conditions. They seem to deliver a more consistent spark and have proven themselves reliable. There have been times, however, when I have wondered whether they are actually needed. Of the standard types, those with a small pinhole orifice and flat base rather than large straight through channel—when clean and dry—seem to channel gas into the breech just as well as hot nipples in my opinion. They do seem to clog faster due to the small channel, but proper cleaning takes care of the problem. The point is, when properly maintained and in good condition the nipple design that comes on your muzzleloader should work well and should not be replaced unless problems dictate otherwise.

There will come a time, however, when all nipples must be replaced. It is not uncommon for nipples to flare or mushroom at the cone after extended use, making it difficult to properly and easily seat caps. Some even become difficult to clean, particularly the fire channel and base. Always examine the nipple before the hunting season begins. If a replacement is needed, make sure to purchase a nipple with the correct thread. The most common is the ¼ × 28 thread, but others exist.

THE IN-LINE IGNITION SYSTEM

When it comes to ignition speed in muzzleloaders nothing beats the modern in-line. A centerfire rifle fires in a millisecond and the in-line is not much slower. Once the trigger is pulled ignition takes place. Unlike the flintlock and sidelock system, there is no delay, no hesitation. The in-line offers the closest thing to instantaneous ignition the hunter can get with a muzzleloader.

The reason for this is the simple genius of its design. The projectile and propellent, the firing mechanism, nipple, and cap are "in line," as the name implies. As already explained, the flintlock has an obvious delay because the primer charge must ignite first and send sparks through the blow-hole into the breech. Spark on a percussion design must travel the length of the nipple, turn 90 degrees, travel through the bolster, and then into the breech. Because the spark is more concentrated and better controlled main ignition is faster, but the distance the spark must travel still results in a slight delay, although hardly noticeable.

With the in-line system, however, the nipple is screwed directly into the breech, directly behind or "in line" with the main powder charge and fires

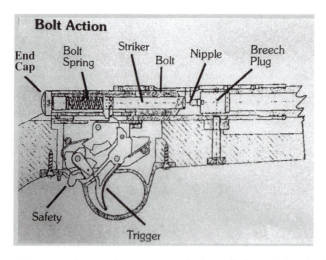

The in-line gets its name because hammer, cap, nipple, and charge and projectile are "in line." Spark from the cap flies directly into the breech which results in fast, very reliable ignition.

spark from the ignition cap straight forward. Equally important, the distance between percussion cap and main powder charge is relatively short. Combined, these two factors help create a quick lock time and shorten ignition time of the main charge.

On plunger-type in-lines the distance the entire plunger must travel once the trigger is pulled, or stroke, is also rather short, from one-half of an inch to three-quarters of an inch from cocked position to cap, depending upon the manufacturer. On bolt-action designs, which came along later and greatly resemble conventional bolt-action firearms in appearance, the smaller, lighter firing pin-type mechanism sits even closer to the cap when cocked, about one-quarter of an inch on most models. The intent here is to shorten the length of stroke and to increase ignition speed even more, which the bolt action in-line does.

All this contributes to the in-line's fast, reliable ignition. For the big game hunter little concerned with the history of the sport, the in-line is the best thing going. As noted earlier, ignition speed in muzzleloading is everything and can mean the difference between bringing home game or not. I own several in-lines. I like them and use them, although not exclusively. Purchasing an in-line is a personal decision, but they certainly have their advantages.

As a hunter and muzzleloading enthusiast, the only problems I have with the in-line design are the common misconceptions about them. They are

In-line ignitions operate with a plunger which is pushed forward by a powerful spring, such as on the T/C FireHawk (top). The CVA HunterBolt operates with a bolt.

easy to clean and maintain and are extremly reliable and efficient. These are wonderful firearms to shoot and hunt with, but it is important to understand them and not take everything you hear about the in-line as gospel.

For example, it is commonly believed that because the in-line receives spark and is ignited from the rear rather than off to the side as with sidelock systems it is more powerful. Not true. Because both blackpowder and Pyrodex burn at relatively slow, predictable rates starting with the first kernel of powder the flame's physical point of entry has no bearing whatsoever on downrange power. There may be a difference in ignition reliability and lock time, but downrange energy is determined by bullet weight not by how fast powder burns in the breech.

Most in-lines also fire using a standard No. 11 percussion cap, the same caps used on a sidelock percussion muzzleloader. Recently, however, so-called "3-way" ignition systems have become popular. This basically means one rifle can be equipped with a standard No. 11 cap, Musket caps, or 209 shotgun primers simply by changing the nipple and breech system. Thompson/Center's Black Diamond in-line and CVA's FireBolt MusketMag series and HunterBolt MusketMag series all accommodate three different sizes of caps. The idea came along when builders started offering "magnum" muzzleloaders capable of handling 150 grains of powder for the purpose of firing heavy loads at greater

Many modern in-lines are designed to accommodate three different caps: The No. 11 cap for standard loads, and the Musket cap and 209 shotgun primer for heavy or "magnum" loads.

range and achieving increased velocities with light bullets. The larger, hotter caps were simply intended to help ignite the heavier 150-grain loads.

But we already know blackpowder and Pyrodex starts to burn and create explosive gases once the first kernel is lit. We also know they ignite at relatively low temperature, far less than the 3,000 degrees delivered by a standard No. 11 cap, and burn at a slow, predictable rate regardless of the temperature that ignites them. The misconception here is that a 209 shotgun primer burns at about 3,024 degrees, not much more than a standard No. 11 cap. So why the need for the centerfire primer? The answer is to generate more gas. As noted, the standard No. 11 cap and 209 shotgun primer burn at about the same temperature but the latter throws about 15 percent more flame which results in better consumption of heavy hunting charges and improved ballistics. It also translates to more positive and even ignition with these heavy charges, but not faster ignition.

A higher volume of gas is irrelevant unless it can reach the main charge, and this is determined by the size of the channel through the nipple and the length of the breech plug. Because the 209 shotgun primer and Musket caps throw more flame and generate more gas, "magnum" in-line makers have been moving towards larger nipples with bigger channels and shorter plugs to allow more to reach the main load.

And what about those 150-grain loads? Do they provide increased bullet speed and performance for hunting purposes? There is a great deal of misleading information out there. Even though a heavy charge will increase muzzle velocity to over 2,200 fps and propel a projectile farther downrange, to reach such velocity light projectiles of around 240-grain are required. These light pistol bullet-sabot combinations are not designed for such high velocities, and at that speed accuracy suffers. A muzzle velocity of around 1800 fps is far better, which means a lighter charge with these light projectiles. These light bullets also shed velocity quickly and in doing so often fail to deliver sufficient energy to reliably and humanely down big game at long range. Accuracy must be maintained, and keep in mind that energy on impact, not speed, kills game.

Also, remember that because of its slow burn rate a charge of blackpowder or Pyrodex needs a definite amount of time to thoroughly burn. Even with the bigger flame from a 209 primer or Musket cap there is some doubt whether the entire 150-grain charge fully burns. Personal tests indicate it doesn't, resulting in more fouling, more muzzle flash, and diminished accuracy. The hunter will have to decide through personal testing whether "magnum" charges are actually beneficial. Based on my own hunting experiences, I have my doubts.

And are in-lines more powerful and accurate than sidelock ignition systems? Here again there is a great deal of misleading information. In-line barrels have a fast rate of barrel twist which is designed to shoot conical and saboted pistol bullets. These bullets have a better aerodynamic design than projectiles with a blunt profile. They slice through the atmosphere better. Because of this, they are quite accurate, but no more than the roundball within normal muzzle-loading range, say out to 100 yards. And power? The jacketed pistol bullet, and conical, normally fired from in-lines have plenty of it, not due to ignition design, but bullet density. The .490 roundball weighs about 188 grains. Many of the bullets fired from in-lines weigh 250 grains or more. Because they are heavier they simply hit with more energy. This is also true because the conical and jacketed bullets retain energy better. In other words, they carry their full weight

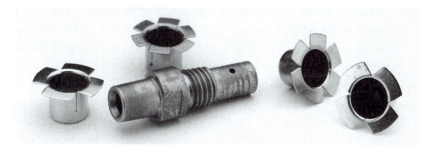

Large nipples are required for Musket caps. These nipples are supplied with each muzzle-loader designed for three-way ignition.

Replacement nipples designed to increase spark to the main charge are available for in-lines. This increase, ignition speed and makes ignition more reliable. This Flame Thrower Nipple from Thompson/Center is one example. It is said to deliver three times the spark to the main charge.

or energy farther downrange. The roundball may lose half its energy around the 50-yard mark, but conicals and saboted pistol bullets retain much of their energy all the way to the target out to 100 or 120 yards. It has very little to do with ignition. Put the same bullet in an in-line and sidelock muzzleloader, with comparable barrels, and you'll get similiar results downrange.

In-line muzzleloaders are capped the same way as sidelock models, by placing a percussion cap on the nipple. The only difference is an in-line-type capper is used. This is basically a straight capping device that fits nicely between bolt or plunger and nipple. Many standard cappers designed for sidelock systems are either too short or wide to fit. Various in-line cappers are now available for standard No. 11 caps, shotguns primers, and Musket caps.

Over the years, the muzzleloader ignition system has continued to evolve. The same is true with the in-line system. We now have the "disc" rifle, a brainchild of Tony Knight of Knight Muzzleloading fame, the same guy who helped usher in the in-line revolution.

The Knight DISC Rifle is an in-line through and through and is still fired using a cap but eliminates the need for a nipple and related capping and decapping tools. Caps are held by a plastic disc which can accommodate either standard No. 11 caps or 209 shotgun primers. Basically, all the hunter has to do before heading into the woods is insert some caps into the disc. When ready to start hunting the bolt-action is cocked and the disc is quickly inserted in front of the firing hammer. To unload, the bolt is uncocked and the disc is removed. If the rifle is not fired the disc and cap can be reinserted and used again. It is extremely fast, convenient, and safe. Currently, the disc system is available on a number of Knight rifles, including the Knight Master Hunter which offers a 24- or 26-inch barrel with 1:28 twist, dual safety, metallic fiber optic sights, Magnum Cross Fire Breech plug which is said to improve velocity by as much as 25 fps, laminated wood thumbhole stock, fluted barrel, and engraved trigger guard.

5

PROPELLANTS

Before discussing muzzleloading propellants two things must be clearly understood. All muzzleloaders, whether flintlock, percussion, or in-line design are intended *only* for blackpowder or blackpowder substitutes such as Pyrodex. It may sound redundant but smokeless powders should *never* be used. This is clearly stated in every owner's manual and should be strictly adhered to. Smokeless powders generate far more pressure upon ignition than blackpowder and even today's high quality muzzleloaders simply are not designed to handle it.

The other important thing to remember is to never exceed the maximum powder charge recommended by the manufacturer. Again, safety is the reason. Each muzzleloader is designed to withstand only so much pressure. To provide a margin for error that limit is generally higher than what is recommended, but to exceed the manufacturer's limit is to court disaster. Barrels have actually blown apart and injured shooters pushing the limit. Never do it. From a shooting or hunting perspective it is never necessary to do so, anyway.

The most popular projectiles these days deliver sufficient muzzle velocity and energy to dispatch big game when pushed by a charge well under the maximum recommended limit.

BLACKPOWDER

Of the propellents used in muzzleloaders blackpowder is the oldest and most traditional. Blackpowder is not a chemical compound, but rather a mechanical mixture of potassium nitrate, also known as saltpeter, charcoal, and sulfur. Saltpeter acts as the oxidizer, giving the mixture its energy, and comprises about 75 percent of the ratio. Charcoal makes up some 15 percent of the mixture and serves as the body, while sulfur makes up 10 percent, binding it all together, and helping to maintain integrity.

It has been estimated that only about 50 percent of this mixture actually burns on ignition. The rest either goes out the muzzle or stays behind as residue. This is why fouling occurs and cleaning is so important. In cases where too much powder is used, such as exceeding the manufacturer's maximum limit, blackpowder that fails to burn can actually become an obstruction with possible hazardous results. Blackpowder is relatively easy to ignite at about 600 degrees Fahrenheit but is sensitive to open flame, sparks, friction, and impact. For this reason it is regulated as a Class A explosive and should be handled with great care. When stored properly—in sealed containers in a cool, dry location—blackpowder will last almost indefinitely.

Blackpowder is available from just two sources in this country. The oldest domestic supplier is Goex. Their product has been around since 1912, although at that time it was produced by the E.I. Dupont de Nemours Company at its Berlin, Pennsylvania plant. In 1970 Dupont ceased manufacturing blackpowder and eventually the Berlin plant became part of Goex, Inc. Today, the Berlin plant is the only blackpowder facility in North America. The other available blackpowder brand is Elephant Blackpowder. It is produced in Brazil and imported and distributed nationally by Petro-Explo out of Arlington, Texas. Elephant Blackpowder has been produced continually since 1866.

Are both blackpowders the same? The answer is yes and no. Both contain the same basic ingredients and ratio of saltpeter, charcoal, and sulfer, are easy to ignite, and burn relatively slowly and at consistent rates. However, Elephant is different in one regard. It has an extremely low sulfate content in the

GOEX is the only blackpowder currently manufactured in the United States. It has been available since 1912.

potassium nitrate brought on by a longer milling process. This brings about low acidity in the powder. Elephant Blackpowder also has a more glazed appearance. The end result is reduced bore pressure and slightly slower velocities. Does this make Elephant inferior? Not necessarily. In fact, velocities are quite consistent with little standard devation, which translates to excellent accuracy and more than enough pressure for dispatching big game. Fired from the same muzzleloader, the competitive paper puncher or ballistic enthusiast using a chronograph is likely to detect a difference, but the hunter should experience hardly any at all. Both are excellent propellents with a long history of good performance and reliability.

Goex Blackpowder and Elephant Blackpowder are available in different grades or various size grain. Both are graded using an "F" system, which represents the size of each grain. For example four F, written FFFFg is the smallest most common granulation, although Elephant Brand offers a five F grade (FFFFFg). Both are generally used for priming flintlock rifles. This is followed by three F (FFFg), two F (FFg) and one F (Fg). For big game hunting many blackpowder users carrying a .45-, .50- or .54-caliber muzzleloader seem to prefer FFg since it provides good velocity, with modest pressures and good power from these calibers with hunting loads. FFFg is also used, but it should be remembered that the smaller the grain the faster it burns. Faster ignition and less fouling might be the result with FFFg but pressure is also lost. This is another

Elephant Brand blackpowder is imported from Brazil. It is available in all popular granulations and is an excellent propellent.

area where some testing and experimentation is called for, but for the three most popular big game calibers pushing heavy loads FFg is a good place to start. Fg blackpowder is best used in shotguns and big bore rifles of .60 caliber and larger.

For big game hunting, blackpowder is a wonderful propellent. There is absolutely nothing wrong with it. It has been used for centuries and because of its historical base remains popular today, particularly among flintlock and sidelock percussion fans. Blackpowder provides consistent burn rates and bullet velocity, is reliable, does not require firm ramrod pressure to provide consistent or optimum performance, is safe to use and carry when handled properly, and has a long shelf life when stored in a cool, dry place. I use it all the time for hunting and target shooting and it has served me well.

One of the most often heard complaints about blackpowder is that it is a dirty propellent with corrosive properties. This basically means more fouling occurs, and a muzzleloader must be cleaned more often between shots. This is true. As noted earlier this happens because not all blackpowder ingredients turn from solid to gas upon ignition and do not completely burn. This is also one reason for all that smoke! Substitute propellents that burn cleaner, require less swabbing between shots, and provide easier cleaning after use have become increasingly popular.

One such example is Clear Shot, introduced by Goex in 1998. Call it blackpowder replica or blackpowder substitute, but after personal testing on the

Clear Shot is a new non-corrosive propellent from Goex. Designed to allow more shots between swabbing, it is available in all popular granulations.

range and in the field Clear Shot seems to display all the best characteristics of blackpowder and other substitute propellants. It is non corrosive and non-hygroscopic, which means it does not pick up moisture in high humidity or temperature variations. Although I have yet to test its ballistics by any scientific means, in the field it seems to offer consistent velocities with hunting loads, and Goex states it offers low pressure, generating no greater pressure than other replicas blackpowder propellants or blackpowder. Clear Shot is 1.3C (Class B) rated by the Department of Transportation, which means it can be shipped and stored like smokeless powder. It also cleans up well with water or solvents.

BLACKPOWDER RULES

- Blackpowder is extremely flammable and explosive. Keep away from heat, sparks, and open flame.
- Sporting blackpowder must be used *only* in blackpowder firearms. Its use for any other purpose is hazardous and not recommended.
- Keep blackpowder away from children.
- Prevent contact with food and smoking material.
- Keep containers tightly closed when not in use.
- Wash hands thoroughly after handling.
- Do not mix blackpowder brands or blackpowder substitutes.

- Do not repackage or purchase or use blackpowder not in its original container.
- Do not dispense blackpowder directly from container into firearm.
- Do not dispense a substantial amount of blackpowder in close proximity to firearm.
- Do not take internally. In the event of ingestion call a physician or poison control center.
- Always store in a cool, dry place. Store in original container.
- Obey all laws and regulations regarding quanitities of explosive and methods of storage.
- Never exceed manufacturer's maximum load recommedation.
- If disposal is necessary, blackpowder must be disposed of in accordance with local, state, and federal laws and regulations. Consult manufacturer for more details.
- Do not dispose of blackpowder container in a fire.
- When loading blackpowder, use only approved loading methods and loading data.
- Use common sense when handling blackpowder.

Note: These same precautions should also apply to all blackpowder substitutes.

PYRODEX

Pyrodex is the brainchild of Dan Pawlak. Although Pawlak's college training was in other fields, he was self-taught in the intricacies of explosives and pyrotechnics and held several patents in the field. In the early 1970's, while working in the movie, fireworks and other related industries, Pawlak grew increasingly dissatisfied with the dangers and performance of blackpowder and became convinced a substitute could be developed. Pawlak eventually teamed up with Mike Levenson, a young man also well versed in explosives, and the two set to work.

Two years later the team developed a propellant light gray in color. It offered less bulk than blackpowder, and though it offered the same basic pressure/time curve characteristics of blackpowder, it lacked many other desired traits. It was at this point the name "Pyrodex" was selected, and though Pawlak and Levenson had more work to do, both were convinced they were on the right track.

In 1974, Pawlak had finally developed a propellant with the same burning characteristics and density of blackpowder. It also offered consistent pressure/time curves but one problem remained. Fouling was excessive which caused ignition problems making it necessary to clean test barrels after every shot. Finally, following months of additional testing and modifications the formula neared completion. Fouling had been reduced well below blackpowder which meant more shots could be taken between cleaning, something Pyrodex remains famous and popular for to this day. The final formula provided consistent shot-to-shot pressure and velocities, and smoke characteristics were adjusted to compare with blackpowder. Ingredients were also added to give Pyrodex the same order once ignited. The color was also changed from gray to black, giving Pyrodex the same appearance of blackpowder. In essence, Pyrodex as we know it today was born and it was first sold to the public in May of 1976. Since then it has been manufactured and sold by the Hodgdon Powder Company of Shawnee Mission, Kansas and is undoubtedly the most popular and widely available blackpowder substitute on the market today.

The wonderful thing about this stuff is that it offers certain familiar attributes of blackpowder. It delievers lots of smoke, cleaning is easy after use, and it can be used volume for volume with blackpowder. In other words, if the proper powder charge for a particular muzzleloader is 80 grains of FFg blackpowder, 80 grains of Pyrodex RS can be used instead without sacrificing ballistic results. Use the same powder measure for Pyrodex that you use for blackpowder. The Pyrodex load will weigh considerably less because Pyrodex is less dense, but for all practical purposes ballistic results will be about the same. Always remember, Pyrodex is measured out by volume, like blackpowder, *not* weight.

Other similarities exists between blackpowder and Pyrodex. Even though Pyrodex has a higher ignition temperature than blackpowder, approximately 730 degrees, consistent ignition can be expected with standard No. 11 percussion caps on both sidelock and in-line ignition systems. Pyrodex does ignite a bit less quickly than blackpowder, and—all guns not being equal—an ignition problem might present itself. If so, replacing the nipple with a nipple designed for modern primers might be the answer. Because of its higher ignition temperature, Pyrodex is rated as a 1.3 Class C solid propellent, the same as smokeless powders, which means it requires a different and less stringent set of shipping and handling standards. Pyrodex can also be used with modern

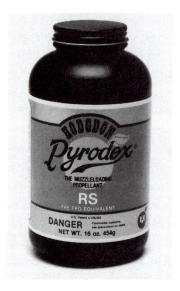

Pyrodex is a popular blackpowder substitute. It is measured by volume just like blackpowder but is rated differently. The RS stands for rifle/shotgun and is the best grade for muzzleloading rifles of .50-caliber and larger.

lubes and cleaning solvents. In many ways, Pyrodex acts like blackpowder, with the same basic ingredients as blackpowder.

But Pyrodex is not actually blackpowder, and there are differences between the two propellents. For example, Pyrodex is a much cleaner burning fuel. The hunter is generally afforded just one shot, but even on the target range I have obtained as many as a dozen shots with Pyrodex before swabbing or cleaning was necessary. This is unheard of with blackpowder. This does not mean, however, that thorough cleaning is not necessary with Pyrodex. It is.

Because it is less dense and slightly more efficient Pyrodex will also provide more shots per pound than blackpowder. In his great book, *Blackpowder Loading Manual* (3rd edition), muzzleloading guru Sam Fadala writes, "Pyrodex yields 93 shots with the powder measure set at 100, while blackpowder yields 70 shots with the powder measure set at 100." I have never actually conducted a similar test, but I trust Sam and his findings.

Like blackpowder, Pyrodex is available in various granulations but has its own designation system. Instead of the familiar Fg system used with blackpowder, Pyrodex uses a more simplified letter system. "P" stands for Pistol, which means its fine granulation is best used in pistols and revolvers. It is equivalent to FFg blackpowder. For this reason it can be used in small-bore rifles such as the .32 caliber and .36 caliber with their typically light powder charges. It can also be used in some large calibers when lightly loaded for small game, but for big game it should be avoided. Pyrodex CTG stands for Cartridge. Because we are primarily concerned here with sidelock percussion and flintlock muzzle-loaders and in-lines, it is sufficient to say Pyrodex CTG is of little interest. There was a time when Hodgdon considered dropping CTG from the line, so the day may come when CTG will no longer be available.

Pyrodex RS is what we are looking for when it comes to big game hunting with medium and heavy powder charges. The RS stands for Rifle/Shotgun. Because it has a medium-sized grain, or kernel, and is equivalent to FFg, RS works well in calibers from .32 to .58 and larger. For those involved in black-powder shotgunning, RS also performs well in shotguns from 28- to 10-gauge.

For years the RS grade was the backbone of the Pyrodex line and remains so today, but RS Select is becoming popular. This is basically a premium grade RS designed to provide better performance for those who want to take things to a higher level. In the Select grade kernel size is more uniform. This affects burn rate which in turn affects how much energy the powder charge delivers. Because Select is equivalent to FFg, rather fine to begin with, and each grain is about the same size, it burns quickly, providing slightly higher energy yields from the charge.

From a hunting perspective each hunter will have to determine whether this slight increase is needed. I have used Pyrodex RS for both paper punching and hunting for years and have found its consistency, burn rate, and energy yield more than sufficient to dispatch game. While I have also used Pyrodex Select from time to time with good results, its advantages in the field were hardly noticeable and the RS grade remains my primary propellent.

Pyrodex differs from blackpowder in other ways, as well. For example, because of its higher flame point or ignition rate it is not generally recommended as a primer for flintlocks. Pyrodex RS is okay as a main charge but even then many flintlockers who go this route, prefer a small amount of FFg downbore first to help ensure and speed ignition. The problem with this when hunting is several propellents have to be carried. A standard FFFFg for priming, FFg next to the touch-hole, followed by Pyrodex for the main charge. Hodgdon says one grade can be eliminated by using a small amount of FFFFg instead of FFg as a kicker. FFFFg is used as a primer anyway and advocates of this method claim it works well ahead of Pyrodex. Do your own experiments prior to the hunting season. If slower ignition is the result, sticking with blackpowder in both pan and breech might be a better choice.

Pyrodex is also available in pellet form. These handy, pre-formed solid charges have all but eliminated the need for a powder horn or flask and because each is nearly exact in volume they provide good consistency and have become extremely popular. Tests both at the range and under hunting conditions have shown Pyrodex pellets are everything they are cracked up to be. They ignite well and provide plenty of muzzle velocity. Overall ballistics were extremely consistent. Because they simply drop down the barrel, reloading time is also decreased. It is important, however, to read the instructions that come in each case before using Pyrodex pellets.

Note, for example, Pyrodex pellets were designed for use only in newly manufactured in-lines of .50- and .54-caliber loaded with a saboted bullet or a conical bullet in conjunction with a fiber wad. Use in sidelock rifles, whether of the percussion or flintlock design regardless of projectile type is not recommended. As Hodgdon puts it: "Due to variations in the size and type of flash channels of such rifles, as well as different rifle bore diameters and conical bullet sizes, hangfires or an improper gas seal of the projectile may occur. These conditions could cause the projectile or a burning pellet particle to exit the barrel in a hazardous manner." Pyrodex pellets should also not be used in Thompson/Center Scout rifles and pistols.

Note that each pellet contains a black ignitor on one end. This is actually inpregnated blackpowder and for best ignition the ignitor end should face the nipple. More important is Hodgdon's maximum load warning. Even

Pyrodex is available in pellet form. It is intended only for in-line ignition systems and comes in different calibers and different granular sizes.

though some magnum in-line manufacturers recommend the use of a number of pellets, some up to 150 grains, Hodgdon specifically disclaims such practice. According to Hodgdon, exceeding their 100-grain maximum load recommendation for .50-caliber muzzleloaders and 120-grain maximum load for .54-caliber muzzleloaders may generate excessive pressure and cause damage to the firearm as well as personal injury.

Originally, Pyrodex pellets were available in just three sizes. Pellets for .50-caliber muzzleloaders come in 50-grain volume equivalent which equates to 50 grains of granular powder by volume and in 30-grain volume equivalent which equates to 30 grains of granular powder by volume. Pellets for .54-caliber muzzleloaders are available only in 60-grain volume equivalent which equals 60 grains of granular powder by volume. In 2001, however, Hodgdon also introduced a 45-caliber 50-grain pellet to complete the list. Keeping this in mind. Hodgdon's recommended maximum .50-caliber load should never exceed three 30-grain pellets, two 50-grain pellets, or one 50-grain pellet and one 30-grain pellet. The maximum .54-caliber load should never exceed two 60-grain pellets. The recommended load for to 45-caliber, 50-grain pellet is one pellet for target shooting and two pellets for hunting. If the manufacturer of your particular in-line muzzleloader has a higher maximum load limit, the decision is yours. Just know that Hodgdon recommends against it.

As mentioned previously, Hodgdon also recommends Pyrodex pellets be used only with sabots and conical bullets with fiber wads. Generally, it is recommended that sabots in .50-caliber rifles utilize .45-caliber bullets and .54-caliber rifles select a sabot that accommodates a .50-caliber bullet. The most successfull sabots, those producing the most consistent velocity and best accuracy, according to Hodgdon, are one-piece and utilize the largest diameter bullet possible for the rifle caliber. The reason for this is that some sabots still on the market were designed several years ago for use with 70-grain to 90-grain granular powder. These sabots may or may not funtion properly when used with the more "energetic" pellets, due in part to the materials used, the overall design of these early sabots, and the large variation in bore diameter, depth, and width, or rifling, and smoothness from rifle to rifle.

As for conical bullets, they may be used with Pyrodex pellets, but to insure successfull performance a fiber wad *must* be used between the pellet(s) and the base of the conical. The wad will provide an adequate gas seal preventing gas from escaping around the bullet. Failure to use a wad may result in excessive leading of the bore, poor accuracy, low velocity, and the possibility of launching a flaming pellet downrange. Fiber wads are available commercially at sporting goods stores and gun shops nationwide and are generally lubricated with a natural lube which assists in creating the gas seal and helps keeps fouling soft and easy to clean. Thompson/Center's Bore Button and Ox-Yoke Orginals' Wonder Wads are two examples.

All this and more is clearly spelled out in the "Warning and Instructions For Use" pamphlet which comes inside each Pyrodex pellets box. As Pyrodex pellets are still relatively new at the time of this writing and users still have questions about them; it is important they be used properly, like all propellents. Read the instructions and follow them. When used properly within Hodgdon's recommended guidelines, these are a handy, reliable, efficient asset to every big game hunter using an in-line.

There are a great many questions surrounding blackpowder and Pyrodex. Which is more corrosive? Which creates more bullet velocity or has a more consistent burn rate? Which is cleaner? Surprising, perhaps, but both are quite similiar. Both perform extremely well under hunting conditions and have done so for years. The best choice for individual hunters is entirely personal.

One other propellent must be mentioned here: Black Canyon. Like Pyrodex, Black Canyon Powder is considered a blackpowder substitute, but with a twist. It is non-sulfurous and therefore non-corrosive. Although bore cleaning is still recommended after shooting it can be done easily with a patch dampened with solvent. The use of water is not recommended. I must honestly state that I have not used Black Canyon Powder to any great extent. For years I have used either blackpowder or Pyrodex and both have served me well. I have conducted no conclusive tests, with Black Canyon but apparently any powder left behind acts as a bore conditioner.

Unlike blackpowder and Pyrodex, Black Canyon Powder is not size graded. It has a large kernel size and should be loaded by weight, not volume. However, because it is 25 percent less dense than blackpowder it can safely be loaded by volume simply by using 25 percent more Black Canyon than either FFg blackpowder or Pyrodex RS. In other words, if you currently shoot a 100-grain charge of blackpowder or Pyrodex, use a 125-grain charge of Black Canyon. Read the manufacturer's warning and instruction label carefully.

One other note, to obtain optimum performance with Black Canyon firm ramrod pressure is recommended. It simply burns better when firmly packed.

6

PROJECTILES AND BARRELS

Walk into a gun shop or pick up a catalog from Cabela's, Dixie Gun Works, Mountain State Muzzleloading, the Log Cabin Shop, or any outlet that sells muzzleloaders and supplies and start looking at muzzleloading bullets—it quickly becomes apparent that there are a great many to choose from. There is the roundball and conicals of various weight and configuration, and then there are sabots and jacketed pistols, even sabots that shoot lead conicals and roundballs. The obvious question for many just getting into big game hunting with muzzleloaders is: Which is best?

The simple answer is the one that delivers sufficient punch to quickly kill the intended target. This means accurately enough and with enough energy to disrupt the nervous system or severely damage the circulatory system. The interesting thing is that each projectile just mentioned above will do just that. All of them! Each is accurate and packs lots of power, but within limits. Also, some perform better depending on their configuration and rifling twist in the barrel. As a hunter who has traveled afield with nothing but muzzleloaders for almost three decades and who has seen his share of big game in various situations, I have come to the conclusion that two basic things are important when selecting a projectile: Understanding what each design will and won't do, their limitations, and accepting the fact that no single design is correct for every muzzleloader or hunting situation.

This does not mean to suggest a host of different projectile types will be needed to handle various hunting situations. It is possible to find a happy and effective middle ground. The basis for that middle ground should be power, how much energy is delivered. It seems many hunters these days are concerned with high muzzle velocity, how fast it takes a bullet to reach the target. If my average shot is around 100 yards I don't care whether a roundball impacts a split-second slower than a conical. What I am concerned about is making sure that whitetail, elk, caribou, or black bear gets hit with sufficient energy to put it down and keep it down. That depends a great deal on where the bullet hits but also on bullet weight, a projectile's cohesiveness, or how well it holds together upon impact, and how much energy it retains and delivers downrange. Projectile penetration is influenced by speed as are range and trajectory, but it is energy that kills game.

When it comes to discussing projectiles it helps, in the beginning, to keep things simple. It can quickly get technical discussing sectional density, ballistic coefficiency, trajectory, concentricity, and the like, and though these topics will be mentioned as we take a closer look at each bullet type, there is no need to dwell on them. The aim here is to get a good picture of what each bullet design has to offer the big game hunter, what works and why. What counts is the end result, which to this hunter means accurate shots, humane kills, and meat in the freezer.

THE ROUNDBALL

Let me first say that there is absolutely nothing wrong with the roundball for hunting big game. Although not as popular as they once were, a good deal of meat has been hung on the pole because of these small spheres. In the right muzzleloader, and within accepted range limits, they are as deadly as any muzzleloader bullet out there. I took my very first black bear, whitetail, caribou, and moose with the roundball, as well as several other big game species, and they have performed well, in some situations better than a conical might have. De-

The name Hornady is one of the best when it comes to muzzleloading projectiles. Shown here are Hornady's saboted XTP bullet, Great Plains Bullet, and roundballs.

pending upon the charge and caliber, roundballs fly from the muzzle up to 2000 fps and therefore offer a flat trajectory under 100 yards. They hold together well during flight and mushroom to nearly twice their diameter upon impact, creating a proper wound channel. Roundballs also release energy inside the animal, producing excellent hydrostatic shock. I have complete faith in them.

When considering the roundball for big game, however, it is important to keep some things in mind. A muzzleloader designed to shoot roundballs is required. Because the roundball is a sphere, slides down the barrel at good speed, and is relatively light in weight, not a lot of spin is required to stabilize it in flight. In fact, too much spin could seriously effect accuracy. To keep spin within desired tolerances and to maintain accuracy, a slow rate of twist, or slow rifling, is used in the barrel.

The Hawken brothers rifled all the barrels in their famous guns with a 1:48 twist because it was the standard twist at the time. In their day these frontloaders took lots of game but at a relatively slow muzzle velocity of around 1400 fps. When non-replica sidelock muzzleloaders starting getting popular back in the early 1970s hunters wanted something faster but still accurate. The problem was that as roundball muzzle velocity increases accuracy suffers. To compensate and to maintain proper spin on the ball manufacturers came out with even slower rates of twist in the barrel. Today, the popular Thompson/Center Pennsylvania Hunter, CVA Mountain Rifle, and the Navy Arms Ithaca Hawken all have a 1:66 barrel twist. Lyman's wonderful Great Plains Rifle has a 1:60 twist. All are specifically designed to shoot the roundball. The same is true of other muzzleloaders with the same rate of twist.

One aspect of many roundball guns which is quickly noticeable is a longer barrel. It is not unusual for the roundball shooter to carry a 28-inch or

30-inch barrel. My Lyman Great Plains Rifle is stocked with a 32-inch barrel. Contrary to common belief barrel length does not dictate rifle twist, nor does barrel length have anything to do with bullet stabilization. But it does affect muzzle velocity. In the case of the roundball gun with its slow 1:60 or 1:66 twist, the projectile simply needs more time to accelerate before exiting the muzzle. Barrels designed to shoot conicals or sabots have a fast rate of twist, 1:32, 1:28, 1:22, even 1:20. Upon ignition of the main charge these projectiles increase speed very quickly so a shorter barrel is sufficient.

There is something else to think about when considering the purchase of a roundball shooter: depth of rifling. It effects accuracy. It is a common belief that the primary roll of a patch is to prevent gases from escaping around the ball, a form of gasket if you will. It definitely does, but the patch also serves a much greater roll; it grabs the rifling inside the barrel and upon ignition puts spin on the ball as it slides down the barrel. Without this spin or rotation the spherical roundball would be far less accurate. Quite simply, a patch can better grip deep rifling grooves, and therefore provide more spin, than shallow rifling grooves. The result is better accuracy downrange. On the better shooting roundball guns the cut rifling is typically .007 to as much as .014 inches deep. Keep in mind that the patch must be lubricated to reduce friction and soften fouling.

While on the subject of patches and roundballs, keep one other thing in mind, too. Patchs comes in various thicknesses to compensate for the under-sized ball. For example, the bore on a .50-caliber muzzleloader is .500 of an inch. Roundballs for the .50 can be .490 or .495. Thicker patches can be used to make up the difference, but in most cases accuracy will be better using a ball close to bore size and a thin patch, say a .495 roundball and .010 patch, rather than a thicker patch and smaller ball. Some shooting at the range will be needed to find out what works best, but this general rule often holds true.

As mentioned previously, the roundball offers several attributes which make it a good choice for big game. The fact that is has good muzzle velocity, flies flat, holds together well upon impact, and releases energy inside the animal are among those reasons. But the roundball is not perfect. Its biggest fault is low sectional density. Sectional density is the measurement of a projectile's mass in relationship to its diameter or length. In other words the more weight a bullet has in relation to its length or diameter the better it retains energy. Because the roundball is round, its sectional density is low. For the hunter after big game this means that the roundball slows down and sheds energy quickly. In fact, about

The muzzleloading hunter has a variety of projectiles to choose from. Shown here from left are the saboted pistol bullet, various lead conicals, and the patched roundball.

half its energy has been shed halfway to the target at 100 yards. It also means that the only way to increase kinetic energy is by increasing ball size.

This is important to know because it helps determine what caliber roundball gun is best for certain big game targets. Take a .50-caliber muzzle-loader shooting a .490 roundball. It weighs about 177 grains and leaves the muzzle at good speed, but at 100 yards its energy has been cut nearly in half to about 600 foot-pounds, depending upon the lead purity of the ball. This is just over the 500 minimum pounds of energy needed to humanely dispatch deer-size game. One hundred pounds of energy may sound like a lot, but when hunting game it is not much of a margin to play with. For this reason the .50 caliber is about the smallest roundball muzzleloader generally recommended for whitetails, mule deer, pronghorn, and big game of similiar size.

Now take a look at the .54 caliber shooting a .530 roundball. To begin with it weighs 225 grains, a full 48 grains more than the .50 caliber, .490 roundball. That is considerable. But what counts is the effect downrange. Even though the .54 caliber also sheds half its energy by the time it reaches 100 yards, it still slams into the target with about 1,000 foot pounds of energy, more than enough to dispatch deer-size game and elk, moose, caribou, and black bear which take about 750 to 800 foot pounds of energy to kill. While a lot of game has been taken with the smaller .50-caliber roundball gun, success often boils down to the shooter pulling the trigger and proper shot placement. When shooting a roundball at big game, the larger .54 caliber is a much better choice. If you really want some roundball energy, the large .58 or .60 caliber is even better, although it takes a considerable dose of powder to obtain reasonable velocities and trajectory.

Still, let's keep things in perspective. Neither the .50 or .54 can be considered good for long range shooting. They shed almost a third of their speed and about half their energy at 100 yards, with things dropping off rapidly after that. For this reason a 75-yard shot is considered long with these calibers. Ideally a roundball target should be under 60 yards.

One other thing should be mentioned about roundballs: There are several types available. Some are cast, others are swaged or cold formed, and though the cloth patch is most traditional they can be used with sabots and the "Poly-Patch" from Butler Creek. Because plastic seems to build up on the rifling and does little to soften fouling, many perfer the lubricated cloth patch. Of the swaged or cast types, I prefer the swaged. These balls are more uniform in roundness, weight, and size from ball to ball which helps out in the accuracy department, and they carry no air pockets, spruces or parting lines, making them easier to load.

Whatever type is used, however, only those of the purest lead should be used. Those from Hornady, Speer, Thompson/Center, or Buffalo Bullet are all free of antimony, tin, or non-lead agents. Upon ignition a roundball or lead conical bullet expands in the bore before exploding down the barrel. This is called obturation. Pure lead simply obturates better than those mixed with alloys, and this translates into better molecular cohesion, meaning they hold together better upon impact.

THE CONICAL

There are literally dozens, perhaps hundreds, of elongated projectiles designed for the muzzleloader. For a while it seemed a new one was coming out every day, each said to offer better ballistics, more energy or penetration upon impact, or some other attribute those before it lacked. It got confusing and even now selecting the right conical seems a chore compared to selecting a roundball. After all, the roundball is a sphere and comes in no other shape. To gain weight, caliber must be enlarged.

Not true with the conical. Because of their shape, mass can easily be added simply by making them longer. This means a particular caliber can accommodate bullets of different weights. A .50-caliber muzzleloader, for exam-

The Barne's Expander MZ bullet retains 100 percent of its original bullet weight while expanding at 1000 fps. Available in .50-caliber 250-grain and 300-grain and .54-caliber in 275-grain and 325-grain, the Expander MZ can handle deer-size game, as well as elk, moose, caribou, and bear.

ple can accurately fire a saboted .44-caliber jacketed bullet weighing 240 grains, or a solid lead Maxi tipping the scales at over 400 grains, or anything in between with enough energy to handle big game.

Conicals also come in different shapes. Some are flatnosed, pointed, or hollow-point. Some possess different style bases, flat or hollow. Some have long shanks, some short. Some have grooves for lubrication, others don't. Some are made of lead, others have a lead core and are jacketed with copper, while some modern conicals have no lead at all. Some are a combination of these variations. For example, the Hornady Great Plains Bullet has a hollow base like a Mini, but has a long shank with multiple grooves for lubrication and maximum bearing on the rifling like a Maxi. There is much cross-over in conical bullet design these days, but the important thing is they all work and work extremely well.

Sound confusing? It's not really. In the end it will take some time at the range and testing in the field to discover which you prefer for hunting big game. It does help to know, however, how these things work and why they perform the way they do. To help simplify things let's take a look at each design separately for the purpose of comparison, and then take a look at why they work.

THE MINI

This name is a bit deceiving, suggesting the Mini is smaller in weight or size than the Maxi or standard, but this is not necessarily true. It is call "Mini" because it is generally smaller than caliber size, not lighter in weight. Lyman offers a .54-caliber Mini that weighs a respectable 425 grains. It's one heck of a slug, one I have used successfully on caribou, elk, and bear.

But the Mini is slightly smaller than caliber. This allows it to be easily loaded even in a fouled bore. The concept here, however, is rather interesting. If the bullet is undersized, what prevents gases from escaping on ignition? The answer is the hollow base. Upon ignition of the main charge the thin wall of the base, or "skirt," expands outward against the bore. This presses the main body of the bullet, or "shank," against the rifling, creating a seal. In essence, the diameter of the Mini enlarges, and while it goes down the barrel smaller than bore it comes out larger than bore. The Mini is available with a hollow point or solid nose and typically has a flat nose rather than pointed. It also comes with grooves for lubrication and can be purchased commecially pre-lubed or un-lubed. The Mini is easy to load, performs well ballistically, and because it is all lead and its mass offers good penetration, holds together well and delivers good energy upon impact in bone or tissue. It is a good big game projectile.

THE MAXI

Maxi design is different from the Mini in two ways. Here again, it has nothing to do with bullet weight or density. There are same caliber Minis and Maxis out there that are of the same weight, or close to it. What sets the two apart is the base. While the Mini base is hollow, the Maxi base is flat.

The Maxi is also close to bore-size; not actually bore-size but close. This makes pushing it down the barrel easy with today's modern lubes, although not as easy as the Mini. When rammed down the barrel it actually engraves or cuts into the rifling to form a light gas seal. Upon ignition, bullet upset, or obturation, takes place. The bullet actually mushrooms against the bore, creating

The Maxi-Balls from Thompson/Center are popular with big game hunters wanting a solid lead projectile. These bullets offer good energy and penetration. They are available from .45-caliber (240-grain) up to .54-caliber (555-grain).

an extremely tight seal which in turns helps promote excellent bullet accuarcy downrange.

Prime examples of the Maxi are those by Lyman in .45 caliber (245 grain) and .50 caliber (370 grain) and those offered by Thompson/Center. The T/C Maxi is available in .45 caliber in 240-grain, .50 caliber in 320- and 370-grain, .54 caliber in 365- and 430-grain, and .58 caliber in 555-grain, which is a huge chunk of lead! They are snub-nosed and have grooves for lubrication. Like the Mini, the Maxi-ball is a good big game bullet. It provides plenty of power, nice expansion and penetration, and good accuracy.

Thompson/Center has expanded on its Maxi-ball with the Maxi-Hunter. It still has a flat base, but multiple grooves for lubrication. The biggest difference is in the nose. Instead of being solid, it is slightly hollow for maximum expansion. At the time of this writing the Maxi-Hunter is available from .45-caliber (255 grains) all the way up to .58-caliber (560 grains). And, as might be expected in today's cross-over bullet designs, there are some Mini bullets that have Maxi characteristics. The CVA Deerslayer or Buckslayer, Bullet is just one example. It is near caliber size and has a pointed nose but a hollow base. It is designed for high velocity, long-range accuracy and optimum expansion. In .50 caliber, they weigh 300 grains and in .54 caliber 375 grains, making them a good choice for big game. Based on personal experience in the field, both sizes work very well.

These Buckslayer bullets from CVA offer good aerodynamic design, yet have a thin skirt and the hollow base of the minie. Available in .50- and .54-caliber and up to 300 grains, these lead bullets offer good range, power, and performance.

THE STANDARD LEAD CONICAL

The basic conical is very popular with a large number of big game muzzleloader hunters, and for good reason. For one thing they are long, some a full inch or more depending upon the weight. This fact helps provide excellent velocity and energy downrange which promotes excellent penetration, very important when stalking big game.

Much of the standard conical's length is shank. Some are slightly tapered for easier loading, others are straight, but in either case the longer shank is important because it helps align the bullet with the bore as it is rammed down the barrel and allows much of the bullet full contact with the rifling as it slides down the bore upon ignition. Both translate into increased accuracy. The base of these bullets is flat, just like the Maxi-ball. It, too, expands upon firing but not nearly as much. A great deal of obturation is not required here because so much of the bullet's shank comes in contact with the rifling. The standard conical also comes with a flat nose or more rounded nose. Some are rounded and slightly hollowed. While neither is as fast as a conventional bullet with its pointed nose (few muzzleloading projectiles are) within normal muzzleloader hunting range they speed along extremely well. Depending upon the rifle, muzzle velocities of 1500 fps and 1600 fps are quite possible with these bullets, fast for a slug weighing 400 grains or more.

I like standard lead conicals and use them a lot. The results over the years on everything from deer to moose and elk have been quite satifactory, and chances are I will continue to use them. I see no reason to change. They shoot extremely well, are accurate, transfer energy well, and hit with a punch and hold together extremely well. They are not known for great mushrooming well, and though they seem to work best on bone, they will open somewhat and transfer energy on muscle and tissue.

OTHER BULLETS

There are other types of bullets that fail to fall into a standard category for muzzleloaders or were not intended for our purpose but nonetheless do quite well. These would include primarily lead pistol bullets, jacketed pistol bullets, and bullets specifically designed for muzzleloaders which generally fall in the conical category but are not made of lead, or are in some way slightly different than standard conicals.

Thompson/Center's Break-O-Way Sabot shoots both lead bullets and copper-jacketed pistol bullets (insert). Upon leaving the muzzle the sabot "breaks away," leaving only the bullet to continue down-range. Both bullets are available in .50- and .54-caliber.

Those in the first group all require sabots (pronounced sah-bow), plastic cups which for all practical purposes do the same thing for these bullets the patch does for the roundball. Sabots come in various sizes which means that by using them it is possible to shoot smaller than caliber-sized projectiles with relative ease. For example, by using a .50-caliber sabot, .38-caliber or .45-caliber bullets, and anything smaller than .50 caliber, can be fired. Also, because it is the sabot which actually grips and rides along the rifling while the bullet itself does not touch the inside of the barrel, sabots make it possible to use copper-jacketed and the newer all-copper bullets such as the Barnes Expander-MZ Muzzleloader Bullet. Because copper is much harder than lead and cannot be wedged against the rifling to form a seal, the sabot does it instead.

The question is, why would you want to use a small pistol bullet in a large bore muzzleloader? After all, for the most part these bullets are not designed for great speed, and size for size are not more powerful than standard lead conicals, or even the Mini and Maxi-ball. The answer seems to be better accuracy, but not due to speed. These projectiles actually have slower muzzle velocities than the roundball, but they are more aerodynamic, allowing them to slice through the air with a flatter trajectory.

Let's take a closer look. Are these pistol bullets, copper-jacketed bullets, and the new all-copper types as good as advertised? Simply put, they are pretty darn good. They zip along at good speed, some up to 1,900 and 2,000 fps, depending upon the charge. This is still relatively slow compared to cartridge guns but faster than most handguns for which they were originally designed. With their speed, hollow points, and controlled expansion technology, these

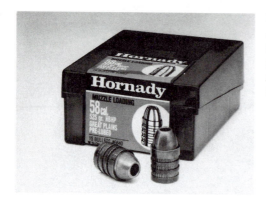

The Hornady Great Plains bullet in .58-caliber (525-grains). This is a big piece of lead that hits with a lot of power. It is excellent for grizzly and brown bear and other very large game.

bullets open up, or mushroom, well at muzzleloader speeds. They also penetrate well, and combined with their good mushrooming capabilities, provide plenty of punch. The only thing to keep in mind is that jacketed pistol bullets and lead pistol bullets have been known to penetrate right through the chest of some big game because they travel too fast. The fact that they do expand well helps, but my experience has been that they seem to perform much better when hitting bone rather than soft tissue, just like standard lead conicals.

While pistol bullets were originally designed for another use (muzzleloaders just borrowed them), there are other types of modern muzzleloader projectiles available designed specifically for the muzzleloader. The Barnes Expander-MZ bullet is a good example. Supposedly this is the first all-copper bullet created for the frontloader. What makes the Expander-ML different, if not unique, is its ability to mushroom upon impact at speeds between 1,000 fps and 1,900 fps while maintaining original weight.

There is also the Black Belt bullet from Big Bore Express. It has no grooves for lubrication because it doesn't require it. Instead, the close to bore-size Black Belt has a slightly over-sized plastic cup around the base which, like a sabot, acts as a gasket and cuts into the rifling to provide spin or rotation. The Black Belt is a good shooting bullet and well represents the modern lead conical.

If all these conical bullets have anything in common it is that they were designed to be fired from muzzleloaders with fast rifling. Remember the roundball gun and how the light-weight roundball needs only a 1:66 twist in rifling to maintain accuracy downrange? Conicals are much heavier, and to achieve good stablization they require a lot of spin. Without it they will not fly with any degree of acccuracy. If you want to shoot conicals, go with a barrel rifled with a rate of twist from 1:20 up to 1:32.

As to which conical bullet to use, no one can answer that question for you. It takes time at the range to see which performs best, which your muzzle-loader seems to prefer. Pick up a few of each, keep records, and before long they will tell you quite clearly. On a personal note I will say this: For the purpose of hunting big game I tend to lean toward the heavy projectiles, particularly on the big-boned, fat-covered, and heavily muscled critters. On deer-size game lighter bullets work well, but on the big boys I want good penetration and lots of power and this is best delivered by bullets of 300 grains or more.

WHY CONICALS WORK

Why conicals work so well has a great deal to do with weight, or sectional density. Because these bullets have more weight in relation to their diameter they are far better at retaining speed and weight to the target. Although conicals will also shed roughly a third of their speed at about the 100-yard mark just like the roundball, they still hit with more power and offer better penetration.

While conicals are great projectiles for big game, they also have their limitations. There are some things to keep in mind when considering certain types. For example, the Mini, Maxi-ball, and standard lead conical fly better to the target than the roundball because they offer a better air-cutting aerodynamic design. However, when compared to the modern jacketed pistol bullet or all-copper muzzleloading bullet the aerodynamics of these bullets, or ballistic coefficiency, is not extremely impressive. This is because they are still blunt and push a lot of air, while the modern projectiles are more pointed.

It is interesting to note, however, that trajectories of the roundball, Mini, and Maxi-ball are about equal. Keep in mind that the Mini and Maxi exit the muzzle much slower than the roundball. While they may retain energy better at long range because of their heavier mass, they lose enough speed to compare with the roundball in terms of trajectory at about 75 yards. The advantage these conicals do have over the roundball is power at longer range. If the hunter can launch a Mini or Maxi and hit the target in a vital area at 100 yards or so, deer-size game should be cleanly taken. Still, a 100-yard shot for these conicals is stretching it because of trajectory limitations. The standard conical shoots a little flatter, which is why I prefer them, and pistol bullets in sabots shoot flatter still but lack the downrange power of standard lead conicals. It depends upon the shooter, of course, but as a general rule 125 yards is a good

CVA's PowerBelt copper-coated bullets offer an oversized plastic base that creates a gas seal in the bore. Unlike sabots, PowerBelt bullets are full-caliber-sized, easy to load, and claim not to require cleaning after every shot. They are available in .50-caliber from 295-grain to 348-grain and in .54-caliber in 348-grain.

shot for any of these conical bullets. Even after more than 30 years of hunting with a muzzleloader, I still like to get as close as possible to my target regardless of the projectile being used.

The point here is that there is no perfect muzzleloading bullet. Learn what each will and won't do in your gun by shooting various types and then make your choices.

7

LOADING UP AND SIGHTING IN FOR HUNTING

One of the most important items purchased with every new muzzle-loader is the owner's manual that comes inside the box. This little manual is your bible, the rules to live and shoot by if you will. If you are new to muzzleloading, with little or no experience, the best thing you can do is sit down and read it cover to cover before even attempting to fire your new muzzleloader.

The manufacturer supplies all kinds of helpful hints and features about the rifle itself, getting started, important things to do and not to do, information on cleaning and maintenance, safety systems, the ignition system, even propellents and projectiles. Information is also supplied on recommended load data. One manual I recently received with a new bolt-action in-line had 28 pages of information. In this chapter we will expand on some of the information these booklets provide, but the importance of reading and studying the manufacturer's manual cannot be stressed enough.

LOADING UP

All muzzleloading rifles load the same way, from the front or muzzle. It should be rather obvious, but the powder goes in first followed by the projectile. But before we even get to this point there are certain things to take care of to insure fast and reliable ignition and consistent accuracy. Whether brand new out of the box or from the gun cabinet, a muzzleloader must be clean to perform the way we want it to. Muzzleloaders from the factory are often covered with a thin layer of oil, even grease in some spots, to protect them. Muzzleloaders at home collect dust, may develop rust after prolonged storage, or may have a coat of oil inside the bore from the last cleaning. It all has to be removed before taking them after game.

This is easily done. The bore and nipple on percusison models, and the blow-hole on flintlocks, are the most important. Let's start with the barrel. The bore is best cleaned with a solvent engineered to take away oil, grease, old fouling, dust, and other undesireables. There are a good many solvents on the market these days and we will talk more about them in the next chapter. The important thing to remember is that you don't need a great deal of this stuff to clean the bore. It works very well and a moistened patch used with a cleaning jig will do nicely. Even then it should be followed up with a dry patch to remove any leftover dirt or solvent. A clean bore affects accuracy, and when hunting bullet placement is vital.

Many hunters prefer to fire their muzzleloaders with a dry bore believing it improves accuracy. I agree, but I like to "condition" my barrels, whether they

An owner's manual comes with every new muzzleloader and includes important information on loading, firing, and safety. Always read the manual thoroughly before using your new muzzleloader.

are new or have been used for years. Conditioning does not seem to increase velocity or power, and there is some discussion that a damp bore may effect consistency between shots, but I have experienced no great deviations in hunting situations within normal muzzleloader range. What conditioning does do is cut down on friction, making it easier to load larger-than-bore sabots and conicals. It also makes swabbing, when necessary, and cleaning much easier.

Conditioning is done by using one of the many wonderful lubes commercially available such as Bore Butter from Thompson/Center, Wonder-Lube from Ox-Yoke Originals, or Pyro-Lube from Hodgdon. These lubes do several things which will be covered in more detail later, but for our purposes here they ease loading, make it possible to shoot several times between swabbing, make cleaning easier, and help protect steel by dispelling moisture. A little dab of this stuff inside the barrel during storage goes a long way. I even use it on the outside of my barrel. It seems to work like wax on a car which is a plus when hunting in wet conditions. No great amount is required inside the barrel or out, just enough to cover the steel.

Once the barrel is clean, move on to the nipple. Remove the nipple and make sure the nipple seat and channel are clean and free of grease or oil. A pipe cleaner works well for this task. The vent through the nipple should also be checked. A nipple pick or pipe cleaner should be used here. Nipple picks are commercially available and will come in handy during the cleaning and maintenance process. On flintlock systems, make sure the blow-hole is clean.

It is also important to make sure the hammer on sidelock ignition systems strike the nipple (or frizzen on flintlock systems) squarely. This can be easily checked by holding the hammer with your thumb, gently squeezing the trigger, and allowing the hammer to slowly drop into place. It should come to sit squarely on the nipple, or, in the case of flintlocks, the flint should hit the frizzen evenly. This has been mentioned before, but failing to ensure proper cap or primer discharge may delay ignition of the main charge, resulting in poor accuracy or even a misfire or hangfire.

Finally, dry fire a cap or two on percussion muzzleloaders. This further dries and cleans the nipple vent and channel into the breech. As an added precaution, remove the nipple a final time. At times, dry firing actually deposits debris from the cap in the nipple, which defeats the whole process.

We are now ready to load the rifle. Hammers are best set on half-cock. This allows air in the barrel to vent out the nipple when powder is supplied. Since we are not interested in full power or consistency at this point start off with a small powder charge. Using a volumetric powder measure, start out with 50 or 60 grains. This is more than enough powder to expel the projectile and give you an idea of how things work and feel, which is what we want at this point. Once the powder has been measured out, set the can of powder aside, away from flame or the shooting area. Grip the rifle near the muzzle, lean it away from the body, and dump the powder down the barrel.

Next comes the projectile. If shooting a patch and roundball or solid lead conical, remember the patch and lead bullet must be lubed. I prefer pre-lubed conicals since it makes things easier. Patches also come pre-lubed, but if not any one of the lubes mentioned earlier works well. Dispense a little on the patch, spread it around evenly, and center it over the muzzle. Keeping the muzzle leaning away from the body, the roundball is then centered on the patch. Conicals and sabot loads can simply be started down the barrel using thumb pressure. The important thing is to keep these elongated bullets as straight as possible, in line with the rifling. A ball starter is used to drive the projectile further into the barrel, the ramrod is then used to push it all the way down the bore, seating it on top of the powder charge. Seating the bullet on the charge should be done with steady,

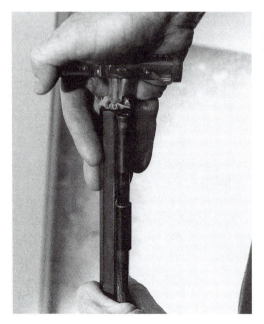

This pre-loader also serves as a ball starter on this patch and roundball.

consistent pressure. Provide a little extra pressure to make sure the bullet is fully seated, keeping in mind a gap between charge and projectile can be dangerous and that both blackpowder and Pyrodex burn more consistenly under pressure. Once the bullet is fully seated return the ramrod to its proper place beneath the barrel.

There are two important things to keep in mind when seating a muzzle-loading projectile. Keep the muzzle leaning away and never lean the body over the ramrod. Never! If gripping the ramrod proves difficult or sufficient pressure cannot be achieved, one of the T-type loaders offered by CVA, Traditions, or Thompson/Center, or a loading tool like the KaDooty from KaDooty Manufacturing or the Power Rod from Ashley Outdoors works well. These will be covered in more detail later in this chapter.

The second thing to remember is that the projectile should descend smoothly and with uniform pressure to the powder charge. Ramming or "beating" the projectile may cause deformities in the bullet which, when discharged, may affect accuracy or damage the bore. If your muzzleloader is properly cleaned and maintained seating should not be difficult.

The muzzleloader is now loaded with powder and bullet, and except for a cap, or primer in the pan on flintlock systems, is ready to go. To load a cap, pull the hammer (sidelock systems), plunger or bolt (in-line systems) all the way back and—keeping the rifle safely pointed downrange—place a cap on the nipple. The percussion and in-line systems are now ready to fire.

Priming the flintlock system is a little more involved. Outdoor writer Dave Ehrig of Pennsylvania has been described as one of the most knowledgeable teachers in the art of shooting and hunting the old-fashioned way. Dave definitely has more experience hunting with flintlock than I do and his book *Black Powder Whitetails*, suggests the following after pouring a half pan of FFFFg blackpowder (FFFg will do in an emergency) into the pan. "Close the frizzen and tap the powder away from the touch hole by tapping the rifle on the opposite of the lock. This will speed ignition by creating a flash of light and heat into the powder train, rather that a slower fuse-type burn of the priming powder."

Keep in mind frizzens can cause misfires if wet or oily. "Even the oil from your skin is enough to prevent sparks flying from the surface," Dave writes. This can be prevented by keeping the frizzen clean with rubbing alcohol. Enough said.

SIGHT SYSTEMS

We could spend considerable time on this subject, as well as sighting in, but since your owner's manual will explain how to make necessary adjustments for windage and elevation we will offer just a few tips.

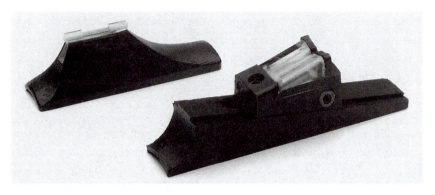

Fiber optic sights such as this Illuminator II sight system from CVA are becoming popular on muzzleloaders. These systems are now standard on many in-lines and replacement versions are available for non-replica sidelock muzzleloaders. Fiber optic systems are excellent in low-light conditions.

Muzzleloading rifles these days come with various sight systems. My Lyman Great Plains Rifle carries a buckhorn rear sight that can be adjusted for elevation and a blade sight dovetailed into the barrel that can be adjusted for windage. It is an updated version of the fixed buckhorn sight common on muzzleloaders of old, and it works well. Of the common sights on muzzleloaders I would have to say this is the most basic. My Thompson/Center Hawken Custom, however, is more advanced, and has an adjustable open sight. These are one of the most common sight systems on today's non-replica muzzleloaders. The rear sight is fully adjustable with screws for both elevation and windage. On the front is a bead-style blade sight.

Another popular sight system is the open adjustable ramp-type. My Knight MK-85, Gonic Model 93 and CVA FireBolt all carry this type of sight. Elevation is increased or decreased by sliding the sight up or down a ramp, while windage is adjusted by moving the sight left or right in a dovetail. This type of sight is also common, primarily on modern in-line rifles but also on non-replica sidelock percussion muzzleloaders.

Muzzleloaders come with various front sights. The "bead" type is popular on modern in-lines, while the "blade" is common on many non-replica sidelock muzzleloaders.

Both types of sights are available today with the benefit of fiber optics, which gathers exisiting light and directs it to specific neon bright points in both rear and front sights. They work very well under low-light hunting conditions. Traditions has their Fiber Optic Sight, Thompson/Center their Tru-Glo system, and CVA their Illuminator and Illuminator II optic systems.

Several other sight systems are also common. One is the open, fully adjustable flip-down type. The rear sight is permanently attached by screws to

Open sights are common on modern in-line and non-replica muzzleloaders. This type of sight adjusts for windage and elevation.

the barrel but is adjustable for windage and elevation by screws. It flips down to accommodate scopes. My Thompson/Center FireHawk comes equipped with this type of sight. There is also the adjustable ladder open sight. This sight has notches, or a ladder, which increases or decreases elevation by raising or lowering the rear sight. On the lowest notch the rifle hits low, on the highest it hits high. Often this type of sight sits in a dovetail notch in the barrel which allows for windage.

Two other types of sight systems are worthy of attention: the receiver, or peep sight, and the scope. Receiver sights rarely come from the factory as standard equipment, but many manufacturers offer them for particular muzzleloaders because they remain popular. Receiver sights are also available from gun shops and sporting good stores.

Receiver sights were popular with buffalo hunters of the old west because by nature these big animals often stood still for long periods and allowed shooters to get a good fix. But the whitetail of today and other big game animals rarely stand still, at least for long. Although these sights are very accurate, many modern hunters believe receiver sights do not perform as well when trying to get a quick, full sight on moving game.

I do not necessarily agree. The biggest problem is that most shooters and hunters today don't use these sights properly. Many try to consciously center

Peep sights are popular among big game hunters and various types are available. This version attaches to the tang on traditional sidelock muzzleloaders.

Buckhorn sights are seen on some muzzleloaders that stick to more traditional design, especially the half-stock Plains rifle. This sight is on the author's Lyman Great Plains Rifle. It adjusts for elevation. Buckhorn sights are typically used with "blade" front sights.

the front bead in the middle of the peep. This not only takes time because the eye must make adjustments but is incorrect. The proper way is to *look through* the peep, put the front sight on the target and squeeze the trigger. The eye will automatically center the front sight in the peep because that is where light is concentrated. It takes some getting used to, but with a muzzleloader that is properly sighted in I have found this sight system no slower than open sights and, in some case, scopes.

And what about scopes on the frontloader? There are definitely two camps here: purists stand adamantly against them while others see no reason not to use them. I fall in the latter category. I strive for the best shot possible when game is in the brush and timber, and scopes certainly help in these and other situations. Several of my in-lines are equipped with scopes, and the older I get the more I appreciate them. It should be noted that scopes are not legal in all states during special muzzleloading seasons so check the regulations where you plan to hunt.

A scope on a muzzleloader must be rugged. Recoil is rather potent, and the last thing you want is the lens to loosen after repeated use. The duplex scope is extremely strong and easy to use with its heavy crosshairs. The thicker crosshairs narrow to thinner wires for precise aiming. Thompson/Center has its own line of heavy duplex scopes called Recoil Proof and Hunter Hawken, and they are excellent. Other fine scopes are available from Burris, Redfield, Nikon, Bausch & Lomb, Leupold, Zeiss, Tasco, Simmons, and others. It all depends on how much you want to spend.

Both sidelock models (top) and modern in-lines can easily be equipped to carry scopes.

Scope power is also important. Non-variable scopes in 2.5X are fine for deer, moose, and bear in heavy brush. Many shots are relatively close, and high magnification is not always needed. A scope of this power also provides good field of view in these situations. However, you might also want to consider a variable scope. On a higher power, they aid in exact shot placement on game at 100 to 125 yards, normal muzzleloading range. Variables offer the option of wide field of view at 2.5X power for close shots, or good magnification at 6X or 7X for pinpointing shots at longer range. They do it all, and for my money are worth the investment.

Nearly all in-lines, carbines, and many non-replica muzzleloaders come from the factory pre-drilled and tapped for scopes. If not, it should be done by a gunsmith. A good set of scope rings or a mounting base will also be required, and these are available from T/C, Weaver, Tasco, and at gun shops and retail stores carrying firearms. While it is quite possible to mount your own scope, best results come from a qualified gunsmith familiar with the task.

Deciding which type of sight system to use is a personal choice. For starters, go with the type that comes with the gun from the factory. They have been tested and are usually more than adequate. The need to change may never a rise. Scopes can be just as useful on a muzzleloader, in many situa-

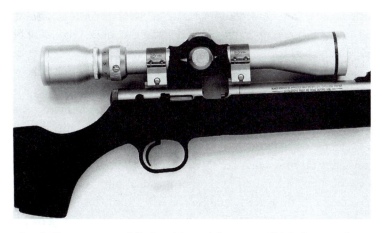

All modern in-lines come pre-drilled and tapped for scopes. Sidelock percussion muzzle-loaders can also be equipped with scopes.

tions, as on a 7mm or .30/.06, and older eyes really appreciate them! Just make sure to check the regulations.

FINDING THE BEST HUNTING LOAD

Once your muzzleloader has been fired the first time you will want to fire it again and again. It will quickly become obvious how much fun shooting these rifles really is, even at paper targets. Keep safety in mind and remember that swabbing between shots might be required, although not so often with Pyrodex.

Eventually, however, you will want to develop the best hunting load for your muzzleloader and sight it in for accuracy. Because we are hunting big game this means developing a load that provides optimum power and accuracy.

Start by picking a projectile type. With roundball guns there is little choice, but in muzzleloaders with fast rifling various conicals and saboted pistol bullets can be used. A particular muzzleloader will shoot each bullet differently, and because we want to achieve not only optimum velocity but consistent accuracy at some point, use the same projectile you plan to hunt with. The same is true with powder granulation; if you start with FFg blackpowder or RS grade Pyrodex stick with it all the way.

Also keep in mind that the maximum load is not necessarily the best hunting load. Maximum load is all the powder you can put down the barrel and discharge safely. Depending upon the muzzleloader design, caliber, and type of projectile, the maximum load may be 90 grains, 120 grains, or even more. Don't get caught up in the belief that the maximum amount of powder will provide the best ballistic results in the field. It rarely does.

This is due to the law of diminishing returns. In his book *Blackpowder Loading Manual*, Sam Fadala, who has made testing muzzleloaders a way of life explains the phenomenon as, "a point at which you load more propellant but gain only more fouling, more recoil, but do not significantly increase the bullet's velocity." If you load 90 grains of FFg and get 1,790 fps, but then load 100 grains of FFg and obtain only 1,798 fps, an 8 fps gain, you have reached the point of diminishing returns. For all practical purposes nothing ballistically is gained with the extra 10 grains of powder. As you begin seriously shooting your new muzzleloader, gradually increase the powder charge by 10-grain increments; you will notice that accuracy will begin to suffer at some point. It may be at 90 grains, 100 grains, 120 grains, or at any point up to the maximum recommended charge. Each muzzleloader is different. But the point at which this happens is your muzzleloader's point of diminishing return, and chances are your best hunting load for that projectile as well. Change projectiles, however, and you have to start all over again, as each will be different. This is why you want to pick your projectile and powder granulation first before developing a hunting load. Once the optimum hunting load is found, I like to load the barrel one more time. With the projectile fully seated and the ramrod still in the barrel, I take a knife and scribe a fine line around the ramrod. I then know when the projectile is fully seated each time. During the excitement of reloading on a hunt it leaves no question and makes things a whole lot safer.

If you're wondering where to begin in finding your optimum hunting load, look at the loading data in your owner's manual. For example, CVA just sent me one of their new FireBolt MusketMag in-lines in .50-caliber. According to CVA's own loading data, the minimum powder charge using FFg powder firing a .50-caliber saboted projectile is 50 grains. The maximum powder charge, the one I do not want to exceed, is 90 grains. I know 50 grains is a bit light for a big game load, particularly when throwing a 245- or 265-grain projectile, so starting at 60 grains I will gradually increase my powder charge in 10-grain increments until I reach the point of diminishing returns. It will probably be either 80 or 90 grains. The point is, the loading data in your owner's manual tells you where to start and where to stop. It also provides guidelines concerning bullet weights. You might want to experiment with different bullets later, but these are a good place to start so take advantage of the available data.

SIGHTING IN

Sighting in a muzzleloader is not difficult, it just takes some time at the range, a little patience for those who have not done much of it, and a clear knowledge of personal hunting range. For example, while a number of new in-lines can handle a 150-grain charge for the purpose of sending a saboted projectile 200 yards out, the question is: is What range do you need for your location and type of hunting? Here in Maine where I do a lot of hunting for woodland whitetails, my average shot is 50 yards, and even when hunting out west for pronghorn, mule deer, or elk or in the far north for caribou long-range hunting is not what attracted me to hunting with a muzzleloader. I might make a 100- or 125-yard shot, but that's about it. I like to hunt close, not launch a bullet downrange just to see if I can hit something. I realize everyone is different, but for this reason and a number of others, such as the loss of velocity and power of many projectiles beyond 100 yards, increased odds of missing or wounding an animal, and my own personal ethics, 100 to 125 yards is about as far I want to shoot at big game.

With this in mind, my open-sight sidelock muzzleloaders shooting conicals or saboted bullets are sighted in for 70 yards, my roundball guns at 50 yards, and my scoped in-lines at 100 yards. Sighting a rifle for accuracy within these limits is relatively easy. One of the most important aspects is understanding how to make sight adjustments. If unclear on the subject review your

Finding the best hunting load for your muzzleloader and sighting in takes patience. If a group similar to this can be achieved, you will be filling tags.

owner's manual, but as a reminder windage is horizontal and elevation is vertical. If your shots are not in the bull, move the rear sight in the direction you want the bullet holes to move. For example, if hitting low and to the left, move the rear sight up and to the right. This is easy with today's modern fully adjustable sights. Scopes are even easier to adjust. Simply remove the turret caps and move the windage and elevation screws in the direction you want to go.

To sight a muzzleloading rifle correctly two things are vital: start close and use a benchrest. Trying to anchor a bullseye at 100 yards right off or at any range offhand will prove frustrating, and there is no way to accurately sight in a muzzleloader standing, sitting or kneeling. It can't be done.

I like to start sighting in .45-caliber to .58-caliber muzzleloaders at about 13 yards. This provides a good chance of hitting paper on the first shot. Fire a three-shot group at the bullseye and make the necessary adjustments. Make sure to load your muzzleloader the same way each time. Use the same powder charge, bullet, and powder type and granulation you plan to hunt with. Now move the target to 50 yards and fire another group, again aiming for the bull. To make things easier concentrate only on windage problems at this point, the left/right adjustments. Elevation (up/down) adjustments can easily be done at 75 yards. Make the adjustments at 50 yards, firing another round if necessary just to make sure. Once in the bull, move out to 75 yards and repeat the process until you are back in the bull.

Except for my roundball guns, I don't mind being sighted in dead-on at 75 yards. In my neck of the woods this is a good shot on deer. In fact, most are under that mark and by sighting in at this range I know my bullet will hit about one inch high at 50 yards, be dead-on at 75 yards and one inch low at 100 yards. I can take game by holding dead-on the chest out to at least 100 yards, because even with this slight variation in elevation and drop I will hit vitals on deer-size game. That's acceptable.

How far can a muzzleloader shoot? Quite a long way, but keep in mind muzzleloader bullets typically drop and lose energy rather quickly, even lead conicals and saboted pistol bullets. Some muzzleloader bullets are being offered to handle 200-yard shots while retaining much of their hitting power and a lot of speed. And we now have muzzleloaders that can safely accommodate a 150-grain charge. It is always a good idea to shoot at various ranges just to get an idea of trajectory but how far you shoot, or should shoot, while actually hunting game should be based on your ability, confidence, ethics, and the situation at hand.

8

MAINTENANCE AND SAFE SHOOTING

Safe muzzleloading, whether at the range or in the field, begins with a clean muzzleloader. Contrary to common belief, cleaning and maintaining a smokepole has never been easier, nor is it necessary to spend hours at the task. With today's solvents and lubes thoroughly cleaning a muzzleloader can be done in a matter of minutes while watching the evening news or a football game. Also, a muzzleloader does not necessary have to be cleaned each time it is taken afield. If you fire it, clean it, especially the barrel. But if no game is seen that day or for several days and the rifle is not discharged, simply wipe away any moisture or oils on the exterior left by contact with skin.

On wilderness hunts, of which I do a fair number each year, my muzzleloader rarely gets the attention it deserves yet only on rare occasion has it failed me, and then only under extreme weather conditions when it might have failed to begin with. One reason it works so well is that it is thoroughly cleaned before leaving home and always well maintained.

What goes on inside the barrel of a muzzleloader upon discharge is amazing. It is also dirty and corrosive. When a muzzleloader is fired only about 50 percent of the propellent is actually used. The rest either flies out the barrel or stays behind as fouling. In fact, a lot of it stays behind. Once fired, blackpowder and Pyrodex leave behind an impressive list of reactive chemicals, including potassium carbonate, potassium sulfate, potassium sulfide, potassium thiosulfate, potthicynate, not to mention carbon and sulfate. By the sound of it you are unleashing a toxic dump when you pull that trigger, and in essence you are. Once potassium nitrate comes in contact with moisture or humidity, for example, rusting can begin in minutes. Sulfur, upon ignition, has the ability to create sulfuric acid. Moisture on any muzzleloader is a big deal.

So what can this chemical reaction do to a muzzleloader? A ring can develop in the bore. This is an area of fouling that failed to get thoroughly removed during cleaning. It never goes away and could in time actually make the bore weaker. The barrel may also pit, creating pockets of rust which in a short time could affect the ease of loading and accuracy. If the lock is not maintained it could fail to function properly, nipple seats can rust and deteriorate which can delay ignition and be hazardous, and a wood stock can soften, even decay, if not properly cleaned. As mentioned previously, rusting can occur anywhere, inside the barrel and out.

There are several ways to clean a muzzleloader these days and we will cover two methods generally considered the most effective, but first it is helpful to know exactly what is available to make cleaning and maintainence a breeze compared to a couple decades ago.

SOLVENTS

There was a time, and not long ago, when the only way of thoroughly cleaning a muzzleloader was with water. It worked and remains popular even today. But modern solvents are rapidly taking. They are fast, convenient, and work extremely well. I use them almost exclusively and have a good stock of the stuff at home and while away on hunting trips.

Solvents are engineered to break down blackpowder fouling, making it easier to remove. On a clean patch or rag, they work as well outside the barrel around nipples and blow-holes as they do inside the bore. Inside the bore they may be applied using a patch or with a fiberglass or brass bristlebrush. A 20-gauge brush for shotguns works very well on both .50- and .54-caliber muzzleloaders. Many solvents are also all natural these days, containing no petroleum-based additives. Thompson/Center's Number 13 Bore Cleaner is a prime

Number 13 Bore Cleaner from Thompson/Center is an all-natural bore cleaner with no pe-troleum-based additives.

example. Some are available in concentrated form, such as WonderLube 1000 Plus from Ox-Yoke Originals. It comes in a 14-ounce bottle but with a 15-to-1 ratio makes 60 ounces of bore solvent. Some solvents are chemical-based. Black Off by Rusty Duck contains ethylene glycol monobutyl esther.

There are a good many solvents already on the market and it seems that every time you turn around a new or improved version hits the shelves. It is not necessary to mention them all. Those covered here have been around for some time, are readily available at gun shops, and can be relied upon to do what is required of a solvent.

Thompson/Center's Number 13 Bore Cleaner has been a favorite of mine for years. It is non-toxic, actually FDA food-grade rated, and does a good job of moving residue without eliminating seasoning in the bore. Black Off from Rusty Duck is also good. It is available in pre-saturated patches, even a handy container complete with tray and brush for depositing and cleaning nipples.

Another top name is Birchwood Casey. Their No. 77 Bore Solvent is one of the best. Not only does it do the job on fouling, it works well on plastic residue left behind by sabots. The same is true of Blackpowder Cleaning Gel from Shooter's Choice. The Hoppe's name is also familiar and their No. 9 Plus solvent is very popular. CVA's Olde Time Bore Cleaner and Patch Lube is said to be made to original U.S. military specs and is a wonderful rust penetrant and fouling remover. CVA's Barrel Blaster Solvent is also quite good. And let us not forget BBC Bore Cleaner from Butler Creek and WonderLube 1000

Black Off from the makers of Rusty Duck Gun Care Products is an effective solvent. The tub on the left is a handy nipple cleaning system.

Plus Bore Cleaning Solvent from Ox-Yoke Originals. Both are all natural, non-petroleum ingredients and do a wonderful job. Finally, there is Spit-Bath from Hodgdon. It works on blackpowder as well as Pyrodex, but most solvents do. Ox-Yoke Originals' Easy Clean Solvent is another good one.

GREASES

We don't use a lot of grease on muzzleloaders but two places where it does come in handy is on nipple threads and the threads of removeable breech plugs. Both areas experience considerable heat and are concentration points for fouling and powder residue. Grease helps prevent these areas from seizing. Whenever cleaning these areas Slick Breech Plug and Nipple Grease from CVA or Thompson/Center's all natural Gorilla Grease will do wonders.

LUBES

I love this stuff! In fact it is difficult to imagine modern muzzleloading life without it. Lubes do so much and are so beneficial I consider them one the most important innovations to come along since the non-replica started the muzzleloading craze back in the 1970s. That may sound like a stretch, but once you realize what the modern lube does you just might agree.

For one thing, lubes reduce friction. It is possible to drive a roundball or lead conical home with other types of lubricant, including saliva, shortening, even petroleum jelly, but nothing makes it easier than modern lubes. Each

Gorilla Grease from Thompson/Center is an all-natural anti-seize lubricant that is excellent for breech plugs and nipples.

time it goes down the barrel on a patch for a roundball or conical a thin, slick protective barrier between projectile and bore is deposited. This helps maintain the crispness of the rifling inside the bore. They continue to reduce friction even upon ignition because they are designed to withstand the 3,000 to 4,000 degree heat of burning blackpowder or Pyrodex. Every time the muzzleloader is fired lubricant is left behind and continues to work.

Lubes are excellent at penetrating pores in the bore, too. They condition or "season" the barrel with each use. These pores are great collection spots for fouling. It is fouling, upon contact with moisture and oxygen, which corrodes a barrel. A well conditioned or seasoned barrel simply offers fewer places for fouling to collect so modern lubes also serve as an anti-corroding agent. This is one of their most important benefits because corrosion can affect accuracy as well as life of the barrel.

Lubes make cleaning easier as well. Not only does more fouling fly out the muzzle upon ignition because the bore is so slick, lubes keep fouling left behind soft. This not only makes final cleaning easier, but allows repeated shooting between swabbing on the range or in the field. On my muzzleloaders, I also use modern lubes on the outside of the barrel. They do a great job of repelling moisture during foul weather and continue to protect during storage.

There are many brands of lubes today. Many of the companies known for solvents also offer lubes. Some are available in a tube or jar, on pre-lubed patches, and carry a pleasant scent. Most are also all natural and biodegradeable. Thompson/Center's Natural Lube 1000 Plus Bore Butter for example was the first all natural lubricant, and this seems to be the trend. Michaels of Oregon makes AppleGreen Hot Shot Patch & Bullet Lube. It is also biode-

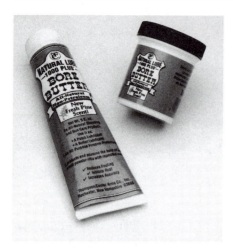

Thompson/Center's Natural Lube 1000 Plus Bore Butter is one of the best lubes on the market. It is available in a natural scent and pleasant pine scent. Lubes help reduce friction and help keep the bore clean which results in less swabbing between shots.

gradeable and smells like apples. Ox-Yoke Originals has its Wonder Lube 1000 Plus and CVA has Slick Load Lube. Hodgdon makes Pyro Lube. It is especially formulated for Pyrodex.

DISASSEMBLING AND CLEANING YOUR MUZZLELOADER

A muzzleloader must be disassembled before it can be properly cleaned. Your owner's manual will provide instructions for how to do this. In some cases this may simply require removal of the barrel from the stock and the trigger assembly from the mortice, often it will be more involved. A growing number of in-line muzzleloaders are designed with a removable breech plug and come supplied with a tool for that purpose. Removal is relatively easy and makes cleaning quite easy as well, one reason why the in-line is so popular.

The muzzleloader must also be unloaded. This seems obvious but should be checked before disassembly. Inserting the ramrod into the barrel is an easy way to see if it is loaded, assuming the ramrod is marked for a fully-seated load as previously recommended. If the ramrod bottoms out above the mark you know it is unloaded and safe to clean. If it stops at the mark on the ramrod it is loaded and the projectile must be removed. This can be accomplished by discharging the firearm, using a CO_2 discharger, or by using a bullet puller. (This is basically a screw-type device that attaches to the ramrod. It is screwed into the bullet which is then manually removed.) Discharging the muzzleloader is the easiest and safest method.

Various accessories might be needed to clean and maintain your muzzleloader. Shown here are a ramrod extension, bullet puller screw, worm or patch puller, clean jag, a thread adapter for converting 10×33 threads on rifle rods to 5/16×27 for use with bore brushes, brass bore brush, and cotton bore swab.

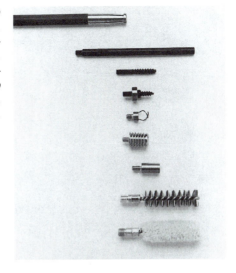

As mentioned earlier, a clean muzzleloader is a safe muzzleloader, and safety is paramount. We all want to live and hunt a long time so cleaning should become part of your hunting routine. It is also part of your responsibility as a gun owner. However, rarely do I give my muzzleloader a thorough cleaning during the hunting season. Before and after, yes. The same is true before leaving on a wilderness hunt and after getting home, but during the home season or while away in the bush a daily swabbing, a check of the nipple, trigger, and lock for proper function, and a wiping of the exterior will generally suffice. Factors such as how many times the muzzleloader has been fired and weather conditions will dictate cleaning. While hunting away from home I al-

Cleaning accessories are available in kits. This one includes cleaning solvent, nipple wrench, brushes, jags, and bullet pullers. These items can also be purchased separately.

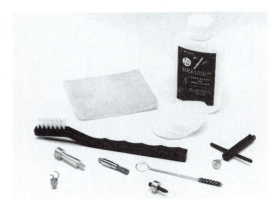

Black Powder Cleaning Gel Bore Cleaner is an excellent solvent for removing blackpowder residue.

ways have my cleaning kit available in camp just in case a full cleaning is called for, but simple daily inspections are the general rule.

It is also a good idea to give your muzzleloader a look during the off season now and then. Wipe off any dust that might have collected and check for

Rust Prevent from Shooter's Choice is a good solvent for preventing, even removing, rust.

corrosion. If the firearm looks like it needs a cleaning, or you simply feel like doing it, go right ahead. A little time and care now may pay off big later.

WATER CLEANING

Water is a good cleaning agent. It works well on both sidelock models and in-lines, dissolving salts left by blackpowder an Pyrodex fouling as well as carbon and sulfur. Water is also cheap and readily available. Contrary to common belief, however, cold water should be used downbore first, followed by hot water. Using hot water first will actually open the pores in the metal and soften and remove some of the lube conditioning, replacing it with water. I much prefer leaving the conditioning in place and removing as much fouling as possible. This is best done by first flushing the bore with cold water. Here are the steps involved when cleaning with water:

1. Remove the nipple (and cleanout screw if present) and place in a container of solvent.
2. Remove the ramrod and set it aside.
3. With the barrel removed from the stock (remove receiver and trigger assembly on in-lines) place the barrel in a small tub or basin and flush the bore with cold water. This can be done by pouring water directly down the barrel or by filling the basin with water and using a 20-gauge shotgun swab or patches attached to a cleaning rod, sucking water up through the nipple hole into the bore. Flush the barrel and suck water into the barrel a couple times.
4. Change to hot water and repeat Step 3.
5. Using a brass or fiberglass bristlebrush, scub the inside of the barrel several times. This will help remove any residue not previously removed.
6. Flush the barrel by pouring water down the barrel one more time.
7. Wet an old toothbrush with hot water and scrub the exterior of the breech around the nipple hole, including the nipple seat and thread, clean out the screw hole and other exposed metal.
8. Wet a pipe cleaner and thoroughly clean the nipple hole into the breech. Do the same with the touch-hole on flintlocks.
9. Wipe the exterior dry. Using dry patches swap the bore. Continue to do so, replacing patches as often as necessary until they appear clean and dry.
10. Wipe all channels, cracks, and crevices dry with patches and pipe cleaners. Dry any moisture that might be present on the exterior of the barrel.

11. At this point I break from tradition. Because I am such a fan of modern lubes I apply a small amount to the bore and the outside of the barrel with a clean patch, restarting the conditioning process. Applying metal preserver or rust inhibitior in the bore is good, but my experience has been that lube is better.
12. Clean the nipple and other screws with a toothbrush. Clean the nipple hole with a pipe cleaner. Wipe dry and apply a dab of Gorilla Grease or other grease. Replace in barrel.
13. Attend to the trigger assembly, wiping away any dirt. Oil lightly.
14. Any brass can be removed and cleaned with brass polish or Flitz.
15. Clean wood stocks and apply a small amount of linseed oil or wax. Reassemble and wipe entire muzzleloader with a clean, dry cloth.

SOLVENT/LUBE CLEANING

Modern cleaning solvents are used instead of water and lubes are used instead of metal preserver or oil inside the barrel and out. The only exception is the trigger assembly and nipple hole. Trigger assemblies are always best oiled, and grease should be used when replacing nipples. Follow all the steps for the water clean-up system, replacing water with solvent. I find this method easier, faster, and much cleaner.

TEN COMMANDMENTS OF MUZZLELOADER SAFETY

These commandments come from Connecticut Valley Arms who, like all muzzleloader manufacturers, preach safety above all else.

1. Keep the gun muzzle pointed in a safe direction.
2. Be aware of your target and beyond.
3. Never rely on a gun's "safety."
4. A gun should be unloaded until ready to use.
5. Always wear eye and ear protection.
6. The barrel should be clear of obstruction before shooting.
7. Handle every gun as if it is loaded.
8. Keep guns and ammo separate and in locked storage.
9. Avoid alcoholic beverages and drugs before and during use of a firearm.
10. Do not alter or modify your firearm. Have your firearm checked regularly by a competent gunsmith. Make sure all parts work properly.

FOUR MISCONCEPTIONS ABOUT MUZZLELOADERS

1. A muzzleloader is unloaded if the cap is removed.

   Although considered unloaded during hunting season in several states (check state regulations) if the cap is removed, as long as the barrel is loaded with powder and projectile the firearm should be considered loaded and should be treated and handled as a loaded firearm.

2. A misfire will not fire after a minute or two.

   Misfire is one of the leading causes of muzzleloader accidents, mainly because the condition is treated casually. When a misfire occurs keep the muzzle pointed in a safe direction until the load has been cleared from the barrel. Misfires occur when the cap or priming powder ignites but the main powder charge fails to ignite. Possible causes: a blocked or clogged vent (flash channel or touch-hole); a contaminated (wet or oily) main powder charge; or no main powder charge. Keeping the muzzle pointed in a safe direction, wait several minutes and recap or reprime and try again. If several attempts fail, removal of the projectile should only be attempted by using an approved method described below.

3. Pulling a projectile is a safe practice.

   Pulling a projectile is dangerous when there is a powder charge behind it. There are several approved methods for removing a projectile from the barrel: Use a CO^2 discharger to blow the projectile from the barrel (Thompson/Center's Magnum Silent Ball Discharger is one of the best). You can also remove the nipple from the breech plug and work a small amount of powder into the flash channel, then replace the nipple, recap, and discharge. The nipple can also be removed and the barrel's breech placed in eight inches of water to soak for 30 minutes. This will deactivate the main powder charge. Use a bullet puller to pull the bullet. For in-lines, with the muzzle pointed in the safe direction, remove the barrel action making sure the percussion camp and any excess fulminate is removed from the nipple. Remove the bolt or plunger, nipple, and breech plug and empty the powder into a safe container. Using the ramrod and cleaning jig with a solvent-soaked cleaning patch, push the bullet from the breech forward and out the muzzle.

4. Blowing down the barrel to clean or clear the vent and extinguish hot sparks or ambers of sparks is safe.

Blowing down the barrel is hazardous. Always keep all body parts away from the muzzle at all times. Point the muzzle only at the intended target.

TEN IMPORTANT SAFETY CONSIDERATIONS WHILE HUNTING

1. Never pour powder directly into a muzzleloader directly from a flask, horn, or any large volume, enclosed container. Measure your optimum hunting load in a powder measure or pre-loader.

2. Use only recommended loading data for the particular model of rifle in use. Different models have different powder charge and projectile capabilities. Improper loading or overloading of a muzzleloading firearm may result in severe injury or death.

3. Never place a cap on the firearm (or prime a flintlock) until ready to shoot. Caps and priming should always be removed when walking, climbing tree stands or fences, transferring the gun from one person to another, or leaving the gun unattended.

4. Never lean or rest a loaded muzzleloader against a tree, wall, vehicle, or other surface. Any fall may cause accidental discharge resulting in injury or death.

5. Never exchange a loaded firearm with any other person. Only the person who personally loaded or witnessed the loading should fire it. This practice will help prevent overloading or doubleloading, both of which may cause injury or death.

6. Never transport a loaded muzzleloader in or on any type of vehicle. A muzzleloader should be considered loaded until powder, bullet, and percussion cap are removed.

7. Never load a muzzleloader until making sure it is empty.

8. Exercise caution when hunting from tree stands with muzzleloaders. Dropping a muzzleloader may cause accidental discharge. Be sure the cap is removed whenever raising or lower the firearm.

9. Never allow the hammer or bolt of a muzzleloader to rest against the cap. Any impact to the hammer or bolt may cause accidental discharge.

10. Never rely on a mechanical safety. Muzzleloaders should always be handled as if ready to fire, regardless of the safety systems employed.

9

BLACKPOWDER AFIELD MADE EASY

Big game hunting with a muzzleloader has certainly come a long way in recent years. The in-line ignition system is perhaps the most obvious and best known example, but other changes have also made the sport easier and more convenient. When I first started hunting with a muzzleloader it was amazing how much paraphernalia was needed just to load and reload the thing. Being a percussion enthusiast, extra caps, projectiles, powder flask, and ball starter were bare essentials. There was also the possibility of a misfire, which meant a nipple wrench and nipple pick to remedy the problem.

Percussion caps back then were generally carried in their original tins. Cap size is no different today, and they are a little noisy in some hunting situations. They can also be difficult to grasp, particularly with cold, wet fingers or in the heat of the moment. Looking back I must have left caps spread from Maine to Alaska. Fortunately, there are tools available today which make carrying caps and capping a muzzleloader a breeze.

Powder was carried in a flask. It was heavy, and when reloading powder had to be measured out in a separate measure. Roundballs or conicals were carried in a small leather pouch which was even heavier than the powder flask. There were other necessary items, too: ball starter, nipple wrench, lube, the list seems to go on and on. I can remember times when my possibles bag seemed to weigh several pounds and each time I went hunting it was like packing for a wilderness excursion. No more. Today it is a whole new ball game.

THE FIELD POUCH

The mountain men of the nineteenth century would never recognize the field pouch most modern muzzleloader hunters carry afield. Their's were generally made of leather and of good size. Everything that could "possibly" be used or needed in a hurry was carried. This ranged from traps to chewing tobacco to flints for starting a fire to extra powder to pemmican for a quick meal. My first bag was made of cotton. I don't recall now where I got it, or even if it was intended for that use. It is long gone now, but it served me well for years.

It has been replaced by a modern field pouch. Mine has a wide loop so it can hang from my belt, zippered compartments that conveniently accommodate everything I might need, and is made of a durable poly/cotton material

This possible bag can be carried over the shoulder. It is made of camouflaged fleece and has one large pocket inside, with hand pockets on the outside for pre-loaders, ball starter, and other implements.

which makes it strong. It sheds water nicely, but just to help I give it a coat of Scotch Guard prior to each hunting season.

A number of companies such as Uncle Mike's, Traditions, CVA, Thompson/Center, even Cabela's, are offering these handy pouches. Depending on who offers them they may be called a "field pouch," "accessories pouch," or "possibles bag." They are based on the traditional bags of old but are much smaller in size. The most popular new models are camouflaged and made of fleece, a combination poly/cotton material, or Cordura nylon. All are relatively rugged and light, and even when fully loaded the hunter barely notices their presence. Some may have a flap with a clip for fastening, others may have zippers, such as the Hunter's Field Pouch from Thompson/Center. Some are a single large compartment, others have two or three smaller compartments. Some even have elastic loops for holding pre-loaders, a ball starter, or anything else that fits.

Pouches with a belt loop are the most popular with today's hunter. They are out of the way, yet keep everything handy. Another popular version has a built-in nylon belt and plastic quick-release snap buckle. Still other pouches or bags are designed to hang over the shoulder such as Traditions' Deluxe Possibles Bag. CVA offers a fleece possibles bag with segregated stations for bullet starter and straight-line capper, internal as well as external pre-loader compartments, a flap to protect a large zippered compartment and a snap lock to keep the cover closed. It can be carried over the shoulder, as a fanny pack, or as a belt pack. Cabela's offers a nice bag made of quiet, water-resistant teflon-coated fleece. The bottom pouch is zippered, and there is a zippered pouch on the back. A large flap covers both the top and bottom compartments.

THE PRE-LOADER OR READYLOAD

For my money the best thing to come along for the modern muzzleloader in recent years is the pre-loader. These handy little tools have virtually eliminated the need for powder flasks, extra projectiles and bullet bags in the field, and with some designs, even powder measures and ball starters. I remember times when I traveled afield carrying all of these items, but no longer. Today, four or five pre-loaders take their place, making things much more convenient.

Though all pre-loaders basically do the same thing—carry a charge of powder measured by volume and bullet—there are several different designs available. My personal favorites are those that serve as ball starter, powder

Various pre-loaders are available. They eliminate the need to carry several extra items afield and make reloading much easier.

measure, palm saver, and have compartments for powder and load. Pre-loaders made of clear plastic make it easier to use the powder measure and check the load visually.

Topping the list is CVA's 4-in-1 T-Loader and the 5-in-1 Loader, offered by Traditions. These pre-loaders are virtually the same, with both easily accommodating a bullet and up to 110 grains of powder for .45- through .54-caliber. The only difference is that the 5-in-1 Loader from Traditions provides a built-in compartment for a No. 11 percussion cap. The CVA version does not. Both can be used as a powder measure, a ball starter, and with the ramrod as a "T-loader" to aid loading and reloading. They are also fairly water-tight. These are the best pre-loaders available. Traditions has a Super Magnum Pellet Quick Loader capable of accommodating three 50-grain Pyrodex pellets and a projectile for hunters using magnum or heavy loads.

CVA's Second Shot Pre-Loader is slightly different. It can still be used as a ball starter and palm saver but is solid black plactic. It is designed to be cut to your normal powder load so no measuring afield is required. Magnum versions for heavy loads are available. For those shooting the roundball, CVA's Rapid Loader is a straight-through tube designed for loading roundball, patch, and powder is one fluid motion. The Universal Fast Loader from Traditions holds a pre-measured charge of powder and ball. It does not serve as its own powder measure but does decrease loading time.

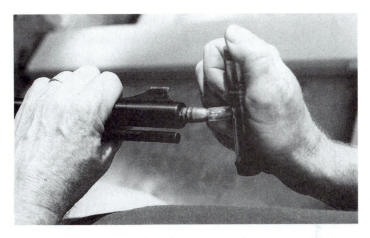

The pre-loader can be used as a ball starter for patch and roundball lead conicals (shown here) and saboted pistol bullets. They make it possible to leave powder tin, powder measure, and ball starter at home.

Thompson/Center's 4-N-1 Quick Shot loader is interesting. It carries powder, bullet or ball, and cap and also acts as a starter in one convenient unit. The starter is like a plunger, activated by pushing down on the top of the loader. It works well, although powder must be pre-measured as the unit does not serve as a powder measure. The Quick-Shot capper compartment is segregated and completely waterproof, which I like, and the unit can be easily converted to accommodate a priming charge for flintlock ignition systems.

T/C's Rain Proof Quick Shot is a smaller version of the 4-N-1 pre-loader, with the same options but without the plunger-style ball or bullet starter. Both models are available in specific sizes or color codes to accommodate .45-through .58-caliber and also come in magnum sizes.

CAPPERS

I used to hate several things about carrying percussion caps afield. On crisp mornings they could make a racket rattling around in their metal container. The tins could be difficult to open with cold, wet hands, to say nothing about retrieving a cap and getting it on the nipple in a hurry.

Fortunately, these problems have mostly been eliminated for the modern hunter by plastic cappers. Three of the best are the Rapid Capper and Tin by CVA, the Combo Capper by Traditions, and Thompson/Center's Star-7 Capper. All have six or seven fingers, each designed to hold an individual cap, and offer a storage tin in the middle for extra primers. They are handy little tools that keep caps readily available, dry, quiet, and easy to fix on a nipple.

Personally, I find the CVA version a little more user-friendly. It is flatter with fewer edges. It simply feels more comfortable in my hand. The CVA capper tin is also slightly larger and holds more extra caps in the tin—up to 20 No. 11—although it only has six fingers while cappers from Traditions and T/C cappers have seven. The latter attribute is not very important, though, considering that in most hunting situations a third or fourth shot is rarely available or needed. The CVA capper is also a fluorescent orange (the Traditions version is green, the T/C model red) making it easier to locate if dropped.

These cappers are generally intended for use with traditional sidelock percussion muzzleloaders, but they do work on some in-lines not mounted with scopes. Most in-line enthusiasts, however, prefer to use a straight-line capper, a rectangular brass tube loaded with a spring that keeps caps "straight" or "in-line" and includes a metal cap dispenser on one end. Depending on the size, each capper holds 10 to 17 No. 11 caps. Most also offer a lanyard on one end making it possible to hang them around your neck.

CVA, Traditions, Thompson/Center, and Uncle Mike's, along with a few others, have in-line cappers to offer. Some are made of brass, others are painted black. Traditions has a black model made of brass for non-glare field use that is really nice. In-line capper's are also available designed for musket

Several types of cappers are available. Shown here are the in-line capper, (top) for use with modern in-line muzzleloaders, and the handy star-type, used for sidelock percussion muzzleloaders. In-line cappers are made of brass or composite material.

caps and 209 shotgun primers. Some are black or clear composite polymer, which makes them durable yet lightweight.

It should also be noted that Dixie Gun Works has their own in-line capper. It holds up to 20 No. 10 and No. 11 percussion caps. Dixie's Capmaster is also interesting. I believe it is the only fully automatic, hard plastic in-line capper available.

FOUL WEATHER HELPERS

One of my favorite times to hunt is under the cover of falling snow. Experience has shown that game is often less nervous and more settled during such periods, and the chances of success can be quite good. Hunting in rain is less desirable, but I've had some memorable hunts during downpours. I have never been a hunter discouraged by less than ideal weather conditions, even when using a muzzleloader.

But some blackpowder enthusiasts are hesitant to venture out under such conditions, fearing the damp, wet weather will increase the chance of misfires. Keeping your muzzleloader thoroughly clean and loading with a fresh charge before heading out each day helps, so do some interesting utensils now available.

Although modern percussion caps tolerate a fair amount of moisture, persistent exposure to the elements can affect their reliability, even causing misfires. CVA's Cap Grippers help prevent moisture from entering around the

The cap grippers from CVA prevent moisture from entering around the cap and help hold the cap in place. They work well during wet weather.

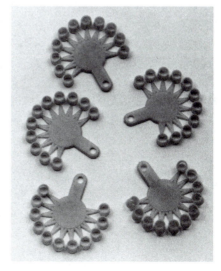

nipple. These useful little devices also prevent cap fragmentation. Traditions and Uncle Mike's offer the same components under different names.

CVA's Cap Covers, a hard plastic cover that fits over the entire nipple and cap, can also be used. They offer an added safety feature and are a good investment even in fair weather conditions.

CVA and Traditions offer flexible, rubber mitts which stretch over the muzzle, keeping moisture from seeping down the bore to the charge. I have used both the cap grippers and covers, as well as the muzzle mitts, in some torrential downpours and blizzards, and they work well. I can't say they were the only reason my muzzleloader fired on demand, but they certainly didn't hurt.

OTHER HELPFUL TOOLS

The sidelock nipple wrench has had a rebirth lately, too. The originals were fairly basic, designed primarily for one purpose: to fit over the nipple and remove it from the barrel. They work well. The newer versions, however, work

This is the deluxe Universal nipple wrench from Thompson/Center. Its long design offers good leverage. The cross bar has a nipple pick and a threaded hole to hold an extra nipple for emergency replacement in the field.

better and, depending on the model, serve more than one purpose. Not only are they larger, making them easier to use, many such as Traditions' Deluxe Nipple Wrench, CVA's Rifle/Pistol Nipple Wrench, and Thompson/Centers' Universal Nipple Wrench come with a nipple pick. Models for larger musket caps are also available.

The ramrod is a standard piece of equipment on all muzzleloaders. They were originally made of wood, but fiberglass versions now come with many in-lines. Fiberglass rods are light, rigid enough for tough loading, yet flexible to prevent breakage, and they are impervious to weather. They are excellent for hunting situations. Thompson/Center makes a polymer-coated fiberglass rod designed to fit most of their rifles and other rifles with 21- to 26-inch barrels. T/C's Hunter's Synthetic ramrods are also quite good and come in 21- to 31-inch lengths in black, or a brown finish for those shooting with non-replica sidelock muzzleloaders.

Quickly sending a bullet home in wet, cold weather, especially when excited, can be difficult. The rod is sometimes slippery, making it difficult to fully seat the bullet. T-handle extensions or palm saver handles can make the rod easier to grip and help apply smooth downward pressure. Thompson/Center makes a dandy T-handle with a wood handle. Traditions and CVA both offer a palm-shaped wooden handle that fits over the ramrod. They are small enough to fit in your pocket for easy access.

What I like better in the field, however, is a ramrod with a built-in T-handle or one that stays fixed to the ramrod even when stored beneath the barrel. It is much faster and one less thing to carry. There are two excellent offerings on the market. Thompson/Center's Power Handle adapts to ramrods and instantly converts them to power rods with pivoting T-handles. When not in use the "T" pivots, allowing the ramrod to slide in its thimbles and the muzzleloader to be discharged.

Ashley Outdoors also offers its Power Rod, which has a handle that flips or rotates into a "T." Reloading is fast and easy, even on stubborn loads or with wet, cold hands. After reloading, the T-handle flips back in line with the ramrod for easy, out-of-the-way storage. The Ashley Power Rod comes in fixed lengths as a direct replacement rod or in a segmented back-up version. I have used the Ashley product for hunting and target shooting on my favorite sidelock and in-line since it first hit the market and have found it to significantly reduce reloading time. Because it helps makes sure the bullet is fully seated, it also helps make muzzleloading safer.

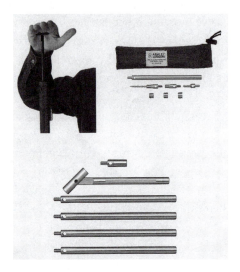

The Ashley Power Road is basically a T-handle on the end of a ramrod. When not in use it flips into the straight position for storage beneath the barrel. It is available in various lengths to accommodate most muzzleloaders.

A couple of other items also help make using muzzleloaders afield somewhat easier. They are called "combo-tools," as they are generally several tools wrapped up in one. One example is CVA's Possibles Tool. The thing is no larger or heavier than a mid-sized pocket knife yet features a knife blade—which surprisingly takes and holds a good edge—a cap remover, nipple wrench, long ball starter and cap holder, short ball starter with nipple pick, male/female adapters for use with a ramrod, wedge puller, and screwdriver.

Thompson/Center also makes a handy device they call a 6-in-1 Tool. It is not quite as versatile as CVA's Possibles Tool, but it wasn't intended to be, and what it lacks in versatility it makes up for in convenience and size. At only 3⅞-inches long it still serves well as a cap remover for both live and expired

This "possibles" tool is made by CVA. It looks like a pocket knife but offers a ball starter, nipple pick, nipple wrench, and other helpful tools.

primers, converts to a nipple wrench, has storage for nipple and caps, and converts to a powder measure, adjusting from 50 to 120 grains. T/C also offers a 4-Way Combo Tool. It works as a capper, decapper, wedge pin puller, and nipple pick.

STANDARD GADGETS

Muzzleloading has come a long way, and the items just covered make taking frontloaders afield a lot easier. In addition to the major improvements, there are certain gadgets that might be of interest. Some I consider necessary, others I seldom use while hunting.

For example, because I am such as fan of pre-loaders I rarely carry an adjustable powder measure in the woods. I do use them at the range when sighting in a muzzleloader or when developing the best load for a new muzzleloader. Adjustable powder measures for rifles are usually made of brass and adjust in 10-grain increments up to 100 or 120 grains, depending on the brandname. Large versions that can measure out up to 150 grains for magnum loads are also available. Traditions is now marketing a Pyrodex pellet dispenser that dispenses two 50-grain pellets at a time.

Powder flasks are something else I never carry afield these days. Just like the adjustable measure, some folks still use flasks for carrying and measuring out powder. Many have spouts of different lengths that meter out different charges of powder. Most flasks are large and made of brass although composite even clear, versions are available. Mine is 6 inches long, holds 12 ounces of powder, and can supply several shots before refilling.

I do carry a ball starter, afield but do not always use it these days, largely because my favorite pre-loaders come with a short stub that starts the bullet down the barrel. I own several, some with a brass short and long starter, others

This powder measure adjusts in 10-grain increments up to 120 grains. The sliding funnel prevents spillage.

This standard ball starter has full brass hardware. The lanyard stud makes it possible to hang this starter around your neck.

with a long starter made of wood with a brass tip. A couple are made of plastic or other composite materials. All have a round handle or knob that fits comfortably in the palm and works well. I personally like the composite starters because they are a bit lighter, non-glare, are are just as strong as the other types. Some ball starters may have a T-handle.

A couple of other items should be mentioned here, not necessarily because they must be carried while hunting, but because they can be used while cleaning or in some emergency situations. I keep them in my cleaning kit when traveling. One is a bullet puller. This is a screw device that attaches to the ramrod and is used to remove a projectile stuck in the barrel. It is not always easy to use and not the safest method of removing a load that will not discharge, but they do work. It is a good idea to use a bullet puller in conjunction with a muzzle guard. This keeps the ramrod centered in the bore and prevents the screw from coming in contact with the rifling.

Some cleaning jags might also be needed. These are metal devices with grooves made of brass that screw into the ramrod and are designed to grip and hold a cleaning patch. They come in different sizes, so the proper caliber-size must be used. To be honest, I rarely use this type of jag. They have been known to get stuck downbore and I have found a cotton 20-gauge shotgun bore swab or the slotted type used on shotguns to work just as well. One thing you should have, either at home or while away in hunting camp, is a worm patch puller. This is another device that screws into the ramrod. It has small wire arms that are designed to hook a patch stuck in the bore while cleaning. These items can be purchased as a kit or individually.

10

MUZZLELOADERS AND WHITETAILS

Without question white-tailed deer are the most sought-after big game species among muzzleloader hunters. And for good reason. They are readily available, have the largest range of all big game, live in varied habitats, reach respctable size in terms of body weight and antler growth, make wonderful table fare, and they are a challenge to bring home. No other big game animal has captured the hearts and imagination of so many hunters.

There was a time, however, when this magnificent animal was not so plentiful. When the first settlers arrived, perhaps 30 million whitetails inhabited the continent. Some areas were home to more deer than others due to habitat conditions, but contrary to common belief they ranged coast to coast, in all of what are now the lower 48 states and into parts of southern Canada, although numbers were rather minimal in the far western states. Our ancestors greatly reduced these numbers as they killed animals for food, the market, and for hides. Habitat destruction also played a major role. By 1646, Rhode Island became the first colony to pass laws protecting the whitetail from hunting during part of the year. Other colonies soon followed. While these laws were largely ignored, they demonstrate the rapid demise in deer numbers early on. By the end of the nineteenth century New Jersey had fewer than 200 deer and deer were scarce throughout New England. The same is true throughout the South and Midwest. By the early 1800s about 80,000 deer were being killed annually on Michigan's Upper Peninsula. A half-century later no deer were found, and by 1900 only about 400,000 whitetails remained throughout the United States.

But their current numbers represent one of the greatest conservation success stories in history. Through massive cooperative programs between sportsmen and state and federal agencies, habitat was improved, relocation programs were initiated, regulated hunting seasons and bag limits were established, and the whitetail experienced a resurgence. Today, some 20 million are with us, and in most areas the population continues to grow. The whitetail is hunted in each state and province where they are present, and in some states seasons are long and bag limits are liberal. As deer seasons were reestablished in states that closed them, or expanded in the 1940s and 1950s, very few hunters took to the woods with muzzleloaders. This was largely due to the cost and scarcity of muzzleloaders at the time. With the arrival of the non-replica muzzleloader in the early 1970s this, too, began to change. Today, along with regular firearm and bowhunting seasons, all but one state, Montana as of this writing, have a special muzzleloader deer hunting season where whitetail deer and other deer subspecies are present. In all states, including Montana, muzzleloaders may be used during the regular deer season.

The whitetail is a magnificent big-game animal and the number one target among muzzleloading hunters. All but a few states now offer a special muzzleloading hunting season on whitetails.

According to Leonard Lee Rue III in his book, *The Deer of North America*, there are seventeen recognized subspecies of white-tailed deer found north of the Mexican border. These subspecies range from the tiny Florida Key deer to the northern woodland and Dakota varities, the largest of the group. Because the Longhunter Society and the Boone and Crockett Club only recognize two for record-keeping purposes we will consider all whitetail as one group and the Coues' deer (pronounced "cows") as another.

I harvested my first whitetail somewhat late in life, at the ripe age of twenty. I had been hunting for a couple years up to that point and had grown somewhat frustrated at not getting a clear shot at game. To tell the truth, I really knew little about hunting deer, I just loved being out there. But on that November morning things changed forever. When that doe came into range, and she was finally mine I felt like the king of the world. Little did I know that I was hooked for life. Each year I take to the woods close to home, or to the prairies of the Midwest, or the rolling plains west of the Mississippi, and each year I feel the same excitement. The funny thing is, despite having nearly thirty years of deer hunting under my belt the learning process goes on. Despite how much I think I know there is always something new to learn. Of all big game, this animal is the most contradictory, the most frustrating, and the one that can be expected to break all the rules and keep you guessing. I love 'em! I am not alone. As many as 10 million hunters take to the whitetail's domain each year, a good number carrying muzzleloaders, and though the majority go home empty-handed, it really doesn't matter. It is being out there that counts.

For many whitetail fans it is not just the hunting that gets under the skin. Hunting is a big part of it, but this animal is a year-round obsession. They are truly an addiction. I am as thrilled at seeing them in the field below the house in July and August, or in September eating my apples, as I am in November and early December. I do hate it when they attack my vegetable garden each summer but am pleased to know that they are not far away. I am in awe by their grace and speed, their ability to outwit me and keep me thinking, by their beauty, and on those occasions when I have brought one home, by their size.

In summer, the whitetail is a reddish-brown, but as fall approaches the summer coat is shed and a thicker, much darker coat takes its place. Southern whitetails, such as those in Virginia, Texas, and Alabama, are typically lighter in color year-round than their northern counterparts in Maine, New York, and Michigan. The darker coats absorb sunlight and help keep the animals warm in winter, while the lighter coats reflect sunlight keeping them cool. White patches are prominent around the muzzle, throat, eyes, ears, belly, and upper inside leg region, and, of course, on the underside of the tail. When a white-tail is alarmed and running away the white flag of a tail is the most prominent feature.

Northern whitetails are also larger than southern whitetails. Bergmann's Rule, one of the four biological laws of natural selection, says that the farther north or south of the equator a geographic race gets the larger the body mass will be. In Maine, several dozen whitetail bucks field-dressing at over 200 pounds are taken each fall. Some tip the scales at 250 pounds or more. Examples in the 140- to 160-pound class are common from northern New England across the northern tier of the U.S. to Minnesota and the Dakotas and parts of Montana and central Canada. Alberta, Manitoba, and Saskatchewan have produced some of the largest bucks anywhere on the continent in recent years. But bucks over 100 pounds or so are front page news in Texas, Alabama, and other southern locals. Bucks between 100 and 150 pounds are considered average depending on the region, but any whitetail over 300 pounds is exceptional. Does typically weigh 25 percent less than males of the same age. Because of their size—not as small as pronghorn, not as large as moose, elk, caribou, and other members of the *Cervidae* family (those who carry antlers, not horns)—the whitetail and the muzzleloader are a perfect match.

They are a good match for other reasons, as well. One is speed. The whitetail has long, slender legs and strong upper leg muscles that allow it to run up to 40 miles per hour for short distances and leap eight feet high from a running start. They can trot and gallop for long periods, but unless pressured or pursued rarely do so. Even when spooked the whitetail has a habit of slowing to a walk after a couple hundred yards and going about its business, often giving the hunter a second chance.

Hunting the whitetail is also challenging due to their sense of smell, hearing, and eyesight. A large portion of the whitetail's brain is devoted to odor reception, and though difficult to judge it, has been compared to the dog's. Whatever the level of the whitetail's sense of smell, experienced hunters know it is keen and learn to deal with it. They know weather conditions affect how well a deer can detect scent, that steady breezes carry odors long distances; that gusty winds disperse odors, making them harder to detect; that calm conditions limit how far odors are carried; that a slight drizzle increases the white-

Whitetail bucks will stick to home ground and familiar travel routes unless pushed hard. This buck was spotted following a known trail the day before the start of the season and harvested by the author on opening day. Pre-season scouting is important to success.

tail's ability to smell, but a steady rain seems to clean the air making odor detection difficult. And this is just the tip of the iceberg. Learning to get within suitable range is one of the biggest challenges the blackpowder hunter will encounter.

But the whitetail isn't blind or deaf, either. The whitetail's eyes are designed to detect motion, and they do so extremely well. The hunter is often spotted first, and it has become an art among hunters to work through the woods at a snail's pace or sit for hours without moving. Because muzzleloading is close-range shooting it helps to blend in with the surrouindings. Stopping by a tree to hide your presence or sitting in some brush to break your silhouette doesn't hurt. Also, when spotted by a whitetail at a distance, or by mule deer for that matter, dropping low is the worst thing to do. All deer feel threatened when an object suddenly disappears. The best thing to do is stand still no matter what the deer does. The same is true when spotted close. If a deer doesn't flee at your appearance it often means it hasn't picked up your scent and is confused. Wait for a shot or do nothing. Even if you don't pull the trigger the deer may simply run off a short distance, circle, or remain in the area and provide a second opportunity later. It should also be noted that deer see far better in poor light than we do. That is why we often hear a deer fleeing at first light or dusk before we see it. They see us first!

As for hearing, it is as sharp as it gets among eastern big game. The ears of a whitetail are big, though not as large as a mule deer's, but they have as much as 24 inches of reception area (mulie ears cover nearly twice

The whitetail is expanding its range in the West, and they are often found in the same country as mule deer. This is a Montana whitetail taken with a modern in-line.

as much). Like a large antenna they can detect a snapped twig at an amazing distance on days with no wind. Hills, heavy cover, rain, even wind and falling snow, interfere with the whitetail's ability to hear, which is one reason why I don't mind hunting in these conditions. I like snow-covered ground or rain-soaked ground even more. It deadens the sound of movement, and though deer can smell much better in humid conditions, at times it is easier to work the wind than remain quiet while trying to cover some ground or make a stalk.

RANGE

Considering the whitetail's plight around the turn of the century it is amazing and fortunate that they are are with us today. But they are. In fact, if we include the Coues' subspecies the whitetail is found in thriving numbers in every state except California, Nevada, and Utah. In these states the mule deer, or its subspecies the blacktail, reigns supreme. In the rest of the country and from southwestern British Columbia across southern Canada to Nova Scotia the whitetail is truly king.

During the rut whitetail bucks will do predictable things. Here a buck trashes a bush, marking his territory and letting females know he is in the area. Successful hunters know when the rut occurs in their area and take advantage of the sometimes foolish mistake, bucks make during the mating season.

For trophy purposes there are good reasons for breaking the various subspecies into several categories with lower minimums for the southern states, but the lack of natural boundaries prevents it. The Coues' whitetail is the only exception. It has been recognized as a separate trophy category ever since the Boone and Crockett Club started keeping records in 1932, although precise boundaries have never been established. Because the Longhunter Society uses the same system as B&C, the accepted area for Coues' whitetail entries are defined as Catron, Grant, and Hidalgo counties in southwestern New Mexico, central and southern Arizona, and the Mexican states of Sonora and Chihuahua. All other whitetail deer are listed under the whitetail typical or non-typical categories.

HABITAT AND FOOD

One of the most amazing attributes of the whitetail is its willingness to reside in a range of varied habitats. It is as home within view of the steel and glass towers of our largest cities as it is in wilderness bastions. This includes the vast northern, central, and eastern forests, coastal plains, the western plains and foothills, the continent's agricultural areas, and the central prairies.

Certain criteria are required, however, namely adequate food, water, and cover. The whitetail can go long periods without drinking, provided its food has a high water content but will frequent water sources more often in drier areas. Hunters visiting semi-arid areas or hunting during periods of low precipitation should keep this in mind. Water holes, hidden springs, and other reliable watering areas are certainly good places to still hunt. Cover is used for protection from enemies, including hunters. It may include a thick hemlock grove surrounded by hardwoods in the Northeast or rugged gullies cutting through an open prairie in the West. Within their home range, deer will have escape routes to and from these protective areas, and they are prime areas to watch.

The same is true of feeding areas. Whitetail are ruminants, or cud chewers. They graze on forbs, buds of woody plants, legumes, agricultural crops such as corn and soybeans, flowers, acorns, fruits, and garden vegetables. Any of these foods present near the transitional zone between two types of habitats make prime whitetail country. Trails to and from these areas, as well as to reliable water sources, should be watched religiously.

GUNS AND LOADS

Long before the centerfire rifle came along the whitetail was being hunted for sustenace and sport with the muzzleloader. In the beginning it was the flintlock and roundball, then the percussion, and now the in-line and saboted-pistol bullet are getting in on the act. No matter what weapon is chosen the whitetail will prove a formidable adversary. They are a challenge even for modern rifles with their greater range and power, and the hunter using a muzzleloader will find their famous qualities greatly enhanced due to the fact that one shot is available and at a reduced range.

Despite its low sectional density and poor ballistic coefficient the roundball makes a good whitetail bullet, particularly in the dense Eastern woods. The roundball offers a flat trajectory, quick expansion, good cohesion quali-

This copper-jacketed pistol bullet is a good projectile for whitetails. Available in 260- and 300-grain, it packs more than enough energy to drop a whitetail.

ties, and releases energy inside the animal. This is exactly what you want in situations where the average shot is under 70 yards. Even in the open country of the West, by concentrating on whitetail bedding areas, places where they feed and drink, and on travel routes, getting within roundball range is quite possible. These are areas that should be the center of game activity anyway. Though the roundball is not the first choice of most hunters these days, I would use a roundball shooter as willingly in Montana or Alberta as I would Maine or Alabama. The options might be a bit more limited and it might be necessary to actually hunt more in the sense of getting closer, getting to know the area and its inhabitants, and being more patient, but that's what hunting with a muzzleloader is all about.

As noted earlier the two most popular roundball calibers are the .50-caliber and .54-caliber. Both will cleanly dispatch a whitetail, even a trophy buck, but of the two the larger .54 is my first choice. Due to its small size and mass the .50-caliber sheds speed and energy more quickly. The .54-caliber roundball is larger, heavier, has more mass, and therefore hits with more energy. It is gen-

This hunter is studying deer tracks in fresh snow. He is carrying a short Bobcat carbine from CVA. With its 26-inch barrel and light weight of just 6 pounds, it is a good choice for close shots in timber or for hunters who cover a lot of ground.

erally accepted that 500 foot-pounds of energy is required to dispatch deer-size game, and there is a better guarantee of getting it with the .54-caliber out to 80 or 90 yards.

Both the solid lead conical and saboted-pistol make excellent deer bullets. They offer good muzzle velocity, have good mass, retain energy extremely well, hold together nicely upon impact, and deliver plenty of power. Either bullet in the 240- to 265-grain range will do nicely on whitetail. If the hunter knows the trajectory of his muzzleloader, either of these bullets will retain enough energy to put a whitetail down with a shot to the vitals out to 125 yards and beyond.

METHODS OF HUNTING

Each whitetail hunter has his or her favorite way of hunting this animal based upon the type of country being hunted, weather conditions, and past experience. Whitetail hunting technique, however, generally fall into four categories and whether we think about it or not, a single day afield can include several of them. These include stand hunting, still hunting, driving, and stalking. I have another technique that I enjoy a great deal that I find very productive in areas with navigable rivers and streams, even lakes and ponds: float hunting. There is nothing quite like being in a canoe at daybreak or dusk drifting on the currents with a muzzleloader during deer season. Because deer drink daily in most cases and expect no danger from water, float hunting can be an extremely productive way to go in the right areas.

Not all muzzleloader hunters hunt from a stand, but I do. Not every day, but in the right conditions it can be one of the most productive methods of hunting the whitetail. In the Northeast where I live a stand often means an elevated stand, either a self-climber, one permanently built in a tree, or a ladder-type. Down in Texas and other open areas where trees are scarce tripod stands are popular. It is important to check state regulations, though, as many states have specific rules pertaining to the use and establishment of stands, the driving of nails into trees, even the use of screw-in steps. Landowner permission, either written or verbal, is usually required to establish a stand on private property. The same is true on large private holdings such as those owned by paper and timber companies. Always know the law, and even if permission is not required common courtesy suggests it be obtained.

Safety is also important. In most cases a stand is 10 to 15 feet off the ground and a ladder is needed to reach them. Stands should be strong and sta-

Extracting a big whitetail buck from the woods is hard work. This buck was taken in Maine during the muzzleloader season with a White G Series Whitetail in .50-caliber shooting a 300-grain lead conical. It field-dressed over 200 pounds.

ble. It is also important that your muzzleloader be unloaded with no percussion cap or priming charge. Slings can be used to carry a muzzleloader into the stand, but I generally lay mine on the ground beneath the stand and use a small rope to pull it into the stand, making sure it is attached to the rifle in such a way that the muzzle is pointing towards the ground as I retrieve it. This can be done by attaching the rope to the trigger guard. Ropes with snap swivels specifically intended for this purpose are available commercially.

Once in the stand comfort and positioning is another issue. The seat should accommodate your size and shape and be positioned so there is room for movement when swinging the muzzleloader to fire. I shoot right-handed so my stand is facing directly at the area I expect to shoot or slightly off to the side. The stand should also be quiet. It is commonly believed deer do not look up. This is not true. Normally, deer have no reason to look skyward, but if a noise or movement from overhead draws their attention they will certainly do so.

Hunting above the ground provides a whole different perspective. While a clear shot may be available at the base of a tree, 10 feet up can be a different story. If necessary remove branches that might obscure your vision or interfere with your point of aim, making sure to leave some camouflage, particularly in back or against the skyline.

One of the big questions when establishing a stand is where to position it. This is best answered prior to the hunting season. Areas where scrapes, rubs, and other sign such as droppings and tracks are heavy should be given top consideration. Places where deer are known to feed and water are good spots, as are heavily used trails. The ideal stand should offer an opportunity to see or at least hear a deer before it has a chance to see or hear you or comes into muzzleloader range, which means being able to view an area out to 100 yards.

Note the prevailing wind when selecting a stand site. Next to locating an active area it is the most important factor governing success. I like to be downwind or crosswind from where I expect to see deer which lessens the chance that my scent will carry to the deer. By checking the wind it is often possible to get deer in extremely close, easily within muzzleloader range. The closest deer I have taken with a muzzleloader was literally below my stand. Also, establishing two stands is often a good idea. Where I live there is a great deal of rolling country and ridges. I put one stand high and another low, keeping in mind that air currents rise in the morning lifting my scent with them and away from approaching deer. In the afternoon the opposite is true. Air currents tend to descend so I hunt the lower stand. Much has to do with wind speed and direction, of course, but at least with two stands more options are available.

One of my favorite ways to hunt whitetail is still hunting. There are times when I simply want to move or see different territory, and still hunting makes this possible. There are also certain conditions during the season when this technique might be better than stand hunting or any other method.

Still hunting, however, takes patience. Lots of it. It is a tactic that must be mastered. To beat the whitetail at its own game it is important to know the area hunted, to cover it at a snail's pace and as quietly as possible. Next to wind direction these are the most important aspects. Make a single mistake, step on a twig, move at the wrong time or too fast, or forget the wind, and chances are it is all over.

A major mistake is moving too fast. I have a favorite piece of whitetail ground not far from the house that is perfect for still hunting. It is an old tote road that makes a complete loop, traveling through a variety of cover. I can go in one direction or the other depending upon wind direction. On a casual summer's hike I can cover the entire route in thirty minutes. But during hunt-

Rubs are common during the rut. They let the hunter know deer are active in the area. This hunter is carrying a Lyman Great Plains Rifle in .54-caliber.

ing season it takes several hours. Clinging to one side of the road for cover, I take a couple of steps, stop, look, listen, and glass with binoculars. After several minutes a few more steps are taken and the process is repeated. In the course of an hour perhaps 150 yards are actually covered. It is a slow, sometimes tedious and trying technique, but it works.

Another reason I like the tote road is that it is quiet. Many sections are covered with pine needles, grass, or moss. There is a section where the road is bordered by hardwoods, mostly oaks and maples, but early in the morning the fallen leaves are usually wet enough that I can walk over them without making a sound. This is certainly true during a drizzle or with several inches of fresh snow on the ground. These are prime conditions for still hunting anywhere. As you move keep an eye on the ground ahead for branches and twigs, avoiding them at all costs. Each step should be placed slowly. This not only helps prevent unwanted noise but helps maintain balance. Always work into the wind or crosswind. Many experienced still hunters like to have the sun to their back if possible. They also hunt with their eyes. They look and scan thoroughly, moving their eyes before turning their heads, moving on only after totally convinced a deer is not in the area.

Knowing the area is important. Successful hunters do a great deal of preseason scouting and by opening day they know the feeding and bedding areas, travel routes, where the scrapes and rubs are, and how best to approach them. During the season they work along the edge of heavy cover and take advantage of tote roads, logging roads, ATV and snowmobile trails and walking paths. They wear garments and footwear that are quiet, and they are always alert and prepared. When carrying my favorite sidelock percussion muzzleloader, for example, I usually carry it across my chest or in such a way that allows my thumb to rest on the hammer at half-cock. I have taught myself to pull the hammer back to full-cock as I raise the muzzleloader into firing position. It speeds things up considerably.

Driving deer generally involves of a group of hunters working as a team. Driving is not legal in every state or province so it is imperative to check the local regulations. In some states laws exist which limit the number of hunters in each party.

Drives work best in areas of thick cover, wilderness areas, and other locales where deer have large areas to roam and the only chance for success is to "drive" them in a certain direction. A group of hunters form a line, perhaps on the edge of a woodlot or corn field and slowly walk towards several other hunters who have been posted at strategic downwind or crosswind locations. By walking slowly the scent of the drivers is carried ahead causing deer to flee along scouted escape routes. Typically, there are more "drivers" than "posters," and to insure safety all hunters are dressed in fluorescent orange. In places where drives are common, posted hunters are stationed on raised stands or high pieces of ground, again as a safety measure.

Stalking is perhaps the ultimate muzzleloading challenge. This is true on all big game, and it is certainly true with whitetails. For me, there is nothing quite as exciting, and challenging to my hunting skills, as glassing from a high vantage point, spotting game, and then slipping up to within muzzleloader range. This tactic works well in large clear-cuts, on the western plains, in the large agricultural areas, and just about anywhere deer can be seen from a distance, particularly where hunting pressure is light. The last thing you want when on a stalk is to have another hunter ruin the game plan. By the same token, rarely have I experienced great success stalking in wooded areas.

It is important to keep an eye on the target for long periods, which is difficult at best in wooded areas, and the opportunity to make noise is simply too great.

The idea is to spend some time glassing, preferably from a high vantage point, facing into or across the wind since stalking into the wind is extremely important. When an animal is spotted the game begins. Select a landmark to pinpoint location, and then select the best route with cover to get within the desired range.

Deer that are bedded are ideal objectives for stalking because they are settled down and are comfortable with their surroundings. A bedded deer also

Bedding areas are good spots to hunt. They are often in thick cover or on south-facing ridges and other areas that collect morning sun. This hunter is carrying a T/C Hawken Custom in .50-caliber.

provides an opportunity to scan for other game that might also be bedded nearby. If other deer are spotted nearby the challenge of getting within muzzleloader range just increased considerably. Deer that are feeding can also be stalked, but they are generally much more alert and easily spooked. If this is the case and a deer flicks its tail, hold tight. This is a sign that it is nervous. Wait until it goes back to feed before continuing the stalk.

Float hunting, or drift hunting, is an ideal way to take advantage of dry conditions, and because deer seldom see or hear you coming, getting within muzzleloader range is rarely a problem. I enjoy it a great deal and am grateful I live in an area where several small, winding rivers and creeks make it productive.

Canoes work great for this type of hunting. They are light, slice through the water with ease, draw little water, are easily maneuvered, and those of 14 feet or more can easily carry two hunters, gear, and a deer. One hunter generally paddles from the stern while the one in the bow does the hunting. The key

Female whitetails are not legal in all states. Where they may be hunted, does can provide a challenge for the muzzleloading hunter due to their size.

here is to maintain silence. Banging paddles, shuffling gear, even human voices carry over water. If possible do little paddling. Drifting is much better. Stay close to the banks and hug the inside bends, slowing as you approach them and sneaking around the corner. After rounding the point, if another bend is within view, cross to the other side to be in better position to round it. While drift hunting can be productive any time of day, morning and late afternoon are especially good.

This is a fun and relaxing way to hunt and, when done correctly, very productive, but keep safety in mind. Wear a life jacket and use caution entering and exiting the craft. Water temperatures during most muzzleloader seasons are quite cold. To lessen noise, old carpet on the bottom of the canoe and covering the gunwales and thwarts helps a great deal. Drift hunting is legal in most states, but check the regulations.

SHOT PLACEMENT

There are several sure shots on a whitetail, or any big game, but the heart/lung area remains the best. A shot to the brain, neck, or spine will usually drop an animal on the spot but the spinal column and jugular vein make up less than 25 percent of the neck area and are risky shots at best with a muzzleloader. The brain is even smaller and is protected by thick skull bone. The heart/lung region is much bigger, and though the deer may not drop on the spot, it is by far the best shot in most hunting situations. Even this large target area is not always easy to hit. At broadside, the heart and lungs are exposed 100 percent but such blessings are rare under 100 yards. When the animal is quartering towards you the area is reduced to 65 percent, quartering away 60 percent, and head-on a mere 35 percent is exposed. From a tree stand exposure is reduced even more.

How much ground will a whitetail cover before collapsing when hit in the vitals? I have had them drop on the spot. On other occasions they have covered 100 yards. There is no way to answer the question with any degree of certainty. I do know that if a deer is walking with no idea of your presence and the heart or lungs are taken out, the chances it will drop or cover less ground are far better than deer on the run. Deer can cover considerable ground with adrenalin pumping through the veins even after major organs cease to func-

Knowing where to look is a key to whitetail success. Old apple orchards are hotspots, especially when acorns and other natural foods may be scarce.

tion. In either case, the chances are good that some ground will be covered because death is not immediate. Once the trigger is pulled note the direction of flight and listen for sounds that might suggest further information, but wait several minutes and let the deer run itself out. Chances are if a solid hit to the heart or lung was made it won't go far. Look on the ground for blood. Blood from a heart shot will be deep red and clear while blood from a lung shot is often frothy.

WHITE-TAILED DEER POPULATIONS/MUZZLELOADING SEASONS

State	Estimated Whitetail Population	Minimum Caliber	ML Season
Alabama	1,500,000+	.40	Varies by area
Arizona	90–95,00 Coues'	.40	Late Sept
Arkansas	750,000	.40	Varies by zone
Colorado	10,000	.40	Varies early Sept/mid-Oct depending upon area
Connecticut	65–70,000	.45	Early Dec
Delaware	25–30,000	.42	Split—early Oct/late Jan
Florida	700–800,000	.40	Varies by zone, generally in early and late Oct/Nov
Georgia	1,000,000	.44	Late Oct
Idaho	N/A	.45	Varies
Kansas	300–400,000	.39	Split—mid-late Sept late Nov
Kentucky	400,000	.40	Split—late Oct Early Dec
Louisiana	750,000– 1,000,000	.44	Split—Late Oct/ mid-Nov/mid-Jan
Maine	350,000	.40	Varies by districts
Maryland	200,000	.40	Split—mid-Oct/mid-late Dec Late Oct. some districts
Massachusetts	80,000	.44	Mid-Dec
Michigan	1,400,000– 1,600,000	.45	Early-mid Dec
Minnesota	1,000,000	.40	Late Nov–early Dec
Mississippi	1,500,000– 1,750,000	.38	Early Dec
Missouri	750,000	.40	Split–early Dec/early Jan
Montana	N/A	None	N/A
Nebraska	170,000	.40	All Dec
New Hampshire	70,000	.40	Late Oct–early Nov
New Jersey	150,000	.44	Varies by zone
New Mexico	15,000 Coues' & Texas whitetails	.40	Varies by zone
New York	800,000	.44	Mid-Oct
North Carolina	800,000	None	Varies by region
North Dakota	150,000	.45	Varies
Ohio	400,000	.38	Late Oct
Oklahoma	300,000	.40	Late Oct–early Nov
Oregon	7,000	.40	Varies by unit
Pennsylvania	1,000,000	.44	Split—Late Oct/Late Dec–early Jan

Rhode Island	8,000	.45	Early-late Nov
South Carolina	1,000,000	.36	Varies
South Dakota	300,000	.44	Varies by unit
Tennessee	700,000	.40	Varies
Texas	3,200,000	.40	Varies
Vermont	130,000	.43	Early Dec
Virginia	900,000	.45	Varies by region
Washington	80,000	.40	Split—early Oct/Late-mid-Dec
West Virginia	800,000	.38	Early Dec
Wisconsin	1,000,000	.40	Late Nov–early Dec
Wyoming	60,000	.40	Varies

Note: Population figures and season dates vary. Check with state fish and game departments for more specific details and possible changes.

11

MULE DEER AND BLACK-TAILED DEER

The mule deer has long been a favorite of mine. The only problem is that I live in the Northeast, and the mulie lives out west. I don't get the opportunity to go after them nearly as much as I would like. When it comes to a challenging muzzleloading hunt, though the whitetail gets all the attention, the mulie is worth the effort, too. This is partly due to the habitat it calls home, which can include some of the most rugged territory in the West. While the whitetail certainly has its millions of fans, the mulie also has its followers, and they are no less dedicated. In fact, if the mule deer was as widely and readily available, I have to wonder if the whitetail would be the only "king" of big game.

In height, a mature mulie buck stands 42 inches at the shoulder, roughly 2 or 3 inches higher than a comparable whitetail buck. Generally, the mule deer is also more powerful and robust looking. While the whitetail can look trim, delicate, almost refined and dignified, the mulie bucks looks like a boxer about to step into the ring. Even the females have a rugged, western look.

The mule deer's body can run close to six feet in length, longer that the whitetail and a bit heavier on average. A respectable mulie buck is good habitat will run 175 to 200 pounds, perhaps 25 to 40 pounds heavier than a whitetail buck of the same age living in good range. Some large mulie bucks tip the scales at over 300 pounds. Whitetail bucks will reach that size, too, but not as often as the mulie. The mule deer is darker in color, and on the face has an obvious black patch in the shape of a "U" tapering down from between the ears to a point midway on the face. The tail is narrow, covered with short hair and tipped in black. The hooves are quite large and more blunt that the whitetail's, which aids them in rugged mountain country as well as deep snow.

But the most distinguishing characteristics of this deer, and the two traits for which they are famous are the ears and antlers. The ears resemble those of a mule, both in size and shape, hence their name. On a large bucks the ears may be eight to nine inches high and nearly half that much wide. On females the ears seen even larger because they are not overshadowed by antlers. In either case, the ears are often one of the first things spotted by hunters in the field.

Mule deer are one of the true big game prizes of the West. This specimen was taken in Montana at 100 yards using a modern in-line shooting a 265-grain saboted bullet.

The antlers are deeply forked, or bifurcated, which means that the points extend from a common main beams rather than fork. The number of points on a mule deer are not necessarily an indication of age since four points plus brow tine of each side are pretty much standard. Rather, antler development and the number of points is related to sexual vitality and dependent on nutrition and certain minerals in the diet, particularly limestone.

The Columbia blacktail and Sitka blacktail are basically the same species. In fact, the mulie was also called the "blacktail," but designation was changed once the difference in size between the two types was recognized. The Columbia blacktail is now considered a separate subspecies, scientifically known as *Odocoileus hemionus columbianus.* The Sitka blacktail falls into the same category, and the primary difference between the two is tied to territorial boundaries, primarily for record-book purposes.

The average blacktail is smaller than the average mule deer. A large buck averages 150 to 200 pounds, but is considerably smaller in body dimensions than many whitetail bucks. Unlike the whitetail, whose largest examples in terms of body size are typically found in the north, the farther north the blacktail ranges the smaller they get. The typical Sitka deer is even smaller and sports smaller antlers than the average blacktail. Although about the same height at the shoulder, the Sitka blacktail is shorter is length and somewhat stockier. The ears on the blacktail are larger than a whitetail's but smaller than the mulies. Antler appearance is similar to mule deer, forming from a main beam. Both have the same black patch on the face.

HABITAT, FOOD, AND MOVEMENT

The mule deer is a child of high, rugged mountain and canyon country. In many western states the use of horses to reach remote areas is popular. Mule deer prefer those isolated rock, canyon and timber pockets where whitetail's dare not go in most cases. Broken hill country offering steep draws, rock outcroppings, gullies and coulee is all prime mulie terrain. Typically, mulies will bed, feed, and frequent areas where vegetation is available, but unlike the whitetail they prefer growth to be sparse. Their bedding areas are generally near low growing brush beneath large, heavily-limbed ponderosa pine, pinon, lodgepole pine or juniper, especially when scattered along a mountainside near the top of the ridge. They often lay near the top where they can see down

The author with a mule deer doe taken in Montana. The muzzleloader is a White G Series Whitetail.

both sides and an escape route is available. These areas should be carefully glassed from a distance when hunting.

The mulie is also quite at home in rolling high desert country, or ranchlands several hundred miles from the mountains. They are found in open sage country but open terrain must offer the type of living conditions are higher elevations: the topography must be rugged and broken and supply cover. It should be noted that mule deer need open space, places where man has had less impact on it habitat. This deer has not adapted well to man's presence as easily as the whitetail, nor does it live as comfortable in close proximity to man. For this reason, the mulie is falling on hard times in many parts of its range. There remain some excellent hunting opportunities, but because of man's encroachment and increased hunting pressure finding trophy bucks is not as easy as it once was.

Like elk, mule deer "migrate" from one elevation or location to another depending on the season. In many locales mule deer will spend the summer in the high country where living conditions are more to their liking and will remain there until the first hard snows pushes them to lower elevations. Prevailing weather conditions, food, water and other factors males locating moving animals one of the biggest challenges facing the hunter. A good guide or out-

A 4x4 mule deer buck taken in Wyoming.

fitter is familiar with deer movements in his area, and for the first-time mule deer hunter this is definitely the best way to go. Generally, October and November are peak hunting months.

GUNS AND LOADS

The same muzzleloader calibers and loads recommended for whitetail will usually do nicely on mule deer. However, they are bigger and shots are normally longer, which means a projectile that can reach out with some power should be used. A roundball gun in either .50-or.54-caliber will do the job, especially the large .54, but even then the shot should be no more than 60 or 70 yards. I prefer lead conicals or sabot loads for this animals, anything is the 250-to 265-grain range.

METHODS OF HUNTING

There are several ways of hunting mule deer but most are predicated on getting high and working down. Mule deer usually are found up high so that means the hunter has to get even high, or at least on the same level. It also means a lot of glassing. My experience has been that the best time to glass is early in the morning from dawn until nine o'clock and late in the day. These the times when mule deer will be moving from beds to feeding and watering areas and back again. Glassing also provides an opportunity to keep an eye on an animal, to see where it travels. During midday, mule deer often bed down and this is a good time to make a careful stalk. While glassing, the most successful hunters take note of the surrounding country, familiarizing themselves with the landscape, particularly ravines, canyons, and other areas deer seem to be traveling to, from or through. A good set of binoculars is a must, just like with other western game.

Still hunting can be quite productive in areas where mulie numbers are high and when travel routes are known. Investigate timbered areas and canyons that contain water, food, and cover and river and creek bottoms and coulees, always keeping watch on the high ridges. If the sign is good, sit and be patient.

SHOT PLACEMENT

Mule deer should be hit in the heart and lung region, just behind the front shoulder and just below the midpoint of the body. A roundball, conical or sabot load missing the precise mark by a couple of inches is sure to do enough damage to kill the animal quickly. Solid shoulder hits may knock them down at close range, but I've seen big mulie bucks stagger and keep on going unless smacked in a vital.

RANGE

These three deer are strictly a western phenomenon. Each state seems to have its share of prime mule deer country, but Utah and Colorado currently have more entries in the record book than all others.

Technically, the Longhunter geographic boundaries separating mule deer and blacktail deer are as follows: in British Columbia, "Beginning at the

The blacktail is a member of the mule deer clan. Notice the big ears and black tail. These deer are found in the northwest United States.

British Columbia-Washington border, blacktail range runs west of the height of land between the Skagit and the Chilliwack Ranges, intersecting the Fraser River opposite the mouth of Ruby Creek, then west and up Harrison Lake to and up Tipella Creek to the height of land in Garibaldi Park and northwesterly along the divide past Alta Lake, Mt. Dalgleish and Mt. Waddington, then north to Bella Coola. From there, the boundary continues north to the head of Dean Channel, Gardner Canal and Douglas Channel to the town of Anyox, then due west to the Alaska-British Columbia border, which is followed south to open water. The boundary excludes the areas west of the Klesilkwa River and the west side of the Lillooet River."

In Washington state, "Beginning at the Washington-British Columbia border, the line runs south along the west boundary of the North Cascades National Park to the township line between R10E and R11E, Willamette Meridian, which is followed directly south to its intersection with the township line between T18N and T17N, which is then followed westward until it connects with the north border of Mt. Rainier National Park, then along the north, west, and south park boundaries until it intersects with the township line R9E and R10E, Willamette Meridian, which is then followed directly south to the Columbia River near Cook."

In California, "Beginning in Siskiyou County at the California-Oregon border, the line lies between townships R8W and R9W M.D.M., extending south to and along the Klamath River to Hamburg, then south along the road to Scott Bar, continuing south and then east on an unimproved road from Scott Bar to its intersection with the paved road to Mugginsville, then south through Mugginsville to State Highway 3, which is followed to Douglas City in Trinity County. From Douglas County, the line runs east on State Highway 229 to Interstate 5, which is followed to the south border of Santa Clara County. The boundary then runs west along this border to the east border of Santa Clara County. The line then follows the east and south borders of Santa Clara County to the south border of Santa Cruz County which is then followed to the edge of Monterey Bay."

These lines of demarcation are rather specific but are the only way the Longhunter Society can prevent intergrades between the categories. Basically, all deer from eastern British Columbia, Alberta, and Saskatchewan; eastern Washington, eastern Oregon, Idaho, Montana, North and South Dakota, Wyoming, Nevada, Utah, Colorado, Oklahoma, Texas, New Mexico, Arizona, Nebraska, Kansas and the remainder of California are considered mule deer. All deer west and beyond this boundary are blacktail deer.

When it comes to Sitka blacktail deer, the accepted range and boundary lines are much simpler. They include the coastal regions of southwest Alaska, including Kodiak Island, and the Queen Charlotte Islands of British Columbia.

12

ELK: THE MOST REGAL BIG GAME

Anyone who has hunted the American elk, or "wapiti," will agree that this is one of the most inspiring and impressive critters they have ever set eyes on. It is a common debate around high country campfires that the elk is also the most engaging and best all-around game animal on the continent. I don't know if I would go that far. I have hunted enough big game of various types to conclude all have attributes that make them special, but based on personal experience I will say this is truly an impressive animal and that hunting it can be demanding yet extremely rewarding. It is an adrenalin and emotional high and joyously addictive. I reside in the East, far from prime elk country. But if I lived in such places as Colorado, Montana, Wyoming, or nearly two dozen other states and western provinces where this noble deer is found and hunted, it would be one of my prime targets.

There are several aspects about the elk that make it a serious hunting quest. Among them is its appearance and size. The Rocky Mountain elk (*Cervus elaphus nelsoni*), one of two species recognized by the Longhunter Society—the other is the Roosevelt elk—is the largest round-antlered member of the deer family on the planet. A large American elk can tip the scales at 600 to 800 pounds on the hoof, stand five feet at the shoulder, and run four feet or more from brisket to hams. Among members of the worldwide deer family, only the moose is larger. The female, or cow, a respectable and beautiful trophy in its own right with a muzzleloader, is smaller, but a large one may still weigh around 600 pounds.

In outward appearance, the American elk is generally brownish-gray or tan with a darker face and neck area. There is a yellowish patch on the rump that because of the elk's darkened tones, can be prominent on some animals. A number of Western guides I have hunted with call this patch a "sunflower." As it moves and through timber or open meadows the elk truly displays a regal air. It has an intelligent look about the face. The eyes are large and sharp. When glassing a bull a hundred yards downwind, it feels as if he knows you are there and is looking straight into your soul. Only when hunting bear have I had my heart beat so fast, or had breath come with so much labor.

The elk is blessed with sharp senses. Its eyesight is among the best of the big game. Its sense of smell rivals that of the whitetail and its hearing is extremely keen. On several occasions it seemed to me this animal had a vacuum cleaner for a nose, able to suck in scents and smells a mile away. Whatever the case, the elk is gifted in all sensory departments. This necessitates glassing from considerable distance, not only to locate game but to minimize the chance of being spotted and to gauge wind and ascertain the best line of attack.

But perhaps the most impressive, awe-inspiring characteristic of the mature bull elk is its headgear. I have hunted caribou with success on the barrens of northern Quebec and Labrador, moose in the black spruce forests and bogs of Newfoundland and in the woodlands of Ontario and elsewhere, and I have observed some truly large whitetail and mule deer bucks, but nothing quite compares to the set of antlers atop the elk's darkened brow. On a truly large American bull elk, these massive, sweeping, spiked antlers can have main beams extending five feet or more towards the heavens and an inside spread of three and a half feet, perhaps more. Some of the tines can easily extend 15 to 18 inches in length. Due to its size the rack of an elk is highly visible in open country, even in some timbered situations. In fact, it is often the first thing drawing the hunter's attention and the one attribute above all others that has made the elk one of the most sought after big game animals on the continent.

The country elk call home is also a primary reason why hunting them is such a joy. The alpine slopes and valleys through much of its range make even

Elk are a challenging quarry with a muzzleloader. Heavy roundballs of .54-caliber and larger, heavy lead conicals, or saboted bullets are recommended. This magnificent bull was taken by Dr. Gary White of White Muzzleloading/MTT in New Mexico using a White Super 91 in-line.

a hunt that does not fill a tag a worthwhile experience. Packing into a remote elk camp by horse, traveling through some of the West's last great wilderness areas, many of which remain virtually untouched, is an ultimate hunting experience. You cannot enter this country and not be changed in some deep and personal way. Just hearing a bugle on a cold autumn morning makes a trip worthwhile. It is one of those magical sounds, like that of the loon, wolf, or whippoorwill.

The other elk of interest to the hunter is the Roosevelt elk *(Cervus elaphus roosevelti)*. This trophy category was established by the Boone and Crockett Club in 1980, and was adopted by the Longhunter Society, as well. In terms of body weight, the Roosevelt elk is often heavier than its cousin inhabiting the backbone of the Rockies and surrounding environs. It is not uncommon for a large bull to tip the scales at 1,000 to 1,100 pounds or better. Not all bulls are of this size, of course, and many run about the same size as American elk bulls, but the Roosevelt elk is known for its large body and impressive weight.

It is also known for its smaller, rather compact headgear. The main beam of a large American elk can run, close to five feet or more, while on a trophy Roosevelt elk the main beams often measure between three and a half and four feet. The primary points are also shorter. On the American elk the main points can be up to 20 inches, but on a truly large Roosevelt elk they may be just over 12 inches, perhaps in the 13-inch to 15-inch range.

RANGE

The comeback of the elk is another American success story. Before the arrival of the white man elk ranged over much of what is now the United States. At times, prior to about 1800, populations existed in what are now called the prairie states, the southern Appalachians—in Tennessee and Kentucky, for ex-

A monster 6x6, bugling during the rut. The comeback of the elk is one of America's great wildlife success stories. (Credit: Neal & Mary Jane Mishler.)

ample—even in New York and southern New England. Elk were so common settlers named new towns, cities, and counties after them. Today, the word elk is used as a place name in at least 27 states. The rapid settlement of these areas, however, contributed to the loss of vital habitat, and along with over-hunting, brought about the elk's rapid demise. By the time Lewis and Clark departed St. Louis on their great western exploration, elk were pretty much gone east of the Mississippi. By around 1900, it was estimated that as few as 40,000 existed on the continent, primarily in isolated mountain pockets of the West.

Today, despite continued loss of habitat and rangeland in many areas and other pressures from humans, the elk is doing well. Controlled hunting, good management by the respective western states and provinces, and programs and public awareness sponsored by organizations such as the Rocky Mountain Elk Foundation have played a major role in this resurgence. Populations fluctuate depending on wintering conditions and other factors, but current population estimates are between 800,000 and 900,000 elk, in 21 states and provinces as far east as Michigan. It should be noted that hunting licenses and permits in many states are allocated by a draw, and in some states and most provinces hunting is limited to residents only. Interested elk hunters should check with individual state or provincial game departments for details. Do so early, well in advance of your hunt, as demand in draw states is traditionally heavy.

The primary elk states and estimated populations include: Alaska, 1,000; Arizona, 35,000; California, 8000; Colorado, 175,000; Idaho, 150,000; Michigan, 1,200; Montana, 90,000; Nevada, 2,500; North Dakota, 700; New Mexico, 25,000; Oklahoma, 1,200; Oregon, 110,000; South Dakota, 3,000; Utah, 50,000; Washington, 60,000; and Wyoming, 90,000. Traditionally, the premier elk states have been Colorado, Idaho, Montana, Wyoming, Oregon, and Washington, not necessarily in that order. In recent years, New Mexico and Arizona have come on strong for trophy elk.

In Canada, the primary elk provinces and estimated populations are: Alberta, 18,000; British Columbia, 40,000; Manitoba, 7,000; and Saskatchewan, 10,000.

According to the Longhunter Society, for record-keeping purposes, the established geographic restrictions for Roosevelt elk include Del Norte and Humbolt counties in northern California; Afognak and Raspberry islands, Alaska; west of I-5 in Oregon and Washington; and Vancouver Island, British Columbia. All elk harvested in other states and provinces are considered

American elk. Minimum Longhunter entry scores for American elk are 255 for typical entries and 265 for non-typical. The minimum score for Roosevelt elk is 225.

HABITAT AND FOOD

The American elk of today is an inhabitant of the mountains and open parklands. Contrary to common belief, this great deer does not necessarily require large wilderness areas to live, providing man leaves him alone. In fact, although often found in rugged country, elk also thrive relatively close to civilization where conditions permit. In many areas throughout the West, however, man has done a good job of fencing off access to winter feeding grounds along many migration routes. In other areas once productive habitat simply has been destroyed or altered to the point that elk no longer feel welcome, and they have moved on.

In general, wherever the range provides expanses of grassy hillsides and parklands for grazing and browsing and heavy timber for cover and bedding, elk will prosper. Keep in mind, the elk is considered both a browser and grazer, but usually prefers grazing, so valleys, river and creek bottoms, and areas offering wheatgrass, bromegrass, fescue, and needlegrass are prime feeding areas, particularly when they are off the beaten track. The American elk will also dine on willow and pine, among others. Canyons and hidden mountain valleys, even those at 8,000 to 9,000 feet, and other areas offering this combination are always good possibilities, as are areas burned over by forest fires that are sprouting new grasses and saplings. Literally thousands of square miles of such habitat still exist throughout the West. Unfortunately, as man continues to encroach on parts of it, elk are increasingly found farther back, and often higher, in some of the most remote and rugged mountain country on the continent.

This is particularly true for some of the biggest trophies. Fewer do-it-yourself hunters tred into the high country, and for the most part it remains the domain of the outfitter in many prime elk locales. Hunting pressure is lower and elk live to an older age. To a large degree, along the rim of the Rockies is where the big boys are, and to find them the hunter must go up top to seek them out.

The Roosevelt elk is an inhabitant of dense rainforest-type habitat. They are an amazing animal, and the country they call home is just as amazing.

Hunting among its dense growth can be an experience in itself. Alder bottoms and lofty cedars covered with moss, dense spruce ridges and valleys, a moss-covered forest floor, along with countless streams, creeks, and rivers, contribute to an unusual landscape. Rain and inclement weather during elk season seem to be a daily occurance, providing a special challenge to the blackpowder hunter. Unquestionably beautiful and perhaps some of the most unique land on the continent, it can be demanding to hunt. Devil's club, blueberry bushes, and aspen are among the Roosevelt elk's favorite foods, all of which are abundant through their far western range.

GUNS AND LOADS

When hunting with patch and roundball no attempt on elk should be made with anything smaller than a .54-caliber; the larger .58-caliber is even better. At close range, say 50 or 60 yards, a .50-caliber will do the job, but such close shots are not common in elk country, and even then it is questionable whether sufficient power will be delivered to do the job cleanly and humanely. Some enthusiasts say yes, but I remain skeptical at best.

Even with conicals and sabot loads, a heavy bullet, something of at least 250 grains, should be used, preferrably something 275-300 grains. With a bullet of this weight one of the .45-caliber sabot loads, even solid lead conicals, put to the lungs, heart, or spine may very well do the trick, but I would still recommend the larger .50-caliber or .54-caliber, and would make a point of getting within 100 yards if at all possible. I would also recommend a bullet with good expansion qualities, something like the Barnes Expander-MZ, the Hornady Great Plains bullet, the Thompson/Center Maxi-Hunter, or Big Bore Express' Black Belt Express, in hollowpoint or flatpoint. The elk is a huge, powerful animal. Don't underestimate them, or overestimate the ability of your muzzleloader.

For a charge, go with the maximum your gun will take, providing it performs well with your chosen load. You want some bullet speed, good penetration, power, and internal expansion.

METHODS OF HUNTING

There are several ways to hunt elk, with bugling and stalking the most common. Of the two bugling is by far the most exciting. There is something mystical, something that touches the very depths of the human soul, about the high-pitched wail of a bull elk calling to a mate on a crisp autumn morning. It can be heard for miles as it echos off hills and canyon walls.

Unfortunately, the bugle is something seldom heard by most elk hunters. This is due in part to the fact that in many heavily hunted areas the mature bulls have grown wise. They have learned that being too vocal often draws danger, and I have heard many guides and outfitters state that the sound of bugling elk is not as common as it use to be. Undoubtedly, this is more true in some places than others, for I have been witness to bugling bulls on more than several occasions.

Also, the bugling season, or rut, generally takes place in September across much of the elk's range. While many gun seasons throughout the west do take place during this month in some management units and zones of certain states and provinces, the general gun season usually takes place after the rut, practically nullifying the thrill and challenge of the bugling tactic. However, a rambunctious young bull, even more mature bulls in some cases, may still be willing to answer the call, so give it a try. You never know, and there is nothing to lose. In those areas where the hunting season takes place during the bugling season, using an artificial call can be both challenging and productive. Like calling moose or "rattling" a whitetail buck, it is an aspect of the hunt which makes the endeavor truly exciting. The best time to bugle an elk is generally early in the day, often around sunrise on cold, crisp mornings, preferrably when the wind is still and things are quiet. It does little good to bugle in windy conditions, unless you are positive that a bull is near. Even then bugling may be a risky venture. Generally in such conditions, as well as in fog and heavy rain, elk are bedded or bunched together and don't move. Calling at these times often raises more suspicion than anything else. Good calling locations include high ridges, rim country, the head of canyons and the edges of hidden grass valleys surrounded by timber. The hunter should be well concealed but have a good view of the surrounding area, and it is important to achieve the right pitch and not to call too much.

Elk primarily move early in the day, from daybreak to just after sun-up and late in the day from dusk to darkness. It is also during these hours when they bugle most and are most actively feeding. These are good times to watch the openings, the grassy valleys and vales, and other primary feeding areas. From about nine or ten o'clock in the morning to about four o'clock in the afternoon, however, they are generally in the timber or other cover bedded down. This is a good time to stalk coniferous forests and aspen.

Stalking is a slow, meticulous, often difficult method of hunting this animal for they are easily spooked, and elk can detect danger by sight, sound, or smell from considerable, sometimes unbelievable, distances. It is vital to move slowly, silently, keeping an eye on the wind. Hunt with your eyes, just as you would when stalking whitetails. When stalking, either on foot or by horse, it is often best to start up high, allowing a chance to scrutinize the country below. A good set of binoculars are a must whenever hunting this animal, since elk are often first spotted at considerable distance, sometimes appearing as mere grayish spots or shapes out of contrast to the landscape. Keep an eye on brushy and timbered bottoms along the edges of valleys and other openings, ridges and canyon rims, saddles between rolling hills or mountains, and especially high, heavy timbered areas on the sides of mountains, slopes, and ridges.

Finally, keep in mind that reaching some the West's best elk country often means putting your butt in a saddle for some long hours of horseback riding. Good elk country is increasingly found far back in the high mountain country, where the largest bulls stay until pushed to lower elevations by snow or poor weather. Elk are free-roaming critters, found here one day, perhaps five miles away the next, so horses are not only used to reach camp, but to actually work the surrounding country each day to scout for game. In many high country elk situations it is not unusual to spend long hours each day in the saddle. I once rode for days with good friend and outfitter Frank Deedee in the Wind River Range of western Wyoming, and for the first few days my rear-end felt like a raw piece of steak, and I felt muscles and bones I never realized I had despite the fact that I had taken the initiative to do some riding before leaving for the hunt. If horses are used on your hunt, be prepared.

SHOT PLACEMENT

Elk are best hit in the lungs for several reasons, regardless of the type of blackpowder projectile being use. For one thing, the lungs are the biggest vital organ on an elk and therefore offer the biggest target. Aim just behind the front shoulder and you're in the boiler room.

Also, the lungs on this animal are not only large but dense. Even a fast traveling conical or sabot load will generally have plenty of time to expand and do some internal damage. If hit solidly in the lungs, it is rare that an elk will go far. But if not, a lung shot typically leaves a good blood trail. Keep in mind, blood from a lung shot is bright red; dark, heavy blood comes from muscle.

Unless absolutely necessary, shots into the heavy shoulder area should be avoided. I have seen the thick shoulder blade actually stop or turn a bullet, particularly the fast expanding types so popular on deer and antelope. I personally prefer heavier, slower expanding loads. I want some penetration before that bullet opens up. If using a fast-expansion bullet, go for the lungs, always. When the lungs are not visible, such as in timber, aspen, or brush country, a spine or neck shot will bring an elk down, but it has to be a good shot. Despite the size of this animal, neither the spine or neck bone is overly large.

13

PRONGHORN—THE WEST'S MOST ENJOYABLE BIG-LITTLE GAME

O f all western big game, the pronghorn is among my personal favorite, right up there with the elk and mulie. In fact, if I were pressed to make a definitive answer, this speedster of the grasslands would probably head the list. The reason for this is simple: They are just fun to watch and hunt, particularly for the blackpowder enthusiast.

There are, however, other reasons why the pronghorn holds a special place in my heart and why this animal provides a world-class hunting challenge for the blackpowder hunter. One is appearance, it looks exotic compared to other North American big game. Glassing a herd of pronghorn on the rolling prairies and plains of north-central Montana, on the east side of the Continental Divide in Colorado, or on the more arid grasslands of New Mexico must be what glassing a herd of gazelle in Africa is like.

From a distance, the pronghorn appears striped or even spotted. Its white under-belly and brisket gives way to a tan or buff-colored trim, and then a darkened reddish brown on the back and neck. The throat area has bands of alternating white and tan and the rump is white. When alarmed and fleeing the erect white hairs of this patch seem to bloom, and a good eye can see it for miles against the brown landscape of the West. The hair of this animal is stiff and bristly, and like that of the caribou, is hollow and easy to damage when skinning.

The males, also known as bucks, have a black face and a patch on the upper side of the neck. The females, or does, typically lack most or all of this dark mask as well as the patch. The jet black horns of the bucks, the only horned mammal to shed its horns each year, are also longer than those on the females, easily extending above the ears. The horns of the male also hook or curve backward and slightly inward, with one forward "prong," hence the name pronghorn. Contrary to common belief, this is not an antelope but the only species in its distinct family, which is found only on the North American continent.

The eyesight of the pronghorn is perhaps the keenest of all big game. It is said that this animal has eyes comparable to an 8X to 10X rifle scope or binoculars. Whether true or not I cannot say, but based upon personal experience with species in Montana, Colorado, and other areas on both sides of the Mississippi, I have little doubt they have the sharpest eyes of any big game. They use this eyesight, as well as speed, to elude danger. Within a few days of

Pronghorn travel in groups, with the biggest bucks often bringing up the rear. Notice the buck just in front of the doe, watching his harem.

birth, the young can run for short distances and as young adults may reach speeds close to 60 mph. In comparative terms, the cheetah is faster in a sprint or short run, but the pronghorn is a marathoner, capable of maintaining a speed of 35 to 40 mph over long distances. It is an incredible sight to watch a herd blaze across an open plain, there one minute and literally gone in a trail of dust the next. In size, an average buck may run 3½ feet at the shoulder, with a monster hitting 4 feet, and perhaps from 47 to 56 inches in length from brisket to butt. Bucks run between 100 and 130 pounds, perhaps a little more in exceptional cases. An average doe runs about three-quarters that size, a small target, indeed, in both cases.

RANGE

The pronghorn is strictly a western phenomenon. At one time it ranged over nearly all of the western United States, extending as far east as the western sections of Minnesota, Iowa, Missouri, Arkansas, even Louisiana. Running north to south, it extended well into Saskatchewan and Alberta in Canada, and deep into Mexico. It is believed that original populations throughout the West numbered more than 20 million, second only in numbers to the bison. Shortly after the turn of the century, however, this native American seemed doomed. Its habitat was rapidly being plowed under or otherwise altered, and cattlemen, fearing pronghorn would compete for grass and rangeland, often shot them on sight. This animal was not accustomed to barbed wire, and the fencing of former habitat greatly reduced its range. Even today, it is rare that a pronghorn will jump a fence, scooting beneath it instead. In earlier times, buffalo kept prairie grasses short, allowing sagebrush and other brush pronghorns like to flourish. With the bison gone, grasses choked out the more desirable forage.

Today, the native range of the pronghorn is much reduced, as are its numbers, but through careful management it is doing extremely well. It is presently found in approximately sixteen states and two Canadian provinces and widely hunted, although in some states only by draw. In many states, hunting is as simple as purchasing a license, and in some managements units of some states, hunters are even allowed more than one animal. The hunting in Canada is generally restricted to residents only. Leading states in terms of numbers and chances of taking quality heads include Wyoming;

Pronghorn are small targets and rarely give the hunter an ideal shot. Patience and an accurate muzzleloader are keys to success.

Montana—which would be among my first choices if looking for a record set of horns; Colorado; New Mexico and Arizona—two other top choices—and parts of Idaho. Several other states also offer pronghorn hunting, including California, parts of Oregon, Utah, and North and South Dakota. Any animal taken from states or provinces where pronghorn may legally be hunted are eligible for the Longhunter Society, provided they make the Society's minimum score of 63.

HABITAT AND FOOD

The pronghorn is a resident of open prairies, the sagebrush and grass-covered rolling plains and tablelands, even the deserts. Generally, only extremely arid, badly eroded areas are avoided. In many areas, some of the best pronghorn country will be found in the transitional zones, where flat prairie meets rolling hills, scattered pine, and rimrock. They like areas with water, although they do not necessarily need it close by. Potholes and other known drinking areas are popular sitting and waiting areas and are actively hunted. It is not uncommon for this animal to range and feed far from a water source, traveling several miles to drink each day. In locales where agriculture is present, pronghorn will take advantage of alfalfa, barley, and other crops. Away from these areas sagebrush, wheatgrass, various weeds and grasses, and other browse plants are sustaining foods.

GUNS, LOADS, AND SPECIAL CHALLENGES FOR THE BLACKPOWDER HUNTER

Despite their relatively small size, a pronghorn can take a lot of lead before hitting the ground. If a shot is misplaced they can travel for miles before they drop. If hit in the right spot, like any animal, however, they are not difficult to kill and may drop on the spot or run only a short distance.

The problem for the blackpowder enthusiast is not killing this animal, but getting close enough to make a good shot. Because of their keen eyesight and the open terrain in which they live most pronghorn are taken at 200 yards or greater. This is questionable range for any muzzleloader, even in-lines with magnum charges throwing conicals and sabot loads, despite what some manufacturers and shooters say. I know blackpowder hunters who have done it, who shrug their shoulders as if it were routine, but I question taking shots that far with a muzzleloader.

So the first challenge is getting within range, say 100 to 120 yards. I have seen a great deal of the West from my stomach and hands and knees while sneaking up on these critters, and I find this cat and mouse game one of the more enjoyable aspects of the hunt. Even if I felt comfortable doing so, and if my rifle was dead on at 150 or 200 yards, taking any animal that far simply isn't my cup of tea. A good antelope hunter or outfitter knows how to use the wind and lay of the land to get within range.

Another challenge is that the blackpowder hunter needs a projectile that will shoot fast—with high muzzle velocity—relatively flat, and hit with some power. This combination is a good possibility up to 100 to 130 yards or so, but after that even a 245-grain conical is going to start dropping fast. Sabot loads are a little better, but a roundball slows down and starts to drop more quickly. Unless hunting over a watering hole, or from a blind where a 60- to 80-yard shot might be possible, conicals and sabot loads are the best way to go. They shoot faster, flatter, and pack more power at greater distance.

The author's brother, Dave, and two excellent Montana pronghorn. At one time pronghorn numbered nearly as many as the buffalo. Their numbers have been greatly reduced, but they still thrive and are hunted in nearly a dozen western states.

A great deal of power is not always needed to kill a pronghorn if a good shot is made. A heavy bullet from a big caliber really isn't necessary, and such a load may prove a handicap because, while carrying more energy to the target, it slows down and begins to drop more quickly. While a heavier load will help beat the wind, which can be a factor in the open "goat" country of the west, I would prefer a bullet that offers a flatter trajectory downrange and one that zips to the target quickly. A medium weight pistol bullet and sabot combination from 245 grains up 300 grains is sufficient. The same is true for solid conical loads, although something as large as the .54-caliber really isn't necessary.

Size is another challenge for the blackpowder antelope hunter. Standing just over three feet, perhaps up to four feet at shoulder, this animal doesn't offer a big target, especially at 100 or more yards. Unless using a scope, getting as close as possible is the best way to overcome this problem. Also, although highly curious, only on rare occasions have I observed antelope standing completely still for long periods of time, particularly when they know man is in the

The author and a female pronghorn taken in Montana. The muzzleloader is a CVA Timber Wolf in .50-caliber.

area. There always seems to be one or two on the lookout, which means the hunter not only has to be a bit sneaky, keeping an eye on an entire group in fear of being spotted, but has to choose his animal, take aim, and get off a good shot in a hurry. Unless feeding, watering or bedded, pronghorn always seem to be moving a little, whether walking, trotting, and running, so the hunter has little time to react in most situations.

Unless you know you will be hunting from a blind and shooting at 100-yard distances or less, select your load, have your rifle sighted in for at least 100 yards, and do some shooting before leaving home at 125 and 130 yards, just in case. Also, practice shooting while lying flat on the ground, sitting "Indian-style," and from other positions. Take a pair of good knee pads and gloves. There is a good chance you will need both, especially in flat, open country where sneaking in for a close shot is often required.

METHODS OF HUNTING

Antelope are hunted different ways, depending upon the terrain. In some locales blinds may be established near feeding and watering areas. This is often the best bet for the blackpowder hunter, since it allows for the closest shots. I once took a respectable buck over a waterhole in New Mexico at 65 yards. Blinds are also used in other areas. I have used light, portable blinds to stalk an animal, nothing more than a camouflaged, three-sided tent-like structure that can be erected high or low to the ground and moved along the ground with ease. Such portable blinds work well Colorado, Wyoming, and Montana. I have also used hay piles, or simply hid behind outcroppings and rock piles.

Stalking can also be productive, but it is necessary to use the wind and terrain to get within range. As noted, antelope are naturally curious, but one sight of a human form and they are gone. Using ravines and gullies, hills, and the general lay of the land is a must. When a herd is spotted, glass the area carefully and plan the best route of attack before making a move. Just remember, chances are your target knows the area better than you do, so work quickly but carefully and be ready to hit the ground if they are spotted unexpectedly, which is always a good possibility. Sitting low to the ground against some rocks or amongst some brush and glassing from a high hill or knoll allows the hunter to spot game at long distances. It also provides an idea of where they are headed and how best to get into position.

In agricultural areas, if permission to hunt can be obtained from the landowner, keeping an eye on alfalfa fields and other crops is always a good idea. Pronghorn will often visit these areas in the morning darkness, or just after, to feed, moving back into the foothills or desert country after a few hours. Evenings are also productive. Watch gullies you suspect are being used for travel and saddles that may be used for crossing from one area to the next. Like elk and mule deer, antelope typically bed in positions where they can scan downward in all directions, or in as many directions as possible, or in the wide open where they can see in all directions.

Hunting is often best early in the day as antelope are out feeding or traveling to and from feeding and bedding areas. The period from noon to about three o'clock can be slow, but by late afternoon they are again out and about. While hunting in north-central Montana a few years ago we would work hard each day until just after lunch, and then lay back and take a siesta like a mountain lion after finishing off a fresh kill. "They won't be moving for a few hours now," the outfitter would say. I thought he was a bit loco, but each day, as if the

Pronghorn get their name from the characteristic "prong." They are indigenous to North America and are a special challenge for the muzzleloader hunter.

outfitter had an alarm clock in his brain, he would awake around two or three o'clock and start glassing. I would stay awake the entire time and continue to scan the area. But sure enough, except for an occasional animal, I saw little game until mid-afternoon. I don't know if this is true everywhere, but in the areas I have hunted mornings and late afternoon to dusk seemed to be the peak periods of activity.

165

When on the move, the biggest bucks, and often the biggest does, typically bring up the rear or trail slightly off to one side. If spooked, pronghorn are prone to circling back through the same area. It may take a while, but it often pays to sit tight and keep your eyes open.

SHOT PLACEMENT

The best area to hit an antelope is in the lungs, behind the front shoulder. A shot to the lungs is the best guarantee these speedsters will not go far. A solid hit with a conical or sabot load can also play hell on bone, so a broadside shot to the front shoulder is apt to knock them down, but I have seen them travel quite a ways carrying a misplaced shot to the rear quarter. Keep the shot up front, to the lungs, heart, or shoulder.

14

THE BEARS

THE BLACK BEAR

It is my humble opinion that the black bear *(Ursus americanus)* is one of the most underrated big game animals on the continent. In many states and provinces this highly intelligent creature was bountied, shot on sight, even poisoned to near extinction by the 1960s. In some areas of its native range it still managed to thrive without the protection of bag limits or closed hunting seasons, while in others the black bear was completely wiped out, primarily in the South. In my own home state of Maine, for example, although the black bear was not completely eradicated, before 1946 there were no laws governing the killing of the animal, and between 1946 and 1957, a bounty of $15 was paid by the state for each one taken, regardless of sex or age. Even as late as 1969, the year the bruin was officially classified as a big game animal, there was no bag limit.

Since then much has changed, not only here in the Northeast but across the continent. In some areas of its ancestral range, primarily the South, efforts

This bear entered a bait area late in the day. Although the animal looks to be of good size, its dark color against the darkening shadows makes this a risky shot.

to bring back the black bear following World War II by trapping and releasing northern bears met with success. In many of those areas "blackie" is now considered a big game animal and hunted. The same is true in some 43 states, 9 Canadian provinces, and 2 territories. It is estimated that nearly half a million black bears are now found scattered across North America, making it the world's most abundant bruin and one of our most available big game targets.

Hunter attitudes concerning this animal have changed, too. Not long ago hardly a head would turn when talk turned to hunting the black bear. It was commonly thought that the animal offered little sport poor eating, and except for a head mount or rug was a poor trophy. Most black bear were taken coincidentally while hunting other game and few guides were in the business of offering hunts specifically for black bear. Today, however, black bear hunting is a popular, highly anticipated event throughout North America. In many provinces both spring and fall hunts are offered. It has also become big business. Some hunts in Canada run as much as $1,500 to $2,000 American dollars with many camps booked a year or two in advance. It is estimated that about 40,000 black bear are now taken across North America annually, making this once lowly revered critter the second most sought after and harvested big game animal on the continent after the whitetail.

I see several good reasons why hunter interest in the black bear has changed. For one thing they are not as dumb as once thought. Their faces have an amazing intelligent look about them, and most hunters who have invested time in hunting them are generally surprised at how sly and cunning the black bear can be. Like all big game, they can appear overly curious, even stupid at times, particularly around food. They can be an easy target around bait areas, but even then blackie can be a challenge and is always a thrill to watch.

Other aspects of the bruin that seems to draw interest is its potential size. Although this is the smallest North American bear species, with the average male running 250 pounds or less, examples in the 300- and 400-pound class and measuring better than six feet from nose to tail are quite possible. A bear weighing 250 pounds is considered a good trophy in many locales, but Newfoundland, the western provinces of Canada, and certain parts of the American west are known for big bears. The largest on record weighed a whopping

Black bear reach tremendous size in parts of their range. This giant was taken in Newfoundland.

800 pounds! Females, or sows, run less, averaging 120 to 140 pounds, although females do grow much larger.

The black bear is also a fine looking trophy once mounted. Although typically black in color throughout much of its range, along the spine of the Rocky Mountains into New Mexico and Arizona and in western Canada, various color phases are possible. Brown, blonde, and cinnamon are most common. In southeast Alaska there is also the magnificent "glacier bear," a black bear that has a splendid blueish hue.

The fact that it is possible to hunt the black bear not only in the fall but during the spring is another factor which has drawn a lot of hunter interest in recent years. Up until the 1970s, and 1980s, many states, including my home state of Maine, offered spring hunting. This has now changed, and most spring hunting in the United States is now confined to a handful of western states. North of the border seven provinces and two territories offer spring bear opportunities. Nova Scotia and Ontario are the only provinces where hunting is

The author (right) after a successful Alberta spring boar hunt. Both boars were taken within two hours of each other on the same stand on the same day, one with a Knight MK-85 in .50-caliber, the other with a CVA Bobcat Rifle in .54-caliber.

limited to the fall. Spring hunting, though controversial in some quarters, offers a chance to travel afield in search of big game at a time when the season on other species is closed. Many hunters also feel that pelts are prime and meat is in better condition in the spring. Bear taken soon after they leave winter dens, from April into early June depending upon locale, carry a better coat of hair that often lacks the rubs and bare spots visible in late August or early September. Because they have used up a great deal of their fat during the winter, it is also my personal belief that spring black bear make for better eating than fall bear.

Despite what is commonly thought, the black bear does provide some wonderful table fare. In fact, it would be a toss up which my family and I prefer more when it comes to elk, moose, caribou, and black bear. When properly taken care of in the field, which means dressing and skinning the animal and cooling it down quickly to reduce body heat and removing as much fat as possible, this is some of the finest tasting meat in the wild. One of my favorite methods is to marinate steaks in teriyaki sauce or Italian salad dressing mixed with olive oil and then cook quickly on a hot grill. It is also excellent lightly brushed with garlic and basil oil on the grill. For those willing to give it a try, one of our favorite teriyaki recipes comes from an old *Better Homes and Gardens* cookbook:

½-cup soy sauce

2 tablespoons cooking oil (we prefer olive oil)

2 tablespoons molasses

2 teaspoons dry mustard

1 teaspoon ground ginger

4 cloves garlic, halved

¼-cup water

Mix all the ingredients together, and marinate the meat for 15 to 30 minutes at room temperature. I usually brush on the excess sauce as I am cooking. This recipe, as well as the Italian dressing, is also good with venison, elk, caribou, moose, and antelope.

RANGE, HABITAT AND FOOD

The black bear is an inhabitant of mixed and conifer forests. It is also found in bottomlands, swamps, rugged mountains, and wooded high country valleys. Considered omnivorous and somewhat nonselective when it comes to what it will eat, it may be found wherever food, water, and cover exists. Black bear are found from the Everglades in Florida up the Appalachian Mountains to New England, as far north as treeline in northern Quebec and Labrador, and from Newfoundland in the east as far west as Alaska and California. Its range also extends down into central Mexico. Surprisingly, due to its solitary nature, blackie may be found in wooded areas relatively close to populated areas.

In general, although black bear populations are found in more than 40 states, some of the largest numbers, and therefore some of the best hunting opportunities, will be found in northern New England, Pennsylvania, along the Rocky Mountains, the Pacific Northwest, and states surrounding the Great Lakes, as well as in Alaska. There is world-class hunting all across Canada, which offers the best black bear hunting in the world.

As earlier stated, the black bear is omnivorous, which basically means it will eat a variety of foods, from meat and insects to berries and grasses and

This paw print suggests a bear of good size. Large black bear are possible in several states and Canadian provinces.

mushrooms. Whatever it finds and wherever it is found, chances are the black bear will stuff it down its throat. In the spring, bears will dine on the first green shoots popping through the snow to help condition its stomach, but carrion is a favorite food to help quickly rebuild protein and fat reserves. Many outfitters use meat in conjunction with various sweets when baiting during the spring season. In late summer, blueberries, raspberries, and other berries, as well nuts, are all eaten. Old apple orchards are always taken advatange of and are good places to hunt. In Alaska and the Northwest, black bear will also take advantage of the salmon runs, much like the brown bear. In Newfoundland and northern Quebec, and perhaps elsewhere across Canada, the black bear is known to be responsible for the killing of caribou and moose calves.

GUNS AND LOADS

The black bear is not overly difficult to kill with a well placed shot. When hunting over bait or with dogs shots are relatively close, anywhere from just a few feet to a few yards. The closest bear I ever shot was less than 20 feet, the farthest slightly less than 50 yards. This animal does carry a thick coat of

This black bear was taken in Manitoba, one of the best bear hunting hotspots on the continent. Like most Canadian provinces, Manitoba offers a spring and fall bear season. The muzzleloader is a T/C Hawken Custom in .50-caliber.

hair, a good deal of fat, and is well muscled and big-boned, so sufficient power and penetration is required. Shot placement can also be critical to down a black bear on the spot.

When hunting over bait or with dogs, guns shooting .50- and .54-caliber roundballs actually make fine bear guns. At 10 to 25 yards the roundball in these two calibers packs enough energy to kill a bear easily when hit in the right spot. The roundball also holds together well and has fair penetration, opening up inside and causing good internal damage, but still dispersing all its energy inside the animal. A .45-caliber roundball might also do the trick at these ranges, but if possible go with at least a .50-caliber, and preferrably the .54.

At longer range, say over 60 or 80 yards when stalking, opt for a conical in the 250-to-300-grain range or slightly heavier, in .45-, 50- or .54-caliber. You want speed and power when you hit this animal at such a range, and you get it with a bullet of this weight when fired from these calibers. You also want penetration, so go with a solid or flat-face bullet rather than a hollowpoint. The same is true of the jacketed-sabot loads. Hollowpoints will kill a bear; I have no doubt about that. In fact, I have taken two black bear with bullets designed to expand. But on large fat-carrying, big-boned and strong muscled animals, say a bear of 250 to 300 pounds or better, hollowpoints may mushroom too quickly and not reach a vital intact. They may also hit bone on the way through slowing and shattering them further. Bears have big, strong bones, even large rib bones, and hollowpoints may cause some injury, maybe even critical injury, but it might not be enough to put them down and keep them down on the spot. I am convinced, even when hunting over bait at close range, that a roundball, solid conical or non-hollowpoint sabot load is the best way to go.

METHODS OF HUNTING

Black bear are basically hunted over bait or with dogs—where allowed—and by spot and stalk. In many states and provinces fall bear seasons take place at the same time as seasons on other big game, so they are taken coincidentally while in search of deer, elk, caribou, and others. Baiting and the use of dogs is not legal in all states, although baiting is the most widely used tactic across Canada and in several states, particularly in northern New England.

Of the various methods, hunting over bait is perhaps the most productive, especially for the blackpowder enthusiast, due to the close shooting range. Personally, I believe it to be the most enjoyable. At times it requires sitting for long periods without making noise or sudden movement, and on occasion it may require some nerve. This animal has been known to be rather brazen, circling stands, even raising up on ladders to get a better look into stands. Bait hunting also gives the hunter time to carefully scutinize an animal before pulling the trigger.

There are, however, a few things to keep in mind when sitting on a bear stand. Upon arrival get as comfortable as possible. You will probably be there a while, and movement is a no no. If you do move, scan the area with your eyes first. Keep you ears tuned for the snapping of twigs or branches. Black bear have a way of appearing silently and suddenly, from out of nowhere, and any quick movement or noise can send them flying. To help me stay as quiet and motionless as possible, it is a custom of mine to take a small paperback novel or crossword book to the stand. I have shot most of my bears over bait while reading Louis L'Amour and other favorite western authors, or while trying to figure a crossword puzzle. It works. It keeps you quiet and motionless, which is

Black bear exhibit different color phrases in some areas of the West. This is a chocolate phase taken during the spring. Notice the thick fur common with black bear taken in early spring.

important when sitting on a stand. Don't smoke, and wear camouflaged clothing, perhaps even a face mask to aid concealment.

Also, when a bear makes the approach, keep your eyes on it, but don't move a muscle or raise your rifle until it has occupied itself with the bait. Once actively feeding blackie drops his defenses and is more concerned with filling his belly than any possible danger. When you do prepare to take a shot, keep your eyes on the animal and raise your muzzleloader slowly. If the bear stops feeding and looks into the woods or in your direction, freeze, continuing to raise your muzzleloader only after it goes back to feeding. Set the trigger as quietly as possible.

SHOT PLACEMENT, GUNS, AND CALIBERS

Despite its potential size, muscle structure, thick layer of hair, and body fat, the black bear is not too difficult to dispatch at distances under 100 yards if the shot is well placed and the projectile is traveling fast enough and is heavy enough for good penetration. The key with this animal is not only proper shot placement, but in reaching the vital organs. Bear can be killed with a shot to the head and spine, but both are relatively small and should be avoided if possible, especially at long range. Once the bear is comfortably feeding on bait, a broadside shot is generally provided, and this is the best angle for a killing shot. In general, I have found the black bear not overly tenacious, but if not fatally hit in a vital organ with the first shot, the opposite is true. A wounded bear in the bush is no picnic, so the first shot better be good!

The best place to hit a black bear with a roundball is in the lungs/heart area, just behind the front shoulder. Roundballs hold together well and flatten well but lose speed and energy quickly. They are best at close range and do more damage in soft tissue rather than against bone. A shot to the lungs and heart will generally put a bruin down nicely under 50 yards.

At greater distances, or if shooting solid conicals or sabot loads regardless of the range, the heart and lung region is still a good bet, but because they travel faster and retain energy it is better to go for bone. Hitting one of the front shoulders is best, since it is not only the biggest hard target but a bear with a shattered front quarter will often go down and stay down, at least long enough for a second shot if necessary. Ideally, the shot should hit the shoulder and continue into the lungs, so a slightly quartering shot is best, which is often possible with black bear over bait.

This monster black bear was taken during a spring bear hunt in Alberta. The bruin weighed over 400 pounds. Notice the wide head, short ears, and wide nose.

A spine shot is a deadly but difficult shot to make. It is not a large target area. If you do make a spine shot, make it high, between the front shoulders. That way if the spine is missed you will hit the lungs. Under no circumstances should any bear be hit in the mid-section or hindquarters.

When it comes to caliber for black bear, I would consider the .50-caliber the minimum when shooting roundballs. The .54-caliber shoots a larger, heavier ball and packs more punch. When shooting conicals and sabot loads, the .50-caliber is sufficient but a projectile in the 250 to 300-grain range is recommended.

THE GRIZZLY AND ALASKAN BROWN BEAR

RANGE

The magnificent Alaskan brown bear *(Ursus arctors middendorffi)* and the grizzly *(Ursus arctos horribilis)* are two of nature's greatest creations. To gaze upon one is like setting eyes on a great beast straight out of the Stone Age.

Second only to the polar bear in size, the brown bear can reach weights up to 1,500 pounds. The average boar is smaller, running 800 to 1,000 pounds, with a length often exceeding eight feet, and a massive head and shoulders. Sows are generally smaller, running about 600 to 700 pounds. I once glassed a large specimen, or what I believed to be a large specimen, for about an hour while fishing along the Alagnak River, on the Alaska Peninsula, and even from a considerable distance it was somewhat unnerving. This is an incredible creature. Even the paws of this animal are big: Hind feet can measure a full six to eight inches across, and up to a foot or more in length!

The grizzly, on the other hand, is generally smaller than its coastal brother. Although still big by black bear standards and just as impressive as the brown bear in outward appearance, an adult male "griz" runs between 350 and 400 pounds, perhaps a bit more. Bears up to 700 pounds have been recorded, but very few. This bear can have a length of six to seven feet, and a shoulder height of three to three and a half feet. It is easily identified by its dish-like forehead and the prominent hump rising between the front shoulders. The brown and grizzly can also be differentiated to a certain degree by color. The Alaskan brown bear is generally more uniformly brownish.

The grizzly is generally lighter, darkening to brownish-black along the spine, upper limbs, and ears. It is also "grizzled," with white or silver tipping of its hair on the upper parts of the body, especially along the back. They appear yellowish at times, and some may appear a shade of gray, or even blackish, but will still carry the light-tipped hairs.

Historically, the grizzly bear roamed over much of western North America, from Alaska south to the Great Plains and California. Today, however, there are less than 1,000 or so south of the Canadian border, primarily in the Yellowstone country of Wyoming and remote regions of the northern Rockies, such as Glacier National Park. The largest huntable populations are found in western Canada, most notably western Alberta and British Columbia, the Canadian territories, and Alaska. Alaska probably has more grizzly bears than all other areas combined, with most found north of the sixty-second parallel into the Brooks Range. In layman's terms, the grizzly is considered an "inland" bear, while the Alaskan brown is considered a coastal bear. For hunting and record-keeping purposes, a line of segregation has been established primarily due to the fact that coastal bears reach much larger size.

According to the Longhunter Society, bears north and east of the following boundary are considered grizzlies: "Beginning at Pearse Canal and following the Canada-Alaska border northwesterly to Mt. Elias on the 141-degree meridian; then north along the Canada-Alaska border to Mt. Natazhat; then west along the divide of the Wrangell Range to Mt. Jarvis at the western end of the Wrangell Range; then north along the divide of the Mentasta Range to Mentasta Pass; then in a general westerly direction along the divide of the Alaska Range to Houston Pass; then westerly following the sixty-second parallel of latitude to the Bering Sea."

HABITAT AND FOOD

Like the black bear, both the grizzly and brown bear can be considered opportunistic feeders. The griz is typically found in upland mountain country to treeline and on open tundra, although in parts of Alaska and British Columbia they are know to descend to lower elevations to take advantage of salmon runs. Primarily, however, they feed on grass, various berries, fruits, leaves and bark, rodents and other small mammals, insects, carrion, and fresh meat when they can get it. The brown bear eats many of the same foods but feeds heavily on protein-rich salmon throughout its range, a primary reason why it reaches such massive size. Look for them in coastal areas and on the offshore islands of Alaska, the latter of which offer some of the finest hunting opportunities.

GUNS, LOADS, AND SHOT PLACEMENT

Both the grizzly and brown bear should be hunted with roundball guns of .54-caliber or larger. The heaviest roundballs possible, pushed by the maximum recommended powder charge should be considered. When shooting conicals and sabot loads a heavy 325-grain or larger solid point will do the trick if hit in the right spot and at the right range, but I would feel more comfortable with a heavier, faster .50-caliber to .58-caliber pushing a 385- to 525-grain bullet. It takes a lot of bullet to stop these critters, so go heavy rather than light, and push it with a maximum charge.

No muzzleloader is powerful enough unless the hunter can shoot it well. I would much prefer to accompany a hunter carrying a .45-caliber rifle loaded with a 350-grain elongated bullet who can put the bullet where he wants at 100 yards than a hunter using a .58-caliber and 500-grain bullet who can't hit the broad side of a barn at the same distance. Each of these bears can be tough to kill and it takes a good shot to knock one down for keeps. In general, I would recommend the largest caliber muzzleloader and heaviest conical or sabot load the hunter can shoot accurately. Also, it is imperative that the first shot counts and can be quickly followed with a second shot if necessary. Be prepared to reload quickly or have another gun standing by.

As for shot placement, both the brown and grizzly should be shoulder-shot if possible. This means the front shoulder! Both can cover a considerable amount of ground, and do considerable damage, with a broken hindquarter. The best shot in my opinion is at a quartering angle which breaks the near shoulder, penetrates into the chest cavity taking part of the lungs or heart and continuing on to the far shoulder, hopefully smashing it as well. It takes a lot of lead and powder from a muzzleloader to do this much damage, but breaking at least one front shoulder is important.

METHODS OF HUNTING

Brown and grizzly bear are generally hunted by glassing and stalking often with the hunter posting in a high position and glassing preferred areas, perhaps over a caribou or moose carcass or areas rich in blueberries or along a salmon river, depending on the season. Once a bear is spotted the best line of attack is designed, keeping in mind that bears have a keen sense of smell and relatively good hearing. Proper consideration of wind direction is critical when stalking any bear, particularly these two.

In early spring, usually with snow still covering the ground, brown and grizzly bears are often found in open grass country getting their stomach and digestive tract back in order. Keep an eye on valleys, grass ridges and slopes, tundra, coastal flats, game trails and crossings, river and creek bottoms, or any dead caribou or moose sites. These areas are also good in the fall, as are areas with abundant blueberries. Salmon rivers are excellent areas for browns in the fall, while the griz seems to favor alpine pockets such as high basins and valleys.

15

MOOSE: OUR LARGEST DEER

Moose are truly impressive beasts to look upon in the wild. They are the largest member of the deer family, and though not the most graceful looking among the deer clan, the human spirit cannot help but be impressed, perhaps even awed, at their sight. Since my early days as a fly fisherman sharing remote Maine trout ponds with them, the moose has been one of my favorite animals. In later years, as I hunted them across the continent, my respect for them as an adversary grew with each new encounter, and I now consider them one of my favorite targets. I have killed several, and each time I am simply awed by everything about them.

One of the most impressive aspects of moose is their size. They seem to tower over everything, and in their presence a human body seems rather small and trivial. Even the females, or cows, are big. I have seen examples in Alaska which no doubt would have tipped the scales at close to a half-ton, and though the typical cow in the "lower 48" and across Canada runs smaller, generally between 500 and 700 pounds, they are still impressive.

The males, or bulls, are even more so. Those in Alaska *(Alces alces gigas)*, the largest of the three groups officially accepted by the Longhunter Society and other game record-keeping groups, can reach 1,700 to 1,800 pounds and stand more than seven feet at the withers. Animals in the 1,200- to 1,500-pound class are not uncommon in some of the best hunting areas of their range. In total height, an Alaskan moose can reach a dozen feet from the ground to top of antlers.

The smallest of the group is the Shiras moose *(Alces alces shirasi)*. A large bull can reach 1,200 pounds or so and stand six feet at the shoulder, with the average running between 800 and 1,000 pounds. They are also somewhat shorter. The more common Canada moose *(Alces alces americana)* typically falls between its two cousins in terms of size and height. A respectable bull will run from 1,000 to 1,200 pounds, although larger examples are quite possible.

Another impressive and attractive attribute of this game animal is its headgear. Moose carry the largest and heaviest antlers of any North American

This massive moose presents a real challenge for the blackpowder hunter. With a well-placed shot from a heavy conical or saboted bullet, even an animal of this size will hit the ground.

big game. On some Alaskan moose total antler width can be better than six feet from tip to tip and weigh 90 pounds. Antlers on the Shiras and Canada moose are typically smaller, in the four and five foot range, respectively, on large bulls, but they are still hefty. It is almost unbelievable to think such massive racks are shed and grown anew each year.

Despite their size, however, moose have some other assets working for them that make them challenging adversaries for the hunter. Like all deer, they have a keen sense of smell, and playing the wind is essential to success. While I have observed many moose that simply stand and stare at a motionless hunter when the wind is right, once human scent is detected they head for cover in a hurry. With their long legs moose can travel surprisingly fast. And when escaping danger nothing seems to stop them. I have had moose travel at top speed through cover a human would have trouble navigating, an amazing sight considering their bulk and headgear.

This animal also has good hearing, so moving with as little noise as possible is important. Also, I believe moose possess better eyesight than generally given credit for. It may not be as keen as a whitetail's, but they seem to be able to spot hunters and detect danger from considerable distance, undoutedly due in part to their great height. They detect motion equally well. In general, while the eyesight of the moose can be considered less than perfect, it is a big mistake to underestimate it.

RANGE

Moose are a northern species, found from Alaska east to Newfoundland, with Prince Edward Island being the province in Canada having none. In the United States, moose are found in the northeastern states, including northern New England and New York, in some states surrounding the Great Lakes, and in nearly a dozen western states. The species is not hunted in all states, and in some hunting may be limited to residents only or hunted only with permits issued by draw. In Canada, however, moose are pretty much open game in each province and to all hunters, residents and non-residents alike. Licenses are generally purchased through licensed outfitters. The exceptions are in New Brunswick which issues hunting permits through a draw and Nova Scotia where hunting is restricted to residents only. In both provinces moose populations are rather small compared to Newfoundland and provinces to the west.

According to the Longhunter Society and the Boone and Crockett Club, moose are segregated into three groups, each having its own specific geographic restrictions. They are as follows:

Alaska-Yukon Moose: includes trophies from Alaska, Canada's Yukon Territory, and Northwest Territories.

Canada Moose: includes trophies from all of Canada, except the Yukon and Northwest Territories, Minnesota, and Maine.

Wyoming (Shiras) Moose: includes trophies taken from Utah, Idaho, Montana, Wyoming, Colorado, and Washington.

HABITAT AND FOOD

Throughout their range moose prefer areas offering a combination of woods, open valleys, and meadows. They are often found near water, lakes, ponds, rivers, and streams. Bogs and other wet areas are also considered prime moose country. Like all deer, the best moose range will offer good cover, good

This bull moose looks worth taking. However, it is still partly hidden by brush. The moose is not yet aware of the hunter's presence and is moving in the right direction. Patience should yield a good shot.

browse and grazing areas, and plenty of water. Moose, like the whitetail, benefit from areas regenerating after a fire, since they take advantage of tender new
growth. Such areas also provide good cover, since the animal's dark color cam-
ouflages well with the blackened stumps and trees.

As for foods, the diet of moose varies according to season. In late spring
and summer aquatic vegetation will always be taken advantage of, and moose
will often be found around lakes and other water sources well into the fall as
long as such foods are available. During a warm fall, these areas can be especially productive since not only do they offer food, but they help moose escape
flies, mosquitos, and other insects. Areas offering willow and other tender
browse, such as maple, mountain ash, birch, aspen, and balsam are prime
hunting ground. Moose will also feed on meadow grasses. Moose also like
high timbered areas, especially high promontories offering easy access to these
areas. Look for them to move down and feed late in the day in mountain areas,
remaining there through the night and moving into the more timbered areas
with the rising sun, much like elk. In locales when hunting pressure is not
high, moose are apt to be spotted feeding in open terrain at any hour of the
day, although early morning and late afternoon to dusk are generally prime
spotting times.

GUNS AND LOADS

All moose are large, big-boned, muscular critters. It takes plenty of
power to penetrate to a vital organ, or to break bone, and a bullet should
offer plenty of internal damage. You will want a big caliber pushing a heavy
load.

When it comes to caliber, depending upon the range and shot provided,
I would not hesitate to nail a large bull with a .50-caliber loaded with a roundball, but the target would have to be under 60 yards and standing broadside for
a shot into the lungs. No scenario is a guarantee when hunting big game, however, and a .54- caliber or larger would be strongly recommended when shooting roundballs. Even then the closer the better. Go for soft tissue when shooting roundballs.

When shooting conical or sabot loads, however, those in the 300- to 400-
grain weight class will do the job nicely. Lighter conicals and sabot loads will
do the trick, but regardless of caliber I prefer a heavy bullet. Both the .50- and
.54-calibers are fine moose guns if a heavy enough projectile is being pushed.

This moose was taken with a Thompson/Center Renegade.

METHODS OF HUNTING

Moose are hunted in different ways depending upon the location and terrain. In those areas where the rifle season takes place during the rut, generally sometime in mid-September to early or mid-October, calling is a popular method. Of the various methods, this is my personal favorite as it is both productive and exciting.

Calling moose is much like bugling elk. I have seen guides in Canada use traditional funnel-shaped horns made of birch, while others have used calls make of rubber pipe about one and a half inches around and perhaps a foot or so long. Some guides claim moose can also be called by simply cupping the hands and making a series of low grunts. I have never seen it done with any degree of success, but have little doubt that in the right scenerio, a bull might take some interest.

Whatever device is used, the idea is to imitate the sound of a willing female. As it is with elk, calling can be quite specific and demands a certain de-

The author took this respectable moose in Newfoundland with his T/C Hawken Custom. A close stalk was necessary, but only one shot was required from the .50-caliber rifle.

gree of skill. When done poorly or at the wrong time it can prove more damaging to success than helpful. Ideally, the hunter should be positioned slightly away from the caller with gun ready and calling should be done by a guide, outfitter, or someone familiar with the technique. Guides and outfitters will also know the best times and places to call, such as early in the day and late afternoon when bulls are most active. For the blackpowder hunter, calling is perhaps the best way to get a moose in close. When bulls are in full rut, it is not uncommon to get an animal within 50 yards or less if conditions are right.

Although not as exciting as calling, and perhaps more demanding because it involves a great deal of walking, glassing and stalking can also be productive. I have used this technique in Newfoundland, Ontario, and Wyoming with good success, and based on these experiences and those of guides who use it almost exclusively, knowing where and when to look are the keys to success. As with most antlered and horned big game, moose are most active during the early and late hours of the day, except during the rut when they can be seen at any time. Rising early and getting on a high overlook or other observation point helps. Once an animal is sighted, the stalk begins, using the wind and terrain to your advantage. Concentrating on bogs, high or low meadows, burned areas, water sources, and other obvious feeding areas will all be productive.

Another productive method of hunting the moose is by boat, or canoe. This is a popular technique in Quebec and Ontario, both of which are blessed with water and plenty of moose. Again, the hunt typically starts early in the day, and as the hunter sits with rifle ready in the bow, a guide or companion does the paddling in the stern. Move slowly, stick close to shore, particularly when moving around bends and points, and make no noise. Although the hunter is at an advantage in the sense that moose typically expect no danger from water, he is also at a disadvantage as sound travels easily over lakes and ponds, or rivers and streams with a slow current. Even the hollow sound of a paddle hitting the side of an aluminum or fiberglass canoe can send this critter heading for the timber.

SHOT PLACEMENT

My experience has been that the only place to hit a moose is in the lungs, behind the shoulder tip. The lungs are huge and provide the largest vital target of any game animal on the continent. Aim just about anywhere

Female moose, called cows, may be hunted in many states and provinces. This one is large and is offering a good shot into the heart and lungs.

from just in back of the shoulder tip to about twelve inches back and about the same distance down, and chances are you will hit your mark. The front shoulder blades are extremely thick and heavy. They have been know to actually turn or stop even some magnum centerfire loads. Although I have no proof to substantiate it, and though manufacturers may argue the point, I have doubts that even the new "magnum" in-lines could damage the front shoulder on a large bull enough to completely knock it to the ground.

But the lungs are another matter. Even a clean lung shot with a round-ball can put these animals down at 50 or 60 yards, and a shot from a conical to this area will do quite nicely. Despite their size, when hit in the right area they are not difficult to kill. Poorly hit, however, they can run for miles even when bleeding profusely.

Head shots are equally risky considering the thickness of the skull and the small target area. There is also the chance of ruining a trophy set of antlers. The same goes for the neck, which is comparatively small and consists of 18 to 24 inches of tough, dense muscle and bone.

Keep things simple and go for the lungs whenever possible, regardless of the projectile used. It is the best shot you have on these massive animals. De-

Moose are not always easy targets despite their size. This young bull is partially obscured by cover, making it a challenging and risky shot.

189

pending upon the hit and its severity, the beast may buckle and go down immediately or head for parts unknown, necessitating a slow, careful following of the blood trail. If it is a well placed shot, however, chances are it won't go far. When solidly hit in the lungs, moose react much like whitetails, covering some ground in a hurry then trying to seek cover, or they drop on the spot. Make sure to reload quickly, and have a second shot ready before taking up the chase. When approaching a downed moose, stay clear of the headgear and have that muzzleloader pointed at the animal until it is known for sure that the animal is dead.

SPECIAL CHALLENGES FOR THE BLACKPOWDER HUNTER

Size is really the factor here. Moose are truly massive. Although not as difficult to dispatch as some other big game in my opinion, considering that the lung area is the primary target, getting a good shot is critical. A shot anywhere else on this animal is taking a risk of not killing the animal cleanly, or not finding it without a lengthy stalk on a blood trail. The last thing the hunter wants is to track a moose a mile or more, since it means a more difficult job getting the prize back to camp or out of the woods. Take your time, wait for your shot, and make it count.

Of all North American big game, moose are perhaps the most time-consuming and demanding to dress, cape, and retrieve from the field. I have seen experienced moose guides take several hours preparing an animal for transit, and it is a two or three man job. If on an unguided hunt, hunters should make sure to have the necessary equipment available, including an axe, saws, knives, and plenty of rope. If hunting with a guide, be willing to lend a hand.

Also, consider how you will get the animal back to camp. Some guides use horses, four-wheel drives or all-terrain vehicles, but I have also backpacked moose out in quarters. On a big bull a single quarter can weight 150 to 175 pounds! It is work, so have a pack frame on hand, and be prepared to make several trips even if hunting with an outfitter or guide if other tranport means are unavailable. With moose, the work truly begins once the trigger is pulled and the animal is down, so make sure you are prepared.

16

CARIBOU: AN ELEGANT TROPHY

The whitetail was the first big game animal I challenged with a muzzle-loader, and the black bear came second. The third species I took was a caribou, and since that first bull buckled and dropped on a sandy beach along Quebec's Caniapiskau River it has been a favorite target. I have traveled to the northern domain of this animal at least a dozen times over the years, and each trip is something I've cherished.

There are several things that make a caribou hunt, and the caribou itself, special. This is true not only for the blackpowder enthusiast, but for any nim-rod who picks up a rifle or bow and heads to the northland. As I write these words and recollet past jaunts in quest of this prize I realize it is the open, sometimes treeless, and seemingly lifeless country itself that keeps drawing me back. The way I look at it, the caribou, is, in many respects, just an added bonus, and even if the northland were absent of its great herds, it would still be a magical place.

Like no other place I have ever hunted, the home of the caribou stirs the human soul. There are still places that few humans have ever seen, and among countless other thoughts, it makes the visitor wonder what the rest of the continent was like before the white man set foot in it. It is beautiful, humbling, even intimidating and a bit scary at times. It can be a gentle and pleasing landscape, or it can unleash some of the worst weather conditions to be found anywhere, all in the same day or within a matter of a few hours. It can seem void of inhabitants or it can reveal more life than most other places on earth. And it can show you things, make you feel and realize things that few other places can.

Standing on a rocky rise, overlooking a river valley and its surrounding barrens that stretch in cold, hard glory as far as the eye can see can make one feel rather insignificant. It was on such a pinnacle, literally surrounded by thousands of miles of emptiness, that I learned at a young age how trivial man is, that he is but a fleeting thing, and when gone, the barrens and tundra the caribou call home will continue to exist as they always have.

But no matter how the north country strikes the visitor, it is the caribou that draws the biggest amount of interest among all who go there. I have seen

The author and his record-book Quebec-Labrador caribou, cleaned and ready for shipment home. The muzzleloader is a CVA Timber Wolf in .50-caliber, complete with synthetic stock. It is ideal for the harsh weather conditions of the north country.

herds in Alaska and northern Quebec numbering into the thousands, moving like waves on the ocean. Though you try to pick out a respectable target, there are so many at times that it is difficult to keep your mind on what you are doing. It is an incredible sight in this day and age, yet one soon learns that few things follow the norm in the caribou's domain, and their vast numbers are just one example.

In Quebec and Labrador, the famous George River herd and other scattered herds are estimated to total about one million. There are so many of them, in fact, that each hunter is legally allowed two animals, and as of this writing there are rumors in the wind the bag limit may be increased to three. In Alaska, the population is undoubtedly larger, and combined with smaller roaming numbers across the top of the continent and in Newfoundland, the caribou as a whole represents perhaps the largest free-roaming population of migrating big game on the planet. Reminiscent of the great buffalo herds that once roamed the American West, caribou move on a never-ending journey from calving to wintering grounds along ancient trails that have been cut into the tundra for hundreds of years. They do so almost lethargically, as if mindless of where they are going or why. When they get to where they are going, they simply turn and start all over again, influenced and governed only by the season, available food, and an ancient calling.

In appearance, caribou are striking creatures. Caribou are among the most pleasing big game to observe and they are certainly one of the most graceful. Caribou walk with long, effortless strides, generally with head held slightly low, but when they run it is with head held high and level, as if trying to balance their massive headgear. And they can cover some ground. I have observed large bulls more than once navigate the side of steep hills and mountainsides as if running on level ground. In some cases it would have taken a well-conditioned man several hours or more to cover the same distance. The stamina and ability of these animals to cover great distances with relative ease is simply amazing.

The reason for this, in part, is due to their long, spindly legs and hoofs. Proportionately, caribou have larger "feet" than any other antlered game. The hooves of a 300-pound bull caribou may be wider and perhaps twice as long as a 600-pound bull elk. They are somewhat roundish, with a cushioned bottom that helps them travel over rock provides support on spongy ground and snow. The caribou also has hollow hair. Not only does it serve as insulation against northern winters, but provides great buoyancy, and with their large hooves for

This caribou is an excellent bull, but is it a trophy? From this angle it is difficult to tell, but it is worth a closer look. Notice the spread and long points. Estimating game in the field can be difficult, but patience and a good pair of binoculars are a great help.

propulsion, caribou are perhaps the best swimmers of all antlered game. I have seen them a mile away from shore in large northern lakes.

The coloration of caribou varies. Generally, the farther north they are found the lighter it gets; the farther south the darker its color. I have noticed this variation on more than one occasion. With some exception, the woodland caribou of Newfoundland have a tendency to be somewhat darker than counterparts in the Torngat Mountains and Korok area of northern Labrador and Quebec. Much of the body of both sexes is brownish to gray, depending upon the area, with white or light highlights around the feet, tail, and parts of the face. I have observed some animals that appear almost entirely white. Males more than females display a whitish or bleached mane on the underside of the neck; on some the whole neck area may appear white and turns even whiter with the coming of winter. A truly large bull may stand 50 to 60 inches at the shoulder and run 400 to 450 pounds, but most average between 3 and 4 feet at the shoulder and weigh 200 to 300 pounds. Females are considerably smaller.

Sitting atop this magnificent animal is a set of antlers that match its physical grace and splendor. Both sexes are antlered, but adult bulls, especially those of trophy caliber, carry the largest racks relative to body size of any deer in the world. It is not uncommon for large bulls to have antlers equal in length and width that equal or surpass shoulder height. The antlers may sweep back and then curve upward over the head, or sweep slightly outward and then up and forward. Whatever the case, the antlers generally sport impressive points on mature and more developed bulls, with noticable palmation of the "bez" points, brow "shovels" and antler tops, on most varieties. It should be noted that there is great variation in antler size and formation among the various caribou groups, one reason why the species has been segregated into five categories for the purpose of record keeping.

Despite its many aesthetic virtues, it is commonly reported that the caribou is not the most intelligent or wily of big game. In fact, the species is considered to be dumb, particularly when compared to the whitetail, mulie, pronghorn, and even moose and elk. I believe this is due to the fact that caribou do not live in such close proximity to man, and therefore simply do not feel as threatened when a two-legged creature is encounted. While I have stalked to within 20 or 30 feet of large bulls when the wind was right, I have had them spook at 200 yards, indicating, at least to me, that they do have a good nose and don't particularly like the smell of man. I question, however, whether the caribou's sense of smell equals that of moose, and believe it is nowhere as keen as a bear's. This is a most curious animal, one equipped with

The author watching a herd of caribou pass by a small lake. Although a respectable bull was in the crowd, the long shot over water was not taken.

generally poor eyesight. When moving slowly and using the wind and cover to your advantage it is possible to get quite close, an advantage for the black-powder enthusiast.

Another characteristic that might prove advantageous at times is that caribou seem to have a short attention span. Even when spooked they may bolt 50 to 100 yards, stop, and then look back or simply start walking off as if forgetting what all the commotion was about. They may even circle back to check you out a second time, or move in a parallel direction, providing an opportunity for another shot. I have, on occasion, even used the caribou's curiosity to my advantage. Check the wind and take a position behind a rock or boulder, and wave your hat or arms. This tactic will at times interest the animal enough to bring it closer, often surprisingly close.

RANGE

Historically, caribou were found in many areas where they are no longer present. Maine had them, as did New Brunswick and Nova Scotia and many states in the upper Midwest. Today, however, this magnificent animal has retreated to the far north, and for all practical purposes its range is circumpolar. There is no hunting of the species in the lower 48 states, and from a hunting perspective its southernmost limit is the fiftieth parallel, which cuts through the province of Newfoundland on the Atlantic coast of Canada. The largest numbers are found between the fifty-fifth parallel north to the seventieth parallel, above the Arctic Circle.

Taxonomically, all caribou on the North American continent are the same, and several subspecies—the woodland and Quebec-Labrador versions, for example—carry the same scientific classification of *Rangifer tarandus*. Historically, there were just three varieties for record-keeping purposes, and according to the Boone and Crockett Club, "the classification of the different species and subspecies of the world was in disarray." With this in mind, and due to differences in size, antler structure and geographical separation, B&C established new categories, totaling five in all, to make record keeping easier and to give attention to certain species which typically do not grow as large or sport the same antler size as their counterparts. The segregation is purely for hunting and record keeping and is not based on taxonomic differences. The Longhunter Society currently recognizes the same five groups, despite the fact that the natural range of some "subspecies" overlap.

This caribou is offering a nice broadside shot. Despite its good spread and mass, it lacks long points that contribute greatly to trophy scoring.

For example, the Quebec-Labrador category was first established in 1968, but these caribou are actually of the Barren Ground clan, with about the same body size and antler size and configuration as counterparts in Alaska and the Yukon. The Central Canada Barren Ground caribou is also of the Barren Ground group, but this later category was established in 1984 to give recognition to animals inhabiting Baffin Island and the mainland of the Northwest Territories. These caribou are smaller in both body and antler than others in the Barren Ground group. The so-called mountain caribou is actually a variety of woodland caribou, basically the same as those on the island province of Newfoundland.

So now, the hunter has five categories of caribou from which to choose. According to the Longhunter Sciety the boundaries of segregation are as follows:

Barren Ground (Grant's): Includes caribou only from Alaska, Manitoba, Ontario, Saskatchewan and northern Yukon.

Central Canada Barren Ground: Includes caribou taken on Baffin Island and the mainland of the Northwest Territories, east of the McKenzie River and west of Hudson Bay.

Mountain Caribou: This separate variety of Woodland caribou is found in British Columbia and Alberta. In 1980 Boone and Crockett expanded the boundaries of this category to include specimens taken in the Mackenzie Mountains of the NWT and southern Yukon.

The specific boundary begins in the Yukon at the intersection if the Yukon River and the Alaska/Yukon Territory border. From there it runs southeast and south along the Yukon River upstream to Dawson, then east and south along the Klondike Highway to Stewart Crossing; then east following the road to Mayo, then northeast following the road to McQuesten Lake; then east along the south shore of McQuesten Lake and then upstream following the main drainage to the divide leading to Scougale Creek to its confluence with the Beaver River; then south following the Beaver downstream to its juncture with the Stewart River, then northeast following the Stewart River upstream to its confluence with the North Stewart River and on to the boundary between the Yukon Territory and the Northwest Territories.

Specimens taken *south* of this line are Mountain caribou; those taken *north* of this line are classified as Barren Ground caribou.

Quebec-Labrador Caribou: Includes only caribou taken in Quebec and Labrador.

Woodland Caribou: Includes caribou from Nova Scotia, New Brunswick, and Newfoundland. Since caribou are only present or hunted in Newfoundland, this is the only place where caribou of the Woodland variety may be taken for official scoring.

The author and his number one ranked Longhunter Record woodland caribou from Newfoundland. Several dozen time bulls were seen during the hunt, but he waited for this one. The rifle is a Thompson/Center Hawken Custom in .50-caliber.

HABITAT AND FOOD

Except in Newfoundland and other pockets across Canada, the caribou is not an inhabitant of timbered areas during most of the year. They prefer the open tundras and barrens with rolling hills and plateaus above treeline throughout much of their range. This is due in part to their preference for lichen and other mosses that grow profusely in those semi-barren regions.

GUNS AND LOADS

It has been my experience that caribou are not difficult to kill. I have taken them with patched roundballs in .50- and .54-caliber, as well as conicals and sabot loads ranging from .45- up to .54-caliber. Once solidly hit in a vital area, it seems to be routine for them to run several yards before staggering to the ground, or to simply stand there and allow life to drain away.

Of the 30 or 40 caribou I have taken over the years, however, I have yet to knock one off its feet. I have had them stumble and stagger upon impact, only to rise and just stand there or cover some yardage before buckling under. Bull caribou, especially potential trophies, are big-bodied with plenty of muscle and bone, and because you want them to know they have been hit, I prefer the larger .50- and .54-caliber muzzleloaders, and heavy, solid lead conicals. Jacketed projectiles or hollowpoints will do the job, but on game of this size I worry about their fragmenting and the possible loss of power on impact. If you use them with sabots, go heavy, at least 250 to 300 grains.

It is my opinion, based on personal experience, that any solid conical of 300 grains or larger propelled by 90 to 110 grains of blackpowder or Pyrodex will do a better job on caribou. A solid will demolish both muscle and bone. When shooting roundballs, go with the .50- or .54-caliber or even heavier, just as you would with moose and elk.

METHODS OF HUNTING

Throughout much of their northern range, caribou are glassed and then stalked. As when glassing other big game, going high to scan for animals pays the biggest dividends. The terrain is typically more open the higher you climb, and from such a high vantage point it is possible to scan for miles. Because caribou country is so open and extensive, spotting scopes are better than most binoculars.

Unless crossing a river or other body of water, caribou generally travel and eat along high trails, atop eskers, ridges, and over or around the tops of hills. They are not difficult to spot, but glassing them from a high vantage point gives the hunter ample time to make a stalk and get within shooting range.

When making the stalk, choose a route that intercepts the herd rather than trying to following it. I have yet to find a hunter who can keep up with these animals on the hoof. Use the terrain to cut off the herd or individual animal, get into a position behind some rocks or brush, and let them come to you. Also, work into the wind, even if it means making a wide circle. Caribou may be less wary than other big game, but once human scent is detected, they can take on a whole new demeanor. They may either be reluctant to come close or may even change their course, demanding another lengthy stalk. As you would with other game, keep low, move slowly and don't talk once the target gets with 150 yards.

In areas where lakes and rivers are abundant, which includes many locales throughout this animal's range, caribou are also hunted from boats. In fact, even in areas where the plan is to go high and glass, many jumping-off

Good binoculars are necessary in the open prairies of the West and barrens of the North. Here, the author's guide glasses for caribou in northern Labrador. The muzzleloader is the author's Thompson/Center Hawken Custom.

This woodland caribou might be a trophy, but it is moving fast and serious observation might not be possible. Even if it fails to make the record book, it is a respectable bull for Newfoundland.

spots are reached by water. Blackpowder hunters should take note of this fact, since strong winds can work up a serious chop and literally soak everything from head to foot, including rifles. Whenever traveling in this country over water, keep your firearm in a case and make sure you have your raingear.

Keep in mind, too, that caribou country can be some of the most rugged and demanding terrain found anywhere. The barren hills and tundra in the north country can seem small and unassuming at first, but start climbing or walking across this land and reality soon sets in. Wear appropriate footgear, boots with deep treads and hard soles, and take it slow. When I first started hunting caribou I was a young man in my twenties and in good shape. But this country has a way of wearing you down, regardless of age and physical condition. On many occasions after reaching the summit of a small "hill" I felt totally exhausted, and though I recovered easily, as I still do, it gets more difficult on each trip.

SHOT PLACEMENT

As with moose and elk, the best place to target on caribou is the heart and lungs area, just in back of the front shoulder tip. This is especially true when shooting roundballs and, in my opinion, jacketed sabot loads, but even with solid conicals this should still be the primary point of aim. A heavy lead conical may do some damage on the front shoulder, but this area is heavily boned and well muscled, and it is questionable whether even a solid hit in this area will stop a large bull caribou. If possible, be patient and go for the better shot to the boiler room. Caribou are often spotted moving slowly or standing still, and many shots are possible at relative close range, so hitting this vital area is quite possible.

As you would with any big game, avoid shots to the stomach and hindquarters. At close range a shot directly up the rectum can be devastating, although it is a small target and there is the chance of missing to the left or right and plowing into the hams, in which case a big caribou can still cover some ground. Head and neck shots should also be avoided as the target area is small and risks damaging the antlers. I have seen caribou hit with high-powered magnum centerfire rifles run off and never be found.

SPECIAL CHALLENGES FOR THE BLACKPOWDER HUNTER

As mentioned earlier, caribou are not too difficult to kill provided a good shot to the lung and heart area is taken. It is possible to get them relatively close, and they make a fine target for the blackpowder enthusiast. Any father looking to take his offspring on a first wilderness big game hunt might find the caribou a suitable target.

The biggest challenge for the blackpowder hunter can be the weather conditions. Most hunting seasons, across Canada at least, commence in August and terminate, for all practical purposes, in mid to late September, due to travel limitations. Even in August torrential rains and heavy winds can be a factor for the hunter who fails to tend to his weapon and powder. Temperature fluctuations can be extreme. It can be calm, 70 degrees, and sunny at one point, and then drop 30 degrees with rain and blowing wind, all in a matter of hours. As the season progresses, particularly from the second week of September, snow, sleet, even stronger winds and heavier rains are possible and should be expected. When it comes to weather, it can be a real challenge for the blackpowder hunter, but it is at this time of season, and in such conditions, when the biggest bulls really begin to move and make themselves known in many areas.

There is also the terrain. It can be demanding on young and old alike. Long treks, often uphill in rugged country, can be expected. Early in the season, mosquitos, flies, and other biting insects can be horrendous, so be prepared.

17

GOAT AND SHEEP

ROCKY MOUNTAIN GOAT

The first mountain goat I ever saw was in the Olympia Mountains of Washington. I was there on a steelhead fishing trip, and finding the fly fishing action not too productive, I took a ride to the Olympic National Forest. It was a memorable experience, for not only is that lofty region one of the most scenic I have ever seen, I had the opportunity to observe and photograph one of North America's most amazing and challenging big game animals.

Since that day, I have glassed and hunted goat in Alaska and several other places, and I am always intrigued by them. Although closely related to other goat-like animals, including the tahrs of India and New Zealand, the chamois of southern Europe, and the takin of southern China, this critter lives only in North America. We are blessed to have them, for to journey into their domain, which includes some of the most rugged and remote mountain country on earth, and to hunt them, is a thrill and challenge.

Historically, the goat has not reached the level of interest among hunters as other game, nor has it obtained the level of acclaim. This is largely due to its comparison to the more popular sheep, which has received more attention from hunting writers over the years. The sheep also seems more elusive, which in the minds of many simply makes it a more prized trophy.

Indeed, sheep numbers have dwindled in many parts of their native range, particularly in the lower 48. In some states, hunting permits are available to residents only or by draw, in some cases on a "once in a lifetime" basis, and are expensive when compared to other license fees. This is true of goats in many areas, as well. But this species has faired slightly better, and, in general, goat licenses are easier to come by. In Canada and Alaska, along with sheep permits, they can be easily purchased.

The goat is a splendid animal to look upon, just as impressive as sheep in its own way. In many cases, they often run larger in size than Dall, Stone's, and the desert bighorn, and may even exceed Rocky Mountain bighorns. An adult "billy" averages around 250 pounds but trophies can weigh over 300 pounds, and a number of references indicate that larger examples have been recorded. In length, a mature goat may run five to six feet and between three and four feet at the shoulder. The females, or "nannies" are smaller. Both sexes are horned and look similiar, especially at a distance, but the males sport a greater and more pronounced hump at the withers. The males are also more solitary and less apt to be found in pairs or groups.

Mountain goats are white. With age they may appear a creamy white, even yellowish. Only two other North American animals are so colored, the polar bear and the Dall sheep. Comparatively, the goat's hair is much finer, softer, and is actually two layers. The undercoat is almost down-like in texture and thickness and serves as protection against the elements. The outer layer is straighter, much more coarse, and in the fall and winter months is quite long to provide even more protection. It is this outside layer of hair that provides the characteristic beard and thick hair, or "stockings," around the legs, and gives the goat its distinctive look. Both are more pronounced in November, but specimens taken in September and October will sport good examples.

Like most cliff and high country dwellers the goat's legs are short but extremely powerful, and they are sure-footed, able to climb, travel, and maneuver along rocky cliffs, ledges, and other areas sheep would find difficult. The hooves are cloven, with well-spread toes that help them negotiate tough terrain. While sheep are generally running animals, the goat is a slow, methodi-

Beautiful scenery is an added bonus to any mountain goat hunt.

cal traveler. Studying it through a spotting scope or binoculars, the hunter will observe how they walk with chosen steps, often stopping as if thinking things out before making a potentially hazardous move. The head is generally carried low, and when threatened, they move off at a steady yet deliberate pace, selecting their escape route with care.

The goat's horns, although not as long or as massive as the sheep's, seem fitting. Billies seldom fight or spar for females or territorial dominance as do male sheep, so large, strong headgear isn't necessary. The horns are round and black on both sexes, quite smooth, sharp, and brittle. In fact, it is amazing more are not broken or missing considering the goat's rugged living conditions.

RANGE

Mountain goats are found only in the West, and primarily in northern latitudes. They are found in a number of western states, including Colorado, Montana, Wyoming, Washington, and Idaho, but the best hunting opportunities for the non-resident hunter will be found in British Columbia, western Alberta, the Yukon, and southeast Alaska. Because there is only one variety of goat on the continent, no geographic boundaries for record-keeping purposes are necessary. All animals legally taken by means of fair chase are listed in the "Rocky Mountain Goat" category of the *Longhunter Record Book*.

HABITAT AND FOOD

The name mountain goat is more than appropriate for this big game animal. Although it may spend its entire life within a five to ten miles radius of where it was born, much of this time is spent in lofty places, usually above treeline. The best place to look for them is along cliffs, crags, and rocky sides of mountains, typically the rougher the better. They may not necessarily be found at the summit of a mountain or atop a range of mountains, but nine times out of ten they will be found in some the the most rugged country around. In some areas, goat may even be found at lower elevations, in high meadows and valleys, even relatively far down and close to the coast provided cliffs and rock outcroppings are available. Grassy, boulder-strewn slopes, and ridgelines should also be glassed and studied carefully.

As with most wild game, food often dictates where goats are found. They are both grazers and browsers, depending on the season. Their primary food source during most hunting seasons is lichen and other moss, grasses, sedges, and other flora. Look for these foods along cliffs and high ridges above treeline, and chances are you will find goats.

GUNS AND LOADS

The hunter might think elk, moose and caribou, due to their size, are the hardest big game to dispatch with a conventional rifle. My experience, however, has shown that some of the "smaller" game, pronghorn and some mule deer and whitetail, can take more punishment and be harder to kill. The goat certainly falls into this latter category. Pound for pound, this animal can take as much lead as any moose I have ever taken, and I wouldn't be surprised if a grizzly might be easier to put down. This is especially true if the target is aware of the hunter's presence and adrenalin is pumping.

To begin with, their extra layer of hair means that the projectile must penetrate not just one covering but two, plus the dense skin, before hitting bone or a vital organ. Both layers of hair are extremely thick and heavy. These animals are also heavily muscled and strong-boned. For this reason, the heavi-

The mountain goat is found in some of North America's most remote and rugged mountain country. To get there the hunter must be in good physical condition.

est roundball in either .50- or .54-caliber is recommended. A .45-caliber roundball might do it at close range, but considering that the majority of goats are taken at 100 yards or more, I wouldn't trust the smaller sized balls.

As for conicals, again, a heavy projectile should be used, something in the 250- to 300-grain class or larger, and it is my opinion that they should be solids, not hollowpoints. Sabots with lead bullets will do the trick, but although some might disagree, I would not recommend jacketed bullets with sabots since, like hollowpoints, they have a tendency to expand too quickly in thick-skinned or heavily haired game and either never reach a vital or hit without enough energy. When shooting conicals or sabots, the .45-caliber will do the job, but the larger .50- and .54-calibers are better choices.

Goats are especially difficult for the blackpowder hunter as they are generally shot at greater distances than most other game. With conventional hunting rifles, shots of 200 to 300 yards or more are the norm. The hunter carrying a muzzleloader needs to get as close as possible and shoot a projectile that travels flat and fast, and retains good energy even 150 yards or more downrange. This makes conicals and sabot loads a better choice for goats than roundballs.

There is also a belief among some experienced goat hunters that these critters, like some African game, just don't have a system overly sensitive to shock. Whether this is true or not I cannot say. I have no scientific data to support or reject the theory. But for their size, goats can take a pounding. This is another good reason for using the heaviest, fastest projectile your muzzleloader will handle with good accuracy.

Muzzleloaders should be sighted in for at least 100 yards. Get to know the trajectory of your muzzleloader as longer shots might be necessary. Hunters planning a goat (or sheep) hunt should spend considerable time at the range punching paper at long range with the load they plan to hunt with. This is true for us all no matter what we plan to hunt, of course, since it is common for many nimrods to spend far too little time sighting in, firing, and getting to know their guns.

When shooting roundballs for goats and sheep, every attempt should be made to get within 100 yards.

METHODS OF HUNTING

Nearly all goat are taken by spotting and stalking. The same is true when hunting mountain sheep. The major difference is knowing where to look. Mountain sheep often prefer saddles and rolling country between peaks, while the goat is generally found on cliffs and in rougher, higher terrain.

As with any type of spotting, the best approach is to get high, above the target if possible. This can be difficult at times, considering the rough country, but it is by far the best method with goat as they typically look for danger below, not above them. The advantage the hunter has is that white coat is easy to spot, and that goats move slowly, even when danger is spotted in many cases. They often bed, feed, or remain in an area for long periods, giving the hunter who uses the wind and terrain to his advantage time to make a proper stalk. On several hunts, my guide and I have spotted a goat shortly after first light and taken most of the morning and early afternoon to get within range. On other occasions, because the situation made it impossible to stalk them without giving away our presence, it has been necessary to wait a day or two before actually getting a shot. Getting within range of these animals, especially with

The mountain goat is a challenging trophy for the muzzleloader hunter, not only because of the country where it is found but because getting this close is not very easy.

muzzleloaders, often demands patience, and it can be a slow, tedious, difficult, and challenging endeavor given the high, rugged country, but such words define goat and sheep hunting.

Depending on the hunter's stamina and condition, several weeks of pre-hunt conditioning should be undertaken. Don't underestimate what this country can demand of the human body, or overestimate what you can do. Just as your muzzleloader should be well sighted in and prepared with the right load, you should be prepared physically.

SHOT PLACEMENT

The best spot to hit a goat or sheep is in the heart/lung area, just in back of the front shoulder tip. Even when solidly hit to these vitals with a well constructed bullet, I have seen them travel a considerable distance before hitting the ground for good. Because goats are often seen traveling or standing parallel to a ridge or steep cliff, they can provide a good broadside shot. In many cases, however, they are spotted facing away, facing towards the hunter, or at some quartering angle. In such a situation, if the hunter feels good placement is possible and the animal is within range, the shot should be taken, but it is often best to wait for a broadside advantage, since a hit anywhere else but the heart and lungs is a gamble. If hit in the rear quarters, even a shot from a large-caliber muzzleloader will not do enough damage to stop a goat.

The same is often true when hit in the front shoulder. This area, on both goat and sheep, is quite solid. It is not as thick and rugged as on a moose, but considering the size of these animals it may be just as thickly muscled and just as strong. To say the least, it takes a solid hit straight on from a well-constructed lead bullet to do terminal damage to the front shoulder and to put these animals down. Head shots should be avoided, since the target is relatively small. Straight-on shots into the chest, particularly with goat, are also risky as they often hold their head low, obscuring that small target area.

SPECIAL CHALLENGES FOR THE BLACKPOWDER HUNTER

Just getting into goat and sheep country can be a time-consuming challenge. In Alaska and many northern locales, flying into remote outpost camps via floatplane, and then taking off on foot, sometimes covering many miles and steep elevation, is not uncommon. In some areas, I have traveled into goat and sheep country by horse, but in Canada and Alaska flying is the general rule. Desert sheep country is often reached by four-wheel drive or horses.

Another challenge for the blackpowder enthusiast is getting within range. Sheep have keen eyes, and the eyesight of the goat is not all that bad either. Their hearing and sense of smell are also good, so staying out of sight, downwind, and as quiet as possible are all key. Considering the rough terrain and open country of the desert sheep, getting within 150 yards or less can be the biggest factor governing success.

These animals can also take a lot of lead. The sheep generally less so than the goat, but all require good shot placement.

SHEEP

Sheep are stunning animals, and no matter how many the hunter sees in a lifetime, it is never enough. There are two basic groups according to horn type, the so-called "thinhorn" variety, which includes the Dall and Stone's sheep, and the bighorns, the Rocky Mountain bighorn and the desert bighorn.

Each of the sheep varies slightly in color and size. The biggest variation in color is seen with the Dall, which is almost pure white. The older specimens, like mountain goat, may appear yellowish or bleached. Stone's sheep are a bluish-black, the darkest of the four subspecies; the two bighorns are brownish-gray. The desert bighorn is the smallest in the group. Large adult males usually weigh 160 to 200 pounds. A big Dall will run 190 to well over 200 pounds, and the mountain bighorn and the Stone sheep can reach 300 pounds, sometimes more. As far as body configuration, the desert variety is more elongated, appearing leaner with slender and long legs. All the other sheep are stockier, with heavier muscle tone.

RANGE

Historically, sheep ranged over a much larger area than what they do today. This is particularly true of the bighorns, which were first sighted by Coronado in 1540. The Rocky Mountain variety was not actually discovered until about 1800, but because they were the first to be discovered by the white man, and because their range included areas desired by settlers for the grazing of livestock—especially domestic sheep—they have suffered the hardest. At one time, bighorns ranged as far east as the western Dakotas and northwestern Nebraska, and south as far as Texas. They may have numbered as many as 2 million. The Stone's and Dall sheep found farther north, and in more remote regions, have fared much better.

Today, for record-keeping purposes, the Dall sheep in considered to range over Alaska, most of the Yukon Territory and Mackenzie Mountains or the Northwest Territories. Stone's sheep occur primarily in northern British Columbia. The Rocky Mountain bighorn is found in the Rocky Mountains northward into western Alberta and the desert variety is found in Nevada, south into Mexico, and eastward into Arizona, southern New Mexico, and extreme western Texas.

HABITAT AND FOOD

Of the four subspecies of sheep, only the desert bighorn can be considered a flatlander. It lives in the low, arid deserts, some of the poorest terrain on the continent, feeding on sparse grasses and other vegetation.

The other sheep live high. In the Rockies some the best hunting terrain will be found at elevations of 10,000 feet, nearly always at or above treeline. In Alaska and parts of Canada, which have their own high country but where the elevation is somewhat lower, good sheep country may begin at 7,000 feet and then go skyward. In general, these sheep like high, rolling terrain with a mixture of rocky outcrops and similar cover. They are often found near water. They are mainly grazers, feeding on grasses, sedges, willows, and the buds of various trees.

GUNS AND LOADS

Basically the same calibers and loads should be used as with mountain goats. However, sheep show less vitality than goats, so some lighter, faster, flatter shooting projectiles can be used. I would still prefer a 300-grain solid lead conical bullet or similiar saboted pistol bullet.

18

ESTIMATING TROPHY BIG GAME

The bull moose stood less than 100 yards away, on the other side of a small waterhole, and he was looking straight at us. Compared to moose I'd seen in Alaska, parts of the Northwest Territories, and even my home state of Maine, my first impression was that he wasn't the biggest moose I had ever seen, but respectable nonetheless. Conservatively, I judged the beast to run in the 1,100-pound range.

Shrouded in fog, its wet, matted-down hair emitted heat waves into the chilled October morning like a blast furnace, and with its head and antlers high against the breaking eastern sky, the monarch had a regal, yet phantom-like appearance. Indeed, here was the king of Newfoundland fir and bog, and guide Todd Wiseman and I had just invaded his realm. Perhaps ten yards beyond the bull was a cow. It's amazing what goes through your head at such times, but I wondered whether we had interrupted a moment of rutting ecstasy. It's funny now that I think back on it, but both animals had that sort of startled, caught-in-the-act expression and didn't quite know what to do. Neither did I.

My guide did, however. It was the fourth morning of a six-day hunt. Todd and I had seen moose each day, mostly cows and calves, but I was carrying a bull-only permit. Although we had also seen a few bulls, they had either been out of range of my .50-caliber Gonic in-line, or the conditions were such that it was impossible to get a clear shot. Todd and I had been dropped off an hour earlier by one of the other guides, and we were going to make a wide loop back to the lodge, taking much of the day to do so. We had quietly snuck through a thick, wet stand of timber and had come out overlooking a huge sopping bog when we came upon the two moose. To say the least, the hunters were as surprised as the hunted.

"Don't move, don't move," Todd whispered from behind me.

"I see them, I see them," came my whispered reply, "but I can't see his entire rack." My view to the head area was partially obstructed by a fir tree about thirty feet in front of the bull. I could see the full body; in fact I had a good broadside shot. Though I was not specifically looking for something to make the record books, I did want something with respectable headgear, and until I could see mass and points my finger stayed away from the trigger.

In fear of startling the animals we just crouched there. "We've got to do something," Todd whispered. "They're bound to spook, especially if the wind picks up." With Todd's warning fresh in my brain, I slowly moved my head and body position to the right to get a better view. I got a full look at the rack, and the minute it came into view I knew it would be going home with me.

The spread was fair, not excessively wide, but enough to get my adrenalin flowing, and the palmation wasn't bad either, at least from my angle of view and at a distance in morning fog. The rack seemed to stand high, an indication that the overall spread would not score many points, but it had some wonderfully long points that clearly stood out. Later, we would count 22 points in all, although only 19 were better than an inch long and would count towards overall score. Looking at the bull, I had a good idea it would not make the record books. But the more I looked at it the more I didn't care. I have never been a trophy hunter, anyway. I like to take respectable game, but I hunt for meat, the challenge of hunting, and the love of being afield, as much as I do horn. The more I looked at this bull, the more I wanted him.

"If you're gonna take him, you gotta do it now," I heard Todd say with rising excitement in his voice. "He ain't gonna stand there forever, me son!"

Indeed. But both the bull and the cow were looking directly at us. I got the impression both animals were trying to figure out what we were and that it wouldn't take much longer for them to do so. We had not made a move for several minutes, and time was against us. The sun was clearing the tree-tops, the mist was starting to break, and I knew if the cow headed for the timber, the bull would, too. I had to make a move.

The gods must have been with me that morning. Keeping my eyes on the cow, I noticed the bull turn its head and look back at his companion, as if asking, "What do you think?" As it did so, reflex took over. I lifted my rifle and put the crosshairs on the Bausch & Lomb Elite 4000 scope just behind the front shoulder, knowing that the bullet would hit dead on at this distance—under 100 yards. The Gonic broke the morning silence like a jet breaking the sound barrier, and through the scope I saw the bull lunge forward. It ran 30 feet and dropped.

When the rack was officially measured several months later, it did not meet any of the North American big game trophy book minimums, including the Longhunter Society, and official record-keeper for trophies taken with blackpowder. At just better than 139 points, the rack was respectable, but it missed the muzzleloading book by just a few points. I had failed to take a record-book moose, but I really didn't care. In my heart, I did take a trophy for I have always felt that any big game animal taken under the rules of fair chase with a muzzleloader, regardless of sex, body size, or what it carries for headgear, is something to be proud of.

When I first started hunting as a youth I learned that hunting in this day and age is a sport, something to be enjoyed, the time afield something to be savored. In later years, as my taste buds for wild game developed, I discovered nothing tastes quite like an elk or whitetail tenderloin or moose or caribou roast. Even black bear, often considered less than edible by many bear hunters, makes excellent table fare when taken care of properly in the field and when cooked right. For the past decade or more meat put on our family table, except for fish and poultry, originated in the wilds, and the thought of eating store-bought meat is enough to make me turn vegetarian.

Big racks and horns do impress me, though, and I have taken some respectable heads over the years—including two, at the time of this writing, for the record books. However, I am far from being what many would consider a trophy hunter. I do not go afield each season determined to get the biggest animal out there. If I see a big whitetail buck, or caribou with double shovels, or mulie that sports big antlers, I will certainly pull the trigger. And yes, there have been times, still are times, when I let some animals pass me by in hope

Bear can be a challenge to field judge. At first glance they all look big. This black bear looks like a good specimen. The hair looks full, there are no signs of rubs or thinning, and its full rounded ears indicate that it is not a younger bear. For the novice hunter or one looking for a rug it is certainly worth considering. From this angle, however, the legs are rather long and the belly is well off the ground, suggesting it is not a massive specimen. The nose also appears long. On large bears the nose is shorter and wider. This bear does not appear to meet Longhunter minimums but it is still a nice-looking animal.

for something larger. But if I should fill my tag with something less than record-book caliber, which has usually been the case, or if my animal turns out to be the smallest in camp, I feel no regret. I love to hunt and eat wild game, and each animal I take is a trophy in my eyes.

Somewhere along the way modern hunters have gone "trophy" crazy. In doing so we have forgotten many of the reasons why we take to the field in the first place. I see nothing wrong in hunting for a large set of antlers, we all do to a certain degree. What bothers me is that it has become "the" thing to do. So much so that novice hunters and those not fortunate enough to be in the right place at the right—which is how most record-book animals are taken anyway—are made to feel less capable. In some cases, it has become the philosophy among hunters that if you don't take something big, if you take a doe or spike-horn, for example, you havn't taken anything at all.

Just about every article published, every photograph accompanying a product in an advertisement, every television show and video, drives down our throats the idea that bigger is better, that smaller, non-trophy game is not worth taking. They all seem to suggest that their product, their technique, will help you get that animal of a lifetime. If it were that easy, every hunter in North America would be in the record books.

A trophy, like beauty, is in the eye of the beholder. I once hunted a spike-horn whitetail for an entire season not far from my home, and though I saw other deer, even a fine six-pointer, I wanted that spike-horn. I had scouted during the pre-season, and just when I thought I had him on opening day he outsmarted me and I didn't get a shot. For the next two weeks we played cat-and-mouse. For his age this was one smart whitetail, and I was bound and de-termined that if I was going to fill my tag that season, it was that spike-horn that was going to do it. On the last day of the season, at a place and time of day when I least expected it, I finally got him, but not until after that bugger put me through hell and made me stop and figure him out. That spike-horn, barely tipping the scales at 125 pounds, didn't make the record books, but in my mind it was a trophy in every sense of the word. I recall few deer that bring back so many fond memories.

We should hunt because we love to hunt, because we love to be afield, and because we appreciate wild game. It can't be denied, however, that game toting large headgear are impressive, and are something that just about every hunter hopes to tag one day. I have to admit that big horns and antlers strike a chord deep inside my being. It doesn't bother me a whole lot not to take the biggest moose, elk, antelope or black bear, but those monster eight and ten-point whitetails, those bull elk with regal sets of antlers, those moose with wide-spread and flat palmations, and those double-shoveled caribou get the adrenalin pumping.

The problem, of course, is that more of us dream about such animals than actually tag them. There are many reasons for this. Many of us do far less pre-season scounting than we should. Many of us are far less patient than we need to be, often taking the first animal that comes along or settling for some-thing less in fear of getting nothing at all. Others—perhaps the majority of us—simply do not recognize a potential trophy or record book animal when we see one.

Because it is impossible to actually measure a game animal before pulling the trigger, the chances of taking a record-book trophy are greatly in-creased if the hunter can differentiate between a really big game head and just a respectable one. While it is debatable whether field evaluations can really be made with certainty using a rifle scope or spotting scope, there is little doubt in my mind that if a hunter knows what to look for, the chances of taking a trophy animal increase. It should be noted that even using the techniques covered here, there is always room for error and even experienced hunters make mistakes.

Field estimating big game is far from an exact science, so studying each animal prior to a hunt is always a good idea. Two good references specifically for hunters seeking a trophy or record book head are *Measuring the Scoring North American Big Game Trophies*, by William H. Nesbitt and Philip L. Wright, published by the Boone and Crockett Club and *The Longhunter Big Game Record Book*, published by The Longhunter Society in Friendship, Indiana. What makes these two books such a valuable resource for the trophy hunter is that both offer examples of scoring system diagrams (not to be used for official scoring) of the various big game species, providing the hunter with a visual indication of what to look for in a potential record-book head. The Boone and Crockett Club book is especially helpful as it has chapters on measuring big game and is loaded with antler and horn characteristics to look for in a trophy. It includes a chapter on field evaluation that, along with supplying even more in-the-field tips on recognizing a possible record, has information on what aspects are most important in achieving a high score.

For example, until I studied the book a few years ago I never knew that development of palmation in both length and width in moose is more desirable when field-estimating and measuring moose than looking for the widest spread. Nor did I know that most record book mule deer have four very long and deeply forked top points, and while some record mulie contenders may also have long, symmetrical brow tines, many of the largest examples have short brow tines or none at all. For the serious trophy hunter, both books have a wealth of information, and should be studied carefully. The Boone and Crockett book is so helpful that I generally carry it with me when traveling in big game country just in case a potential trophy is spotted.

Most guides, outfitters, and experienced hunters are adept at determining the caliber of an animal in the field. Experience has taught me that on guided hunts, however, the guide is not always at hand to size up an animal for the client. The average hunter, particularly those hoping for a real prize, should be familiar with what to look for.

WHITETAILS

Of the two most popular deer species in North America, the whitetail deer and mule deer, the record book whitetail is the most difficult to judge in the field.

For one thing, the whitetail is a brush and timber-loving creature and it is often difficult to see the body, head and antlers for any long period of time. Many times, deer are on the run when seen, and even in open country this allows little opportunity to determine size before pulling the trigger. In his book, *The Complete Book of Hunting*, North American big game expert Clyde Ormand points out that the typical antlers on a whitetail lean a little forward, and the main beams "lie in a flat plane to the viewer making them difficult to estimate."

With one forked brow tine, good inside spread, long tines throughout, and good overall mass, there is no doubt about the trophy quality of this buck's rack. (Credit: Neal & MJ Mishler)

Still, experienced trophy hunters I know insist a whitetail buck can be judged a potential record-book contender if, facing the hunter, the rack exceeds the width of the body. Considering that the average big buck had a body of about 14 to 16 inches wide, this is not a bad method of judging a trophy animal. Some hunters also measure the horns against body features, particularly an uplifted tail, which may stand more than 12 inches over the body, or the vertical distance between brisket and chin. For example, if the antler height is equal to the height of an uplifted tail, or as Ormand writes, "would fill the area between chin and brisket as the buck runs, it is apt to be an outstanding rack."

Field judging any whitetail can be tricky in many situations because rarely do they give the hunter sufficient time. On a typical whitetail buck, however, there will be at least four long symmetrical points, plus beam tip on each side. Some will have five or six or more measurable points. The fourth point (G-4) will surely be six to eight inches long and the previous points will be even longer. Inside spread is important and the antlers will rise high above the head. A non-typical trophy rack is likely to show the same well developed normal points as on a typical rack but with additional points sprouting in various, sometimes odd directions.

The same is true when field judging the Coues' deer, but on a smaller scale. Inside spread is important and anything over 14 or 15 inches should make the book. There will also be at least three well developed points plus main beam on each side.

MULE DEER

Mule deer are a little easier to judge if for no other reason than that they are often found in more open country and can be scoped at greater distances giving the hunter more time to determine size. They are also easier to size because mule deer offer some larger body features that whitetail's lack that can be use to the hunter's advantage, namely the ears.

Mule deer have extremely large ears that sit far apart on the head. When a buck mule deer is alarmed, or stands at attention observing a possible threat, he holds his ears almost straight out but at a slight angle, and they span a distance of 20 to 21 inches between them. If the bend in the antlers extends past the ears, the hunter should take a closer look. This is particularly true if the inside main beams are wider than the ears!

In his book *Hunting Big-Game Trophies*, acclaimed North American trophy hunter Tom Brakefield makes an interesting point concerning the importance of symmetry when it comes to sizing mule deer bucks stating a balanced rack with the same approximate measurements per side, and four long points plus brow points are highly important. Brakefield writes, "When the hunter has to quickly size up a head in the field, especially if the antlers are in silhouette, he invariably estimates the length of the "Y's" that is, the two forks on each side. In those terms the "Y's" should be at least 8 to 9-inches deep for trophy consideration." Even better would be "Y's" in the 10 to 11-inch range.

Mass and total length of the main beams are also important in scoring both whitetail and mule deer, as is uniformity of the tines on each side. Odd number points, four on the left and five on the right, for example, can actually lower total scoring with deductions.

All deer can be difficult to estimate in the field due to thick cover, distance, or movement. It is no different with the mulie. They don't give the hunter a long time to size them up except from a considerable distance.

When opportunity knocks, though, take a look at antler width. If the rack stands tall and is approximately half as tall as the body from withers to the ground you may be looking at a real keeper. Also, if the buck is faced head-on, quartering on walking away look at the ears. They are approximately 20 to 22 inches wide when full extended, and if the inside spread equals or surpasses them, chances are it is a good dear. Trophy mulie bucks will also invariably sport at least four long and deeply forked top points on each side. Long symmetrical brow tines and general symmetry are contribute to the score.

When it comes to the Columbia blacktail, keep in mind the racks are typically smaller. Height is generally a good indicator of long points, which contribute to the score. There should be four of them, deeply forked. Sitka blacktails will often show four points to the side, but sometimes three. Look for spread and good mass in the main beams.

ELK

The elk, one of North America's largest antlered big game is best gauged by comparing antlers to body. First, however, as of this writing most record-book American and Roosevelt elk listed in the Longhunter Record Book, in both typical and non-typical categories, carry at least six points on one side.

Good width and long G4s and G5s mark this bugling bull elk as a keeper. (Credit: Neal & MJ Mishler)

Some list five points on one side and six, perhaps as many as seven or nine, on the other depending upon the category. The number of points count, as do the length, particularly the fourth (G-4) and fifth (G-5) points. They should be close to 16 to 17 inches or better, and 11 to 12 inches of better, respectively, in the typical category. The main beams will also have a long sweeping curve over the shoulders. Most Longhunter records have a main beam length from about 30 inches to more than 55 inches. Inside spreads measure in the same range. Big bull elk often carry their head gear leaning back over their bodies. From the side, if the antlers approach body length or reach the highquarter, take a close look. Viewed from the front, antlers appearing about twice as wide as the body make a good head. If the antlers clear both sides of the body by a foot or so when viewed from the rear, and if carrying the necessary points, particularly the long fourth and fifth points, don't let the animal get away!

Look for the "Y" at the end of the main beams forming the fifth and sixth points. If the "Y's" are evident, estimate how long they are. If the points are in the 5, 6, or 7 inch range the hunter just might be looking at a record-book head.

Finally, look at the third point. This is generally the shortest of the first four points on a bull elk. If the "Y" tines are the same length or longer than the third point, the hunter is looking at a good animal.

PRONGHORN

Because of their small size, speed, keen eyesight, and open terrain in which they are found, pronghorn are among the most challenging targets for the muzzleloading hunter. They are also one of the most difficult to estimate in the field before pulling the triggers, which makes them a double challenge for the hunter looking for a trophy.

Trophy pronghorn, however, can be evaluated in several ways. A reliable method is to compare the horns with the body. For example, if the pronghorn is standing broadside and the horns are one-third the length of the body in height or better, not including the neck, look the animal over closely. It could be a record. Most records in the Longhunter Record Book are greater than 11 inches, but at the length the horns will needs a good "prong" and mass to make the minimum. Something is the 14- to 16-inch class would be more desirable. Also, if the horn spread is exceeds one-half of the body width when glassed from the rear or head-on the animal is good size. Look at the ears, too. If from any angle the horns are three to four time higher than the ears, a trophy buck is at hand.

Even a trophy buck can be difficult to judge in the field at a distance using these guides. A good spotting scope with fully coated optics mounted on a good base in the 20X to 30X range makes the task easier and binoculars will work at close range. There are, however, some other things to look and study that help determine whether a buck is worth taking.

Look at the prongs. They should measure five inches long from the back of the horn, which means it should extend three to four inches from the front of the horn for record book consideration. The base of the horns should also have good circumference. If they look to be 2 to 2½-inches at the base from the side, take a good look. That would equate to a 5- to 6-inch circumference, which is quite good.

Don't worry about inside spread. It looks nice but contributes little to the total score. Most Longhunter records have a spread of about 11 inches or less. What really counts is the prong, horn length and mass.

CARIBOU

Of all big game heads, caribou are perhaps the most complex to score and estimate in the field. For one thing, they all look big and carry numerous points which can be confusing when viewing through binoculars. But more than that, in official scoring there are more than three-dozen factors taken into consideration, as many as 14 measurements on each side, more than any other North American big game. Because of their complexity, hunters are advised to study the scoring charts available in the Boone and Crockett book, *Measuring and Scoring North American Big Game Trophies* or *The Longhunter Society Big Game Record Book*, to see which measurements are critical or contribute most to overall score. In fact, doing so is recommended for all big game.

It should be pointed out, that caribou heads vary greatly in size and configuration, depending on area and subspecies. This is the reason for so many trophy categories and varying minimum scores. Something needed for a minimum or high score in one category might be less important in another, although all caribou are measured the same.

Considering their complexity, there are some indicators that can be used to help determine to a certain degree whether a bull is a potential trophy. For example, if the antlers or a bull caribou appear nearly as high as the body height, take a closer look. Look for the long, important top points, overall spread, the bez, palmation, and overall symmetry. All affect scoring, particularly uniformity of each antlers, or symmetry. Look at the top points first, though. All four should be in the 18- or 20-inch range to make the Longhunter book. Keep in mind, the two longest top points will be added to the score, so the longer the better.

The top palms should be wide, for good mass, and the shovel(s) should be long. A trophy rack also has good main beam length, which can be compared to the body. If the rack seems to be as high over the head as the body is tall at the shoulder, it has the potential of being a good rack. Good bulls have main beam length in the 45 to 50-inch range. Look for well-developed rear points, keeping in mind that only one will be measured and added to the score. If there is only one, it should be long. Look at the bez. They should be in the 15- to 18-inch range. In general, the great the spread the better and anything that extends 10 to 11 inches beyond each side of the body when viewed head on or from the rear is good. Finally, look for mass, particularly between

This series of photos shows how patience pays off. At first glance, this caribou looks good, but I wouldn't pull the trigger on this view alone. A few minutes later, the bull moved, showing good palmation and points and decent spread. Finally, the bull turns again, showing another good angle. It is definitely worth taking.

the brow and bez points, between bez and rear point(s), just below the first top point, and between the two longest top points.

This is a lot to look for. Although caribou often give the hunter ample time to look them over unless a major error is made, in the excitement of the moment it is easy to overlook critical characteristics that help the total score. In a rush just keep in mind beam length, inside spread, and length of the shovel(s) bez, rear point(s) and top points along with symmetry should get most of your attention.

MOOSE

All moose look big on the hoof, and hunters often associate body size with antler size. It is the first mistake in field estimating these animals, one that proves costly once the trigger is pulled.

The first thing to look for is overall spread. Keep in mind, unlike deer, elk and caribou where inside spread is important, moose receive scoring credit from greatest spread. In general, a bull must reach a certain benchmark to make the Longhunter minimums: they are at least 35- to 40 inches for Wyoming moose, 45- to 50 inches for Canada moose and 55- to 60 inches for Alaskan-Yukon moose.

This looks like a nice bull moose, but it lacks palmation and points. Although it would make some fine dining chances are it would not make the record books.

As important as greatest spread is to the score, width and length of each palm is even more important. Combined they contribute more than 50 percent to the total score. For a trophy bull, look for palms that lay or appear flat which contribute to a great spread, rather than palms that appear cupped or bowel-shaped. The number of points is important, too, but keep in mind they must be over one inch in length, and longer than they are wide at the one inch mark to be taken into consideration.

And finally, when viewing a bull from the side, don't pull the trigger until you can see both antlers. One side may look impressive but the other might actually be smaller, have a smaller palm, or lack points, greatly reducing your score. As with all big game, look for good symmetry.

SHEEP AND GOATS

Those fortunate enough to hunt one of the four subspecies of North American sheep should keep in mind that despite slightly different horn formation and size, all can be field judged the same basic way. In general, overall curl depth and mass is what to look for. Keeping that in mind, the ram war-

Goats are best field-rated using the ears, especially when viewed head-on. Generally, if the horns are twice as long as the ears it is worth taking a closer look. Keep in mind that both nannies and billies sprout horns, and nannies may not be hunted in some locales.

rants closer viewing if the horns seem to be of good mass and if the curl is about one-third the animal's height with a broadside view.

The rudimentary observations are important, but as Brakefield states in his book, "Beware if the ram carries rather thin horn, especially if the points are perfect and curve up to the eye level or even above. This will be a young animal, hardly worth shooting." Again, look for good mass and a curve sweeping past the lower jaw with blunted tips going past the eyes, which indicate age.

A good goat can be considered worth a closer look if the horns are about one-fourth the animal's height, not including the shoulder hump. Also, remember a mountain goat's ears are approximately four inches long. Any horns twice as long as the ears or better is worth closer scrutiny. A thing to remember, too is large rams are generally solitary individuals. However, they may hang out in pairs or groups of three, and in this situation it is possible to compare one with the other to better determine size. Goats are equally as solitary, except during the mating season. If the animal is accompanied smaller animals you might be looking at a female. Also, look at the hair. On both sheep and goats older males, those carrying the largest horns, often have an aged yellowish tint.

With this said, some other things should be mentioned, particularly where goats are concerned since both carry horns, and since in some areas it is illegal to kill females and it may be necessary to distinguish a nanny from a billy. In areas were both sexes may be harvested, this is less important and should be given little concern since a large female may carry larger horns than some females. Where only billies are legal, and for those hunters who desire taking only males it is worth knowing that adult goat seen in the company of young, or "kids" is usually a nanny. Again, billies are more solitary, and though they may be in the immediate area, they are apt to be off by themselves.

Early in the season, when the hair is still short, it may be possible to confirm sex by the genitals. This is difficult, however, as many seasons takes place later in the fall when goats have a full body covering, and since many hunters prefer only examples with long hair. If this is the case, keep in mind males have a larger, more pronounced shoulder hump than females. Their hair is also more shaggy, or "wooly" looking, often more yellowish or bleached, and the profile of the billy is more stocky, or chunky, than the nannie's.

The horns can also be used to determine sex. Nanny horns are generally more spindly-looking, and they typically hook back and down more sharply, especially towards the ends. Horns atop a billy are bulkier, and lay back much more gradually along their entire length.

Estimating sheep in the field can in many ways be easier than goats. Along with the aspects previously noted, keep in mind the horns of the so-called "thinhorn" varieties, the Dall and Stone's, tend to flare out more from the head, whereas the heavier-horned species, the desert and mountain bighorns, generally have horns that are more tightly curled. Sizing them up in the field, however, is basically the same.

Whenever possible, view a ram head-on, from the front. As noted in *Measuring and Scoring North American Big Game Trophies*, a ram facing away often looks much bigger than it really is, and even a side view is rarely accurate. A frontal view, though, will clearly show the lowest point of the curl, which on nearly all record-book contenders will drop well below the chin line. The deeper the curl falls below the chin, the better.

In reality, considering the high mountainous terrain in which they are found, the physical demands in reaching it, difficult shots and other factors, any first sheep or goat should be considered a trophy in the eyes of the hunter and hunting world, particularly when taken with a muzzleloader. Even under the best circumstances and under the best conditions these are some of the most difficult animals to harvest among North American big game. When bagged under the rules of fair chase, success is such a testimony to a hunter's determination, hunting ability and marksmanship that not to look with pride upon a specimen simply because it falls short of the record book minimums is an insult.

BEAR

Bear are among the hardest of North American big game to estimate in the field. Unlike the horned and antlered species bears are strictly scored by skull size. Bears are also completely covered by hair, and have a ample supply of muscle, including around the skull. They all look big, and it can be a difficult task estimating a bear in the field.

Certain aspects can be used to the hunter's advantage, however. A bear skull does not shrink with age, it gets larger, so the older bears will have the biggest skulls. Look at the head and compare it with the body. If the bear seems to have a big head, chances are it is a young bear and the skull is small.

You want just the opposite, a bear with a huge body that makes the skull look small. Also, look at the way the bear walks. If it moves with a slow, rolling waddle as if carrying a heavy load, rather than with an easy, light-footed gait, it could be a trophy bear.

I also look at the nose. Young bears tend to have a long, dog-like snout. The nose of an older, more mature bear is often shorter, flatter, and rounder. Look at the ears, too. Ears of young bear appear long and pointed, while those of older, larger bear are shorter and rounded on the tops. In many ways, an older bear looks and acts old: in the way it moves, the speed at which it moves and in appearance.

Take a look at the legs. If they are long, lean, and if the bottom of the stomach rides high above the ground, chances are it is a young, small bruin. On the other hand, of the legs are short, fat and the belly hangs close to the ground, you may be looking at a keeper. Take a look the body, too. Small bear are usually long and lanky; bigger bear seem shorter, fatter, more robust.

On brown bears, look at the neck. The neck on young brown bear seem to be missing, but older, more mature adults have a long, distinguishable neck. Young browns also tend to feed between their paws, while large examples feed further away from the body. Finally, regardless of the subspecies, all large bear seem to carry their head low, as if unconcerned with any danger that might be in the vicinity. Smaller bear tend to carry their head higher.

LONGHUNTER SOCIETY MINIMUM ENTRY SCORES

GAME ANIMAL	MINIMUM ENTRY SCORE
Black Bear	18
Grizzly Bear	19
Alaska Brown Bear	21
Polar Bear	22
Cougar (Mountain Lion)	13
American Elk	255
American Elk (non-typical)	265
Roosevelt Elk	225
Mule Deer (typical)	146
Mule deer (non-typical)	175

Columbia Blacktail Deer	95
Sitka Blacktail Deer	75
Whitetail Deer (typical)	130
Whitetail deer (non-typical)	160
Coues' Whitetail Deer (typical)	70
Coues' Whitetail Deer (non-typical)	75
Canada Moose	145
Alaska-Yukon Moose	180
Wyoming Moose	125
Mountain Caribou	280
Woodland Caribou	230
Barren Ground Caribou	320
Central Canada Barren Ground Caribou	275
Quebec/Labrador Caribou	320
Pronghorn (antelope)	63
Bison	92
Rocky Mountain Goat	41
Muskox	80
Bighorn Sheep	136
Desert Sheep	125
Dall's Sheep	132
Stone's Sheep	132

There are, of course, other ways to estimate game on the hoof, and ability to do so with a degree of accuracy comes with experience in the field. Just like everything else in hunting, it takes time and some trial and error. Reading up on the subject can increase the learning curve. Along with what is offered in these pages, Tom Brakefield in *Hunting Big-Game Trophies*, from Outdoor Life/Dutton, offers some wonderful tips on evaluating heads in the field. The edition I own was published in 1976, and undoubtedly the book is out of print, but check with your local book store or local library.

Clyde Ormand's *Complete Book of Hunting* from Outdoor Life/Harper & Row, also has a complete chapter on the subject. I have the second, revised and updated edition that was published in 1972, and it, too, is undoubtedly out of print. There is also *Measuring and Scoring North American Big Game Trophies*, offered by the Boone and Crockett Club. It can be order by contacting Boone and Crockett Club, Old Milwaukee Depot, 250 Station Drive, Missoula, MT., 59801-2753 or by telephoning 406-542-1888. They are also on the web at *www.boone-crockett.org*.

QUICK REFERENCE GUIDE TO MAJOR CONSIDERATIONS ON FIELD ESTIMATING BIG GAME

Species	Major Considerations
Whitetail/Coues Deer	Inside spread, Beam length, Tine length, Overall mass
Mule/Blacktail Deer	Inside spread, Forth depth, symmetry Overall mass, Beam length
Caribou	Beam length, Inside spread, Shovel(s) length, Bez length, Rear points, Top points
Moose	Greatest spread, Palm width and length, Point total
Bear	See text for major indicators suggesting a possible record
Antelope	Prong length, Overall mass, Overall length
Mountain Goat	Horn Length, Overall mass
Sheep	Curl depth, Overall mass
Elk	Beam length, Antler spread, Tine length, Overall mass

19

GAME CARE AND SELECTING A TAXIDERMIST

At some point, just about every hunter desires to have something mounted. It may be a shoulder-mount of a respectable bull elk or caribou, two of the most impressive mounts ever to grace a wall, or it may be a full-size mount of a black bear or antelope. It may even be a rug to lay in front of the fireplace.

Game mounts are often the biggest or most impressive specimens we take while afield, but they may also be the first animal we tag. My brother, Dave, has a head mount of a doe whitetail, the first big game animal he ever took, and I had a rug made of the first black bear I ever tagged. Neither animal made the record books, and both of us have taken much larger game since, but mounts are memories. They help us relive special times. Each time I look at the various mounts in my living room and office they take me back to days afield.

I do not specifically hunt for mounts, but a good number of hunters do. When I pursue big game two things are always in the back of my mind: keeping that meat in good condition until I get it to the butcher and, if it is to end up as a mount, skinning the animal properly and keeping the cape in prime

A quality mount looks natural and lifelike, such as this black bear.

shape until I get it to the taxidermist. Whether most hunters realize it or not, proper care for meat or mounts begins long before the hunt even starts.

SELECTING A TAXIDERMIST

One of the most important things the hunter can do to help ensure his or her game meat, skins, and antlers are in good condition on arriving home is to talk to a taxidermist before departing for the hunt. This is particularly important if the hunter has never caped an animal for mounting and is going on a do-it-yourself hunt. It is also good general knowledge, since a couple of outfitters and guides I have hunted with in the past were rather rough in their treatment of game. One in particular took shortcuts I didn't appreciate. Had I not been looking over his shoulder and scrutinizing his work, I don't know what I might have ended up with. Talking with a taxidermist before leaving home is part of your investment in the hunt. It takes little time and may very well prove to be one of the most important things you ever do as a hunter.

Specifically, a taxidermist can instruct you in how to properly skin an animal based on the type of mount you have in mind. This will help prevent making any unnecessary cuts that might otherwise have to be mended, thus

The author and his first moose from Newfoundland. The skull has been cleaned for a "European" mount, which will show the horns and skull.

costing more money. A taxidermist should also be able to instruct how best to store capes and meat in backwoods situations, talk about "splitting" the lips and "turning" ears, explain how critical areas around the eyes, nose, ears, and mouth are, and cover other "dos and don'ts" that are essential in obtaining a high quality, good looking mount and fresh meat. I know several taxidermists in my area that supply written instructional guidelines complete with drawings showing the various cuts. Ask if such guidelines are available, but if not, take some notes and make sure they are with you on the hunt for reference.

There are some other things you should inquire about too. They include discussing price, deposits, and time of delivery. One mistake many hunters make is to base their decision on cost. There is no way around it, good mounts that are done properly can be costly. Look on them as an investment. If one taxidermist is charging $195 for a whitetail head mount and another taxidermist several towns away is charging double or triple that, I may look at them all, but chances are it is the more expensive studio or the one in the middle that I will go to. The less expensive taxidermist may be cutting corners, may be new in the trade and not as skilled, or he may be cutting prices to get more work. If you are satisfied with the less costly mounts, go with it. But remember, just like anything else, you generally get what you pay for. Ask about panels, bases, and habitat work, too. Are they included in the price?

Inquire about deposits. One-quarter to one-third down is about the standard. If custom work is being done, a greater deposit is not unusual. Many taxidermists will vary the required deposit depending on several factors, such as the amount of work, total cost, time of delivery, and so on, so don't hesitate to ask.

Good mounts also take time to complete. Depending on the mount it can be as long as 14 to 24 months. It can take half that time to get a pelt properly tanned. Taxidermists that promise completion in six to ten months are generally not in great demand and therefore don't have much backlog. They may also be cutting corners somewhere that could affect the appearance of the finished product and how long it will last. For a good mount from a top, in-demand taxidermist, a year to two years wait is not unrealistic. Speaking from experience, it is difficult to muster the patience to wait that long, and we might ask ourselves why, but I have seen good taxidermists at work, and when they do things right and take those extra steps for a quality mount it is easy to understand why it takes so long.

Ask for references. I generally like to get the names of new clients, hunters who recently had worked delivered, and old clients, those who have had a mount hanging on the wall for several years. By contacting both I learn whether the taxidermist's work stands up under the greatest test of all, time, and whether his quality has slipped in recent months. I also like the names of references who had the same animal mounted as I plan to hunt. In some cases, I have had references invite me to review the mount or mounts. Once making contact, I ask if they are satisfied with the work, if it was delivered on time, and how long it took. Would they use the same taxidermist again? Were there any misunderstandings on price? If it is an older mount, how is it holding up over time? If the mount was shipped when finished, was it packed carefully, did it arrive in good condition, and did the taxidermist follow up to check on its condition and your satisfaction. This latter point does not necessarily reflect on a taxidermist's ability to offer quality work, but it does show whether he or she is concerned about the product and you as a customer.

Also, once selecting the taxidermist you want, let him know when you expect to deliver your game. A good taxidermist is a busy person and many like to prepare for a client's arrival. If you plan to have your game shipped, let him know when it might arrive, how it is being shipped, and by whom. If you live a considerable distance from the taxidermist, ask about having the finished work shipped to you. How is it shipped? Is insurance included in the cost? Will the taxidermist deliver it? At what cost? When you deliver your game after the hunt, get the price, deposit, delivery date, and any other particulars in writing on a receipt.

But before any of this takes place it is necessary to select the taxidermist you want to work with. In many states and some provinces taxidermists have to be licensed by fish and game departments, so a telephone call might get you a listing. Many taxidermists also advertise in state, provincial, or regional sporting magazines and publications, sometimes local newspapers. You might also have a friend who has had some work done, or see a mount in someone's home, office or a sporting goods store. If so, ask about it. Once obtaining a list, make a few telephone calls and ask if you might stop by to see their work and ask a few questions. If so, make an appointment.

Most taxidermists are willing to make time for questions and for reviewing their work, particularly the latter. Not all, however, will go out of their way to instruct in proper field care of game. They may be busy, and some just don't feel it is part of their job. If this is the case, I simply thank them and go elsewhere. There are lots of highly qualified taxidermists out there, and I want one who will make the time. Be courteous and friendly, and explain what you require. Again, make an appointment, make a point to be there on time, and prepare your questions. Don't wear out your welcome. When you leave let him know you appreciate his help.

You should also have some idea what to look for when reviewing a taxidermist's work. To the layman hunter, a taxidermist is simply someone who "preserves" or "mounts" wildlife. In reality, however, a taxidermist is much more. Among their other unique and varied skills, they are expert at skinning and sculpturing. Taxidermists must have an intimate knowledge of the species and its habitat. A certain positioning of the head, expression on the face or about the eye, can mean the difference between a typical mount and one that truly stands out. A master taxidermist is aware of new techniques and materials in the trade, they respect the animals on which they work and care deeply about the finished product.

Without question, a highly skilled taxidermist is one of the most knowledgeable naturalists and wildlife experts there is. Many are avid hunters, possessing a thirst for knowledge about animals that goes far beyond the average sportsman. It is this knowledge, this desire to recreate big game mounts in a true, realistic and dignified manner, that sets a great taxidermist apart from one who considers it a mere job.

When I look at a mount, the first thing I look at are the eyes, ears, and nose. These are the focal points of any mount, and they will quickly indicate whether a taxidermist knows his trade. Do the eyes looked focused? Are they looking in the same direction? Are they clear? Does each eye have a tear duct? Do they look real? Are the ears positioned correctly? Are they in proportion to the head? Is the nose shiney?

Also look at the overall expression of the mount. Does the facial expression look natural and in character? I don't know how many ferocious looking black bear mounts I have seen over the years. The mouth is open in a hostile, snarling, man-eating expression. The black bear is one of my favorite game animals, and I have seen many in the woods, a number from just a few feet away that were looking straight up at me as I sat in a tree stand. Not one had such an expression. It is completely out of character. Why should a black bear be

When studying the work of a taxidermist, look closely at the eyes, nose, and mouth. They should look like the real thing.

mounted this way? A whitetail mount might have the ears turned a certain way, the eyes looking fully alert, the nose flared as if investigating potential danger. If it is a deer, elk, moose, or anterlope mount, are the horns or antlers positioned correctly? Have they been cleaned? Do they look natural?

To answer many of these questions, it is necessary for the hunter to have at least a general knowledge of the species he plans to hunt. Even with limited knowledge, a careful, up-close look at a mount can tell the hunter whether the taxidermist knows his business. When reviewing a taxidermist's work, take some notes and compare them with the work of other taxidermists before making a decision. You will see a difference from one to the next, and in a short time the experience and expertise of a particular taxidermist will become apparent.

Finally, keep in mind that all this takes times. Don't wait until the last minute to select the taxidermist you want to work with. If your deer hunt in Montana is planned for November, start looking in July or August. If traveling to northern Quebec for caribou in August or September, start your search in April or May. If going on a spring bear hunt to Alberta or Newfoundland in May or June, start looking in January or February. Give yourself at least three to four months to find the right taxidermist.

DRESSING AND MEASUREMENTS FOR GAME MOUNTS

For the most part, antlered game require the same basic cuts and skinning procedures when destined for the taxidermist. While most outfitters and guides take care of skinning, and though many are quite good at it, it is always a good idea to know what to do and what not to do if for no other reason than to make sure the guide is doing it right.

In some ways, the fun ends when the trigger is pulled. Properly taking care of game in the field takes some time and effort. Once the animal is down, there are several things the hunter can do to ensure the prize will arrive at the taxidermist in the best possible condition. It all starts will proper field-dressing and getting the animal out of the woods.

In nearly all cases, once the decision has been made that an animal is going to be mounted, only one cut should be made for field-dressing. This cut is from the anus to the bottom of the chest bone. Do not cut the throat, as is the custom among some deer hunters, nor should the area around the brisket be cut. The neck and brisket are areas that are plainly visible on head and shoulder mounts, and cuts to those areas will only have to be mended later. It may also be difficult for even the best taxidermist to obscure these cuts so they will not show in the finished product. Once the animal has been dressed, wipe away any blood or body fluids that may be on the hair. Blood can stain and is difficult to remove, especially after it has had time to dry.

Equally important is getting the animal out of the woods without damaging the hair. Much of the damage to future mounts is done when transporting game back to camp or the truck. It is not uncommon for deer hunters to drag their animal, but when doing so efforts should be made to drag it head first, keeping as much of the head and shoulder area off the ground as possible. Dragging from the head also means pulling with the natural direction of the hair, which is less apt to cause damage. Caution should also be taken when pulling over rocks, fallen logs, and other obstacles. The best scenario is to get the animal off the ground completely, either by carrying it by the legs with the aid of a friend or transporting it on an all-terrain vehicle. On western hunts in remote country, game can be transported back to camp aboard a pack horse. The animal can also be caped and quartered on the spot and backpacked to

At more than 1,000 pounds, moose can be a chore to get out of the woods. Here, two guides are finishing the field-dressing process. The moose will be quartered and carried back to camp.

camp. No matter how you transport it, take caution with the pelt. The taxidermist needs something in good condition in order to provide a quality mount.

Upon arrival back at camp, the work really begins. Many taxidermists prefer certain measurements and photographs to help mount the animal as life-like as possible. When taking photographs for the taxidermist, take at least two of the head, one from the side, and one from the front. Take photos of any distinguishing marks, too.

What measurements should be taken depends upon the type of mount the hunter has in mind. For head and shoulder mounts only, a few measurements are required. For full body mounts even more measurements are required. Most of these measurements are best taken *after* the skin has been removed. The reason for this is to make sure the form on which the mount will be created is the same size as the original animal. Measurements should also be taken before skinning to give the taxidermist a before and after idea of size. Also, certain measurements will not be available after skinning or field-dressing. If the weather is warm and the need to cool game meat is immediate, measurements before skinning are better than nothing, but ideally, measurements after skinning are best.

Whenever possible, trophy or record-book antlers should be left intact and not "split." It is more difficult transporting them this way, particularly

Suggested Measurements
For Antlered and Non-Antlered
Game After Skinning
_____

Neck and Shoulder Mounts

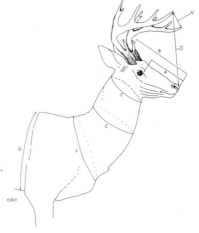

A) Front corner of eye to end of nose.
B) End of nose to back of skull.
C) Circumference of neck in back of ears.
D) Tip of antlers to tip of nose.
E) Circumference of neck around the middle.
F) Circumference of neck in front of shoulders.
G) Circumference of body in back of elbow.
H) Tip to tip antler spread.

Full Mounts

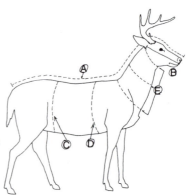

A) Length of body from tip of nose to root of tail, measuring along the back line.
B) Tip of nose to back of head.
C) Greatest circumference of body.
D) Circumference of body in back of shoulder.
E) Circumference of neck behind ears, at mid-neck and front of shoulders.

All measurement are best taken after skinning although measurements with skin on are better than nothing.

when shipped by air, but leaving them whole helps provide a much stronger mount, makes mounting easier for the taxidermist, and provides a more exact reproduction in terms of overall spread. There is also the fact that antlers that have been split are not eligible for the record books. If the antlers must be split it is important to take a measurement of the inside spread (measurement H, Illustration A). This will allow the taxidermist to set the antlers correctly and to obtain the proper spread in the finished mount.

SKINNING GAME FOR HEAD AND SHOULDER MOUNTS

The procedures used to cape or skin an animal depend a good deal on whether refrigeration facilities are available, whether it is possible to get a skin frozen or cooled within a day or two, and if it is possible to keep it frozen or cold during transport to the taxidermist. If so, the job of skinning and preserving is much easier.

First, make a cut (Cut 1) around the chest several inches behind the front shoulders. Typically, I like to make this cut well down the belly, keeping in mind it is always better to give the taxidermist more skin to work with than less. Make a second cut (Cut 2) around each of the front legs below the elbow. A third cut (Cut 3) is made up the back of the legs to intersect Cut 1 around

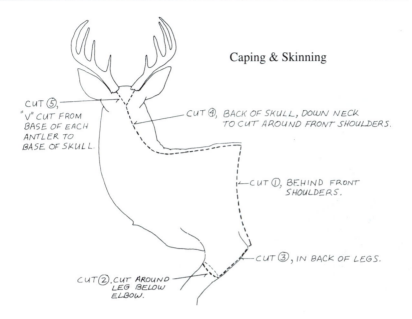

Caping & Skinning

CUT ⑤, "V" CUT FROM BASE OF EACH ANTLER TO BASE OF SKULL.

CUT ④, BACK OF SKULL, DOWN NECK TO CUT AROUND FRONT SHOULDERS.

CUT ①, BEHIND FRONT SHOULDERS.

CUT ③, IN BACK OF LEGS.

CUT ②. CUT AROUND LEG BELOW ELBOW.

the chest. This is followed by a cut (Cut 4) from the back of the skull down the back of the neck, going between the shoulder blades to meet Cut 1 around the chest. All cuts should be as straight and clean as possible and should be made going with the hair grain.

It is now possible to actually start skinning. The type and size of knife used for the chore is up to the hunter. Some prefer a large, one-piece knife with a sharp point, others like a folding knife on the small side, perhaps with a rounded or slightly upturned nose. Personally, 1 have found it easier to inadvertently puncture a skin or make unwanted slices with a sharp, pointed knife. This could be more my fault than knife design, but blades with rounded, slightly upturned noses with a cutting edge going all the way to the tip seem less apt to puncture a skin. Knives that fold should have a solid locking feature to prevent the blade from folding during heavy use. A knife should also be sharp and be able to hold an edge. Skinning an animal takes a toll on any knife, so make sure you keep checking the edge and have a good stone handy.

When actually skinning your game, cut as close to the skin as possible. In critical areas it is okay to take some meat and fat. It can be removed later; most taxidermists like to see capes as free of meat and fat as possible. Starting with the cut around the chest, work towards the head, up to the first vertebrae

Certain measurements will help the taxidermist produce a quality mount. These hunters are measuring the length of the pelt from tip of nose to tip of tail.

where the neck attaches to the skull. At this point, only if freezer or refrigeration is available, cut through the neck with a saw. Clean the skin of meat and fat, wipe away any blood, and then with the cape lying flat on the ground, hair down, fold the cape (flesh-side out) into a bundle working towards the head and antlers. With the skin lying flat, I generally fold the sides in, leaving part of the flesh showing. I then roll the head forward, making sure the area where the neck was cut is touching flesh and not hair. I then fold the sides in so they touch each other, and continue to roll forward, wrapping the skin between the antlers, hair touching hair. Once this is done, I wrap the cape in a burlap bag, game bag, old pillow case, or in cheesecloth, and put it in a plastic bag and freeze or refrigerate.

Contrary to common belief, it does little good to salt the cape if it is to be frozen or kept in cold storage. The salt doesn't freeze and just makes a mess that will have to be cleaned up later. Also, many taxidermists actually prefer the cape to be brought in this way, with head attached, so they can do the delicate work of skinning around the eyes, turning the ears and splitting the lips. Many outfitters and guides are quite skilled at skinning in these areas, and if so, let them do it. But if the hunter is unfamilar with how to do it, leaving the head attached is the best way to go, but only if the pelt can be frozen or kept cold.

This pronghorn has just been caped. Now the outfitter is doing some fine skinning around the eyes. Notice how neat and clean the skinning job is. This will pay off at the taxidermy shop.

If cold storage facilities are not available, which is often the case deep in the bush, or if in camp for longer than a week, it is important the head be completely skinned. It is a slow and tedious job, but critical, and just about anyone can do it if they take their time.

To start, make a "V" cut (Cut 5) from the base of each antler to the cut at the base of the skull (Cut 4). Now cut the lips free of the gums. This is a crucial cut. The most important thing is to retain as much of the lip on the inside of the mouth as possible. To do this, cut where the inside lip skin meets the uppermost part of the gum. If there are any questions or doubts about this, or about turning the ears or skinning around the eyes, make a point to ask your taxidermist before leaving home.

Once these cuts are made, start skinning the head. Work forward towards the antlers, cutting the ears as close to the skull as possible. When the antlers are reached, use a blunt screwdriver to pry the skin away from each base, making sure to get all the hair around the antler base. Work slow, and be careful not to rip or puncture the pelt. Once complete, continue to skin forward until you come to the eyes.

Of the various cuts around the head, the eye area is most critical. The eyes are a focal point on any mount, and along with the headgear, are among the first thing observers scrutinzie. A good taxidermy job around the eyes can also make or break a quality, realistic-looking mount, and it all begins with proper skinning.

A good friend of mine and award-winning taxidermist, Rock Agostino of Creative Maine Taxidermy in Lyman, Maine, once showed me a neat trick that helps prevent the eyelid from being cut. Rock inserts a finger deep into the eye socket to locate the back of the eyelid, and literally cuts around his finger, using it as a guide. The same tactic is used to skin the back of the mouth and nostrils. When doing the eyes, take care to retain as much of the tear duct as possible, and as much of the nostril area inside of the nose.

Once the skin has been fully removed, wipe away any blood, remove as much excess flesh and fat as possible, and skin out the ears, turning them inside-out as you go. Since no freezer or cooler facilities are available, it will be necessary to salt the pelt to prevent spoilage and slippage of the hair. Use non-iodized salt only. Do not use rock salt. Iodized table salt will work if it is the only thing available, but rock salt is too coarse for good penetration. The pick-

Once an animal has been skinned, extra time and effort should be taken to remove excess fat, meat, dirt, and blood.

ling salt that should be used is available at most feed supply stores in 50-pounds bags, and the generaly rule is to be generous with the salt, work it into the flesh, and cover all exposed areas, especially around the eyes, mouth, and ears. On bear, working generous amounts of salt into the pelt is particularly important. The list below offers some guidelines as to how much salt might be required for some popular big game animals.

Species	Cape and Head Only	Whole Hide
Moose	20 to 30 pounds	50 to 60 pounds
Elk/Caribou	10 to 25 pounds	30 to 35 pounds
Deer/Pronghorn/Sheep or Goat 150 to 250 pounds	5 to 15 pounds	20 to 25 pounds
Black Bear	10 to 15 pounds	25 to 40 pounds
Grizzly Bear/Brown Bear	15 to 20 pounds	30 to 50 pounds

Game should be caped and salted as quickly as possible, particularly if the weather is warm. It is really impossible to use too much salt. Use what you feel is necessary, but more is better than less. Also, salt your hide when it is still moist after skinning, and use only salt that is dry. If the flesh side of the hide starts to dry, or is dry, wet it before applying the salt. It is also important that the salt penetrate deep into the skin, so keeping it flat on the ground, work the salt into the pores and flesh with your hands, making sure to force salt into all the nooks and crannies.

Pay special attention to the critical areas around the head: the eyes, nose, ears, and lips. Cover these areas well and work the salt in deep. Also, when salting capes for full mounts or rugs, don't forget to work around the anus. It may be distasteful, but it is an area that spoils quickly. Many hunters start salting their skins by dumping salt in the middle and working outward toward the edges. I like to pour salt around the edges first, working the salt in well, and then move towards the middle. All meat and as much fat as possible should be removed before salting. Salt will penetrate through them, but it slows the curing process.

Once your cape and head are well salted, fold the head down to the shoulder area, fold the sides in (flesh against flesh), and roll it together from the side as you might a sleeping bag. You can place it in a burlap bag, but it is best to store it in a well-ventilated area on a slope, with an open end pointing down, out of the sun or in the coolest place possible. Storing it this way allows the moisture drawn out of the skin by the salt to run off. A well-salted skin can last this way for some time, but check it every day. After a 24-hour period, if additional salt is available, drain the skin, scrape away the remaining salt and add a new application. If no extra salt is available, drain away any fluid the best you can and allow the original salt application to continue its work.

REMOVING ANTLERS AND HORNS

After skinning, the only thing left to be done is removing the headgear from the skull. Compared to skinning the animal and working around the head, this is the easiest part of the process. Remember to leave plenty of skull plate for the taxidermist and to make the two cuts as straight as possible.

CUT WITH SAW FROM BACK OF SKULL, THROUGH EYE SOCKETS, LEAVING PLENTY OF SKULL PLATE.

Using a fine-toothed saw such as a "Wyoming saw," cut from the back of the skull (see illustration) on an angle that takes the cut through the eye socket. Once cutting into the eye socket, make another cut from the bridge of the nose down to the front of the eye socket. The antlers or horns should easily dislodge, and by cutting to the middle or close to the bottom of the eye and in front of the eye, plenty of skull cap is retained for a stronger and more accurate mount. After removing the headgear, clean away any meat or tissue. To "split" the antler make a single cut in the middle of the skull between the antlers.

In some situations, it is necessary to split the antlers for easy transport. This is particularly true with large game heads such as moose, elk and caribou, even some large deer, when traveling by commercial air carrier. I really hate to do it, since it weakens the mount and officially cannot be scored for the record books once split. If it has to be done, measure the greatest inside spread, and make a third cut through the skull in the middle of the antlers.

SKINNING GAME FOR FULL-BODY MOUNTS AND RUGS

Full body mounts of various big game and bear rugs are extremely popular among hunters. If you have an empty wall a rug can certainly fill the void, and though full mounts are more costly, they can fill a corner like nothing else and are a marvel to see.

Slightly different cuts are needed for rugs than for life-size mounts or head mounts, but the same great care and patience should be taken around the head. All that is really needed for rugs is a full cut from the Adam's apple down to the tip of the tail. Next, on the front legs cut along the inside of each leg up to the center line, starting at the paws, as shown in the illustration. On the rear

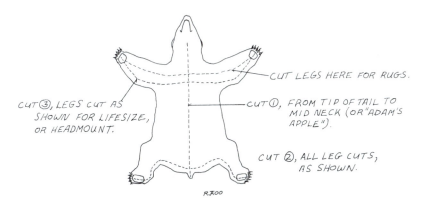

CUT LEGS HERE FOR RUGS.

CUT ③, LEGS CUT AS SHOWN FOR LIFESIZE, OR HEADMOUNT.

CUT ①, FROM TIP OF TAIL TO MID NECK (OR "ADAM'S APPLE").

CUT ②, ALL LEG CUTS, AS SHOWN.

R.ROO

legs cut along the backside of the leg again starting at the paws. To remove the feet, skin around the bone and detach at the ankle or wrist joint. With game that have paws, the cut can start at the wrist joint, or it can continue into the pads. In either case, once the skin is removed freezing is recommended. If cooler facilities are not available it will be necessary to skin the pads to the last joint, leaving only the claws. Once this is done the head must be fully skinned, including turning the ears and lips. Great care should be taken around the eyelids, tear ducts of the eyes, and the nose. Each of these areas should be heavily salted. Remember to take your required measurements on the carcass.

Salting and hanging skins is important when coolers or other refrigeration is not available. Salt prevents spoilage and can be removed later.

When a life-size mount or head mount is desired, make the same cut from the Adam's apple to tip of tail. The four leg cuts are all the same and should be from the hoof or paw along the rear of legs to the center line. The animal can now be skinned. Remove the skull as you would with a rug or shoulder mount, turning the ears and splitting the lips. Salt or freeze the pelt.

While it is important to skin an animal before it starts to spoil or cool, doing a quick job leads to punctures, unwanted cuts, perhaps even injury. Take your time, and if unsure about something before leaving home, talk it over with your taxidermist. The last thing you want is to ruin a good trip by messing up the skinning job. In his book *The Sportsman's Complete Book of Trophy and Meat Care*, a book worth reading if you can find it, author Tom Brakefield gives the following general timeframes for skinning various big game species, based on an average skill level. After some years of experience I agree with them, although hunters doing it for the first time may take longer.

	Head Mounts	Life Size Mounts/Rugs	
Species	**Time To Take Cape Off**	**Time to Take Skin Off Rest Of Body Skin**	**Fine Work On Rest of Head/Flushing**
Moose	2 hours	1–1½ hours	3 hours
Elk/Caribou	1–1½ hours	1 hour	2–2½ hours
Goat/Sheep & Deer	45 to 60 min.	30 to 45 min.	1½ to 2 hours
Bear	1 to 2 hours	1½ hours	1 to 1½ hours

Finally, it should be pointed out that skinning an animal that has had time to cool doubles the difficulty and time necessary to do the job. Skinning is much easier while the animal is still warm and the hide still soft and pliable.

PROPER FIELD CARE OF GAME MEAT

The flavor of wild game is distinct, there is little doubt in my mind that it is of better quality, and better for you, than meat purchased over the counter. There is also a large degree of satisfaction knowing where it came from, how it has been taken care of, and how it got from field to table.

But it must be said that not all wild game to touch my palate had the taste and quality I have come to appreciate. Over the years there have been times when what was placed before me smelled so bad, was so dry or tough, or tasted so bad I simply couldn't get it down. It made me wonder how the animal had been taken care of in the field, how concerned the hunter was over its quality, among other things. The only thing I can think at such time is "What a waste!"

Without question how game is tended afield governs its quality as table fare. When an animal is harvested also contributes. Buck deer taken before the rut, I have found, are often better eating than those taken during or after the rut. The same often goes for elk and moose. Stag caribou taken while still in velvet, in August or early September, generally provide better dining than those taken later in the season who have lost their velvet. And experience has shown me that black bear, which is among my favorite wild game, are better eating when taken in the spring rather than the fall, particularly late in the fall.

But more than anything else, how quickly a game animal is field-dressed, how well it is cleaned, how quickly it is cooled, and how well the meat is kept cool and butchered play the key rolls in how it will taste, and whether a chain saw will be needed to slice through it.

As soon as any big game animal is harvested, it should be field-dressed, drained, and any blood or body fluids wiped away. It is okay to take some pictures, but keep in mind that the minute an animal dies, it starts to break down and body heat begins to give birth to bacteria that if allowed to work too long, can affect the taste and texture of the meat. For this reason, it is a good idea to field-dress and clean the animal immediately after it has been taken, and then stage your photos. When field-dressing, placing the animal on a slope will help drain the body cavity. "Bleeding" an animal by slicing the throat or sticking the brisket serves no useful purpose and actually increases the difficulty of obtaining a good mount.

Cleaning the inside of the body cavity of blood and body wastes, and cooling the body quickly are just as important as dressing the animal quickly. Smaller big game like deer, antelope, and some black bear can easily be lifted manually by the headgear or front legs to help drain the cavity in the field. Back at camp, get the animal off the ground as quickly as possible, and prop open the body cavity. This allows the body to drain even more help facilitate air circulation and the cooling process. A damp cloth can be used to wipe away any coagulated blood and dirt inside the body. I also like to get my deer, antelope, and black bear skinned as quickly as possible, since removing the blanket of hair speeds up the cooling.

In remote hunting areas big game often must be quartered and carried back to camp. Here, guides quarter the hindquarter on a moose taken by the author in Newfoundland. It was necessary to carry each quarter and skin four miles back to camp.

Larger big game species like moose, elk, caribou, black bear greater than 250 pounds or so, and grizzly are more difficult to handle. Due to the amount of body heat these beasts retain after being taken, it is important to dress, clean, and cool these animals as quickly as possible. Even waiting an hour or two can have dire consequences, especially on meat inside the cavity and along the back where body heat is concentrated. This is particularly true of most bear as they carry a great deal of fat which slows cooling and speeds up deterioration.

On many hunts, guided and unguided, I've field-dressed, caped, and quartered these species on the spot, and I believe this is the best way to go. Not only does this allow meat to cool more quickly, it is also easier to clean. It is also easier to bring such large game back to camp in pieces unless you have some transportation help. Anyone who has successfully hunted these animals knows what I mean. My Newfoundland guide and I carried my first moose out on our backs. Getting these animals out of the woods can take hours and the last thing you need is body heat and coagulated blood working on the meat.

One decision that has to be made when quartering game in the field is whether a mount is desired, and if so, what kind. This greatly effects what cuts to make and whether or not to remove the complete cape. Personally, I have seen few full-mounted moose, caribou and elk. Most are head or shoulder mounts, which means only the front portion has to be skinned. The head and antlers can even be left attached to be dressed later. If this is the type of mount planned, the main body in back of the front shoulders can be either skinned or cut with the skin left on. Both have advantages and disadvantages. Fully skinning all quarters allows faster cooling, but it also exposes the meat to dirt and flies if the weather happens to be warm. The hunter, along with the guide, has to decide which way to go based on the situation. If the hair is left on, remove it as soon as possible after arriving at camp.

No matter what choices are made, there are certain things the hunter can do to speed up the cooling process, to keep meat clean, to protect it from flies and maggots, and to improve table quality. The first thing is to get it off the ground, in the coolest spot available, out of the sun. Erecting a tarp over the animal to keep off rain, snow, and sun is a good idea, too. Allowing an animal, or quarter, to lie on the ground helps it retain heat, and the area touching the ground will be the first to spoil. Hanging an animal allows the air to reach all areas, and within a day or two it will begin to stiffen, or form a hard case, which helps protect the meat.

As mentioned earlier, wipe away any dirt, blood, or body waste and fluid. If left, they will draw insects. You can also cut away all fat, particularly on bucks, stags, and bulls taken during the rut, and on bear at any time. The fat on males of the species during the rut and on bear gives meat a strong "gamey" taste and smell and spoils quickly. Also remove any collected blood, membrane and meat parts that might not be worth keeping, and make sure no meat parts not touching other meat. Again, these are the areas where flies collect and maggots form and which spoil most quickly, so get rid of them.

When all this is done, to further protect your meat in camp or while being transported out of the bush, cover it with a cotton game bag or wrap it in cheesecloth. No matter what type of hunt I go on I have one or the other available. Most guides and outfitters do as well. Game bags or cheesecloth allows air to circulate and keep dirt and insects away. Finally, if you plan to be in camp a while, or if the weather is warm, get the meat to a cooler. When meat is clean and has had time to form a case, it will last a surprisingly long time in temperatures below 40 or 45 degrees. But anything warmer than that for more than a couple of days, and the chances for spoilage increase greatly. Whenever time allows, particularly if you have a long trip to pack and carry the meat out of the bush, consider boning it out. This can be done at any time but is easiest

How guides and outfitters handle big game suggests their concern for a hunter's successful experience. Here, black bear are carefully removed and placed in a clean area for skinning.

when the animal or quarters are still warm. Not only does boning help dissipate body heat more quickly, it means the hunter can carry more meat, rather than bone, when packing out is required.

For some, skinning an animal and taking care of the meat is a chore, the worst part of a hunt, but I rather enjoy it. For one thing, it means a good part of the trip—taking an animal—has been a success, and while others are still getting up before daybreak trying to fill tags all day, I am back in camp drinking coffee, relaxing, and tending to my animal. It is a part of the hunting experience that I don't mind at all, and when it comes to quality mounts and table fare, it is an extremely important part, as well.

How meat is butchered also affects meat quality. I am not the best hand at cutting and packaging meat, nor do I have the proper tools and saws which make the task easier. But I have little doubt that cutting and packaging your own game is the best way to go if you have the space, tools, and time.

For one thing, you get the cuts of meat you want. On more than one occasion I have stipulated what size roasts and the thickness I wanted in steaks and chops, and gotten back something bigger, smaller, thinner, or too thick. I think the problem is that butchers get too busy, and simply forget what was requested by individual hunters.

More importantly, when butchering your own game you can take the time to properly remove as much fat as possible and completely bone it out. The fat on game meat doesn't freeze very well, and when left on steaks, chops, and roasts, or when ground into burger in a short time—typically within three or four months—it begins to affect the meat's taste.

Also, the bone marrow of wild game has a quick and negative effect on the taste of meat. It should be boned before cutting and freezing, and I prefer to bone an animal as much as possible in the bush if I plan to take it to a butcher. Like fat, marrow from wild game animals doesn't freeze very well and has a strong, game taste. If a butcher uses a bandsaw to cut through bone and meat, which is quite common with most butchers, and if pieces of marrow get on the meat and remain there, it will impart a strong, wild flavor. Game you butcher yourself is probably cleaner of hair and bone. That same bandsaw that flings marrow into your meat is also tossing fine bone chips here and there, too. And though some butchers are careful to remove hair, most will not be as careful as you.

Still, most of my wild meat is cut by a butcher. The butcher I work with near home has known me for years, and he knows what I like. Though it costs more, he removes nearby all fat and bones from my game before cutting. On trips out west and to Canada, some outfitters and guides will have made arrangements to have the game of their clients cut, wrapped, and frozen for them. That's okay, but insist the fat be removed and the meat boned before cutting. It will undoubtedly cost more, but it will be worth it.

Finally, whether cutting and wrapping my own game meat or having it done at the butcher, I have it vacuum-sealed or double wrapped in freezer paper, particularly with large species like moose, elk, and caribou. They take time to consume and will be in the freezer for a while. When poorly wrapped and frozen over long periods game meat can dry out or "burn" in the freezer. I have found that when vacuum-sealed or double-wrapped it remains fresher for longer periods of time. No matter how well meat is wrapped, however, or how cold the freezer, the longer it remains in the freezer the more flavor it will lose, so eat it and enjoy!

20

GUIDES, OUTFITTERS, AND BOOKING A HUNT

Some of the finest folks I know are guides or outfitters catering to the big game hunter. I respect their high regard for the animals they hunt and the quality of the service they provide. They understand that not all hunters are as skilled at hunting as they pretend to be. It can also be said, of course, that some guides and outfitters are unprincipled, devious, and distrustful people.

For many hunters traveling to a distance place to hunt big game is a dream come true. They fantasize about visiting strange territory, about hunting species they have long read about and perhaps have never seen. They scrimp and save every dollar possible for months, sometimes years, to make their dream a reality.

But when they day comes to leave, are they really ready? Have they done their homework? They have selected an outfitter, but is he the right one?

Each year I am fortunate enough to take a number of big game hunts, and the majority of those hunts are with guides and outfitters. Whenever contemplating a hunt with an operation new to me, I always go through a process that assures me that this is the outfitter I am looking for. It requires some time and the use of the telephone weeks in advance of actually booking the hunt, but it provides piece of mind that when I do make the commitment, I have done my best to guarantee I get the hunting experience I want. Of course, nothing in life beyond death and taxes is guaranteed, and booking a hunting trip with an outfitter is certainly no different. Doing your homework before making a decision, however, can erase a lot of the worry that naturally rises during the process.

One of the first steps in planning a hunt is getting information on various outfitters in the state or province you want to visit. Whenever possible, I prefer to get a list from state or provincial outfitting associations such as the Professional Outfitters Association of Alberta and the Wyoming State Board of Outfitters and Professional Guides. Not all states and provinces have such organized associations, but most do, and upon request they will provide a list of licensed operators. They will also answer inquiries about whether a guide or outfitter you might be thinking about is actually registered and if any complaints have been filed against him. The names, addresses, and telephone numbers of these associations can usually be obtained by contacting state fish and game departments or tourism offices.

If no organized outfitter association exists, fish and game departments can still be of great assistance. In nearly every state and province guides and outfitters must be registered or licensed, and while it is common for such agencies to remain impartial and not make a recommendation, the hunter can at least obtain a list of outfitters and guides that are licensed to operate, thus eliminating the possibility of booking with an outfit working illegally.

The next step is to request information from outfitters. You can send off letters requesting brochures and other information, but that takes time. Although it adds to the monthly phone bill, I usually call to request information. Not only does this speed things up, it also puts me in personal contact with the outfitter. You can tell a great deal by a person's voice and how they respond to your questions, and I have actually booked hunts based on my initial feeling for the person on the other end of the line, by their enthusiasm for their operation, area, and game. If they take the time to ask me what I am looking for and the game I hope to find, if they are straight forward and open and offer to assist me in making my hunt a success, I usually go with them.

Dean Armbrister of Rock Creek Outfitters, who runs antelope, mule deer, and whitetail hunts out of Hinsdale, Montana, is one such outfitter. Dean is the type of guy who will spend hours on the phone addressing every aspect of the hunt, and with such enthusiasm that you can't help but get excited. The

Good guides take the time and effort to familiarize hunters with the surrounding country. This hunter and guide are about to head out for a day's hunt, but before they leave, time is taken to point out where they are heading.

first time I spoke with him I knew immediately that this guy knew his business and cared more about quality than quantity. I booked with him on the spot.

But most hunts are not booked this way. Along with requesting information on the hunt, I ask for a list of references. I always contact several to get a first-hand feel of what the hunt was like and whether everything promised or advertised was delivered. I ask about everything from the knowledge of the guides to game seen, success rates, and game care, to what the accommodations and food is like and if there were any hidden costs or surprises. Other questions will come to mind during the conversation, and helpful observations will often be made by the contact. But two questions I always ask at some point are: "Were you genuinely pleased with the hunt?" and "Would you hunt there again?" If the answer is positive, then there is the good chance you're on the track of a good outfitter and a quality hunt.

One other thing I keep in mind when talking with references, is that most outfitters furnish the names of their happiest and most successful clients. While talking with these people, I ask if they have the names and telephone numbers of others that might have been in camp at the same time they were. If so, I contact them as well. Although these people might be just as pleased, they might supply other information that the initial reference failed to mention. There is also the possibility that they were not quite as happy with the hunt.

Once narrowing down my outfitter list to one or two, I also want to make sure this is the right hunt for me before making a final decision. For example, more and more outfitters across the continent are catering to hunters who use muzzleloaders, but some do not, so I always ask. I also fly to many of my destinations, as do many hunters these days, and I understand the federal regulations governing flying with blackpowder. From past experience, I know blackpowder and Pyrodex can be difficult to find in some locales, so I always ask the outfitter whether propellent is available in his area. Some outfitters, when asked, have even gone out of their way for me and picked up some propellent prior to my arrival, while others have offered on their own.

Don Ayers, of Ayers Outfitters in Alberta, is one such example. While in the process of arranging a spring bear hunt a couple of years ago I had mentioned that I would be hunting with blackpowder. Later Don spoke up and said, "You indicated you'd be hunting with blackpowder, Al? I know the legalities concerning flying with the stuff; let me know what you need and I'll have it here waiting for you." Not all outfitters are this sharp, and some don't care, so you have to. Whatever the case, make sure you bring up the need for powder during your conversation.

Floatplanes are common in remote big game country. Baggage is often limited to 45 to 60 pounds per hunter, depending upon the type of plane used. Be sure to ask. Also, expect delays due to bad weather during September and October in the north country. The author once got stuck in camp for six days because of poor flying conditions.

I also make it a point to ask whether the hunting conditions and terrain are conducive to blackpowder guns. If it is a spring bear hunt over bait in Alberta, for example, or an elk hunt in Montana, I want to know the distance of the average shot. In general, make sure you understand the type of country you will be hunting. Know if it is heavily forested, open and flat, or rolling hills. Even though our modern frontloaders, powders, and projectiles are better today than ever before, and though some us are darn good shots even at long range, blackpowder hunting does have its limitations.

There are, of course, basic questions to be asked about the quality of food and accommodations, what the outfitter supplies, and what you are required to bring, if anything. For example, must you bring a sleeping bag? Is this a catered hunt, or do you have to supply your own food? Who prepares the meals? Make sure you inquire about weather conditions and temperatures at the time of year you are planning your hunt. How about rain gear and insect repellent?

Also, a good many hunts require some hiking or cross-country trekking. Find out how much will likely be involved and make sure you are physically prepared. Nothing can ruin a potentially successful big game hunt faster than not being in shape. While booking a mule deer hunt a year or so ago in Wyoming, outfitter Frank Deedee of Halfmoon Ranch made a point of telling

Hunting camp arrangements vary widely. This is a caribou camp in northern Quebec. The two large cabins are sleeping quarters for the guests. The smaller building in the middle in a common toilet/shower house. The guides' tent is at the end. A separate building is used for meals.

me that we would be covering some rough terrain and asked what kind of shape I was in. "The big bucks here are in some rough country, Al," Frank said, "and we have to work to get them, so be prepared." I was, and though I didn't get my buck it wasn't from lack of trying or from not being in shape. Some outfitters don't mention the physical requirements some of these hunts call for, while others forget or simply assume you can take the punishment. Be sure to ask.

Most of the basic questions are covered in outfitter brochures and information packets, but it never hurts to go over them. One thing I always like to know is how many hunters will be in camp and how many hunters are taken each week.

I have found that success rates are generally higher in camps that cater to smaller groups, say a half-dozen hunters per week or less, rather than a dozen or more. Camps and outfitters who cater to smaller numbers seem to be more concerned about quality rather than quantity, which is exactly what I look for. They also care about not over-hunting their resource. With 15 to 20 hunters in camp each week over a long season it is easy to do just that in many areas.

Don't forget to inquire about trophy care. Is there an additional fee for skinning and taking care of meat, or is it included in the price? Most big game outfitters I have hunted with over the years pride themselves on proper skinning of game and preparing meat for the trip home, but I have heard reports

In some wilderness areas, tents serve as sleeping and dining accommodations. Such camps are common in the West where elk are the prime target. Many bear camps also use tents. Here, a group of hunters enjoy morning coffee on a Wyoming elk hunt. When properly established, tents are warm, dry, and clean.

from some hunters who claim the outfitters they hunted with really lacked in this area. I know enough about capping and boning out game animals to do it myself, and if that is part of the deal, fine; in fact I usually help. But if it is supposed to be the outfitter's job, I want to make sure it is done right and with care. Ask how skins and meat are kept while in camp. Are skins and pelts salted or are cooler facilities available? Ask whether boxes or other shipping containers are supplied for shipment of pelts, hides, and meat.

How about hunting licenses and permits? Does the outfitter assist in securing them, or is it entirely up to you? Are they available over the counter, through the outfitter, or through a draw? If it is a draw, what are the chances of success? Make sure all license application fees and deposits to the outfitter are refundable within a reasonable length of time if you fail to draw a license. States that issue licenses by draw typically return all fees, perhaps minus a small filing or application fee, within 30 to 60 days or so, and most outfitters with a good reputation follow suit. But there are cases when outfitters may be slow to return deposits. Ask when any deposit will be returned if you fail to draw, and ask if you can get it in writing.

Inquire about the best time to hunt, the prime weeks, especially if you are interested in trophy game. Ask the best time to book the hunt. Most will say the sooner the better, and in most cases they are right but don't be pressured into any commitment until sure that this is the hunt you are looking for.

Finally, don't judge an outfitter solely based on cost. A higher priced hunt is not necessarily a better hunt. We all live within a budget, and if a hunt is more than you are able to spend, don't go in debt to book with an outfitter with the thought that his high price is a guarantee of success or of a better hunt. A great many outfitters offer quality game in prime areas for substantially less than other outfitters that may charge two or three times as much. The accommodations may not be as elaborate or offer as many comforts, you may have to supply your own food and do you own cooking, help out around camp, perhaps even cape your own game, and take care of some other services a higher priced hunt might provide. But as long as the game is there, the camp is clean, and the guides and outfitter do their part and get me into good country, I prefer the less expensive route.

Some of the best hunts I have ever been on were those where clients did as many camp chores and duties as the guides and outfitter. Personally, I don't go on a hunt to be spoiled. If I contribute to the hunt and the operation of the camp, it just adds to the experience. I would just as soon do my share, sleep in

Horses are not only used to get hunters into remote country but to get game out. If horses are part of your hunt, plan accordingly and make sure you are ready to spend long days in the saddle.

a tent, clean dishes, cut some wood, or help in taking care of game. Such hunts are often less costly and just as good in quality.

The point of all this: know what you are buying. Do your homework. Don't be afraid to ask questions, and don't buy anything you don't want. In fact, get your hunting buddies together, beat heads, and make a list of questions before you even call. If there is any doubt in your mind about an outfitter, if something feels wrong, or you're not sure about some aspect, get it clear or go elsewhere. Trust your instincts, that little voice inside. It will rarely let you down. This is true while hunting, and I have found it is just as true when booking a hunt with an outfitter. There are a lot of good outfitters across this continent, but it's up to you to select the right one.

Keep in mind that all this investigation and study takes time and lots of it. Don't wait until the last minute. Ideally, any hunt, whether it be a spring bear hunt or a fall elk, deer, antelope, moose, or caribou hunt, should be booked and confirmed by February or March at the latest. In states that require a draw for licenses, some license application deadlines may be as early as February, March, or April. Start gathering names of outfitters and making contact prior to the Christmas holidays, if possible, and be ready to made a decision by the middle of January or early February. After this time you might not be able to book the week you want or even book at all with a popular outfitter.

21

TRAVELING WITH MUZZLELOADERS

The modern hunter is a mobile individual. We have the ability to travel farther, faster, and in more comfort than our ancestors ever thought possible. I don't know how many times over the years I have departed Boston's Logan International Airport in the early morning hours and by late afternoon been glassing game in northern Labrador, Colorado, Alberta, or Alaska. Even if we jump in cars or pick-ups, we can travel hundreds of miles each day, traveling from the East Coast to some of the West's premier hunting grounds in less time than it took the pioneers to travel one hundred miles. It's incredible. And I often wonder as I fly here and there, what the mountain men and early settlers would think about it all.

But while reaching far off places can be quick and relatively easy, it does have its frustrations, potential mishaps, and inconveniences, particularly for the traveling blackpowder hunter. Some advance planning before leaving home, and some procedures once arriving at camp can make things go a whole lot easier.

Some of the biggest problems come when flying to our hunting destinations. I have to say that with all the miles I have flown to out-of-the-way destinations, I have experienced only one unfortunate mishap. This came in the form of lost baggage, and fortunately it was there when I arrived home. Regardless, when it happens it is frustrating, inconvenient, and in some cases expensive. In my particular case it involved a large, hard plastic ammunition-type case. In it I carried all my hunting knives, binoculars, a set of Motorola Handi-Com 10 portable two-way radios, some hand tools, gun cleaning kits and all the muzzleloading paraphernalia I had collected over the years plus other miscellaneous items. Although I was eventually reimbursed by the airline, some of it was irreplaceable, especially a hunting knife given to me by my grandfather.

The next worst thing that happen to me was having none of my baggage arrive. I had flown from Portland, Maine to Billings, Montana via Cincinnati and Salt Lake City, and upon arrival in Billings early that afternoon, not one of the nine bags belonging to my partner and I arrived. We made out the necessary claim forms, and it was promised that as soon as the bags came in they would be delivered to our final destination, some four hours away by car. The airline kept their promise, and at 2 A.M. that morning our bags and gun cases did arrive, but they might not have, and the hours until they arrived were some of the longest and most nerve-racking I've ever experienced on a hunting trip.

There is really nothing the hunter can do about lost baggage. In general, the airlines do a pretty good job at transporting and delivering millions of items on schedule, but lost and damaged baggage does happen. If you travel enough, I suppose it is only a matter of time before the odds catch up with you. There are, however, some safety procedures you can follow that might reduce the chances of it happening to you.

To begin with, carry any expensive items, cameras, binoculars, scopes (and two-way radios) on board as part of your carry-on baggage. You can only carry so much, and only certain kinds of items, but anything kept with you is virtually guaranteed not to be lost. Also, purchasing extra travel insurance can help. It doesn't necessarily mean a larger reimbursement if something is lost or damaged, but it does increase the airline's liability and provides more leverage. And if something is lost or damaged, don't be afraid to send a letter off to the public affairs office of the airline, even if efforts are made to settle the claim. Be polite, but express your feelings and how your faith in the airline might be restored. Following deregulation, airlines seem more willing to keep customers happy and satisfied, so don't be bashful, make yourself heard!

Some airlines have a policy of not transporting guns, so when making reservations, either on your own or through a travel agency, make it known that you are going on a hunting trip and will be shipping firearms. Airline reservation clerks, once this is known, will generally inform you of any special procedures or requirements. If not, be sure to ask.

One thing they do usually tell you that makes a big difference is to get to the airport early and check in. This is particularly true if flying internationally, such as to Canada, but also if traveling within the United States. Whatever the case, plan to check in at least a solid hour, if not more, before departure.

In a good many cases the earlier you check in, the shorter the lines at the ticket counter for that particular flight. Also, the earlier you check in, especially with firearms, the better chance you have of getting those guns on board. With all the increased security at airports these days, checking in firearms takes more time. It used to be that all you had to do was fill out a tag attesting to the fact that the guns were unloaded and off they went. Today, however, these same tags have to be signed and it is not unusual for clerks to want to look at the guns just to make sure. This takes more time. Keep any keys to gun cases handy and don't tape your cases closed, as many hunters do, until after they have been checked at the counter. Chances are you will just have to remove the tape, which delays getting your baggage checked in. When I finally do add some security tape, generally gray duct tape, I wrap it around and over the locks of my cases. Even when locked, I have had cases come off the luggage conveyors with the locking mechanisms sprung open. Whether from human hands or rough handling, or poor locks I cannot say, but it does happen, and I have found taping over them makes a big difference.

Good, solid gun cases are also important. I have used the popular Gun Guard cases for years, with excellent results. They are injection molded, rugged, piano-hinged along the entire back, and offer thick foam padding. Other quality gun cases include SKB, Doskocil, Field Locker, and Gun Master, offered by Carry Cases, Inc. of Milford, Connecticut. Most are carried by Cabela's, Gander Mountain, L.L. Bean and retail stores such as Wal-Mart and K-Mart. Any case you purchase should be durable, have locks and, ideally, egg carton-type foam on the interior to hold firearms securely and safely. As with all your baggage, make sure your gun cases have a name tag with your address and telephone number, or better your name and particulars plainly and boldly visible right on the case. During the height of hunting season, it is amazing how many gun cases go through an airport and how alike they all look.

If heading for Canada and departing from a U.S. airport, make sure you declare firearms at Customs before departing. The same is true if you reside in Canada and are heading into the U.S. It only takes a few minutes, but this is another reason for arriving at the airport well in advance of departure time. To speed things up, have the serial number, model, and make of any firearm with you readily available. I usually have mine written down on my airline travel itinerary, which I always keep handy. Firearms should also be declared at Customs when traveling into Canada by vehicle, and visa versa. Stick the small white declaration form in your gun case beneath the foam padding; it will be valid as long as you own that gun and can be used again.

As for other baggage, I have found it much easier to travel with soft duffle bags rather than hard or soft suitcases. For one thing, you can get more in them, and they pack easily in the trunks of cars or the bed of a pick-up. I have found them even easier to stow in float-planes or helicopters when hunting remote areas. Canvas bags, such as the standard military types are fine, but I prefer some of the newer designs offered by Predator Sporting Equipment of York, Maine, or those offered by Cabela's or L.L. Bean. They are much more rugged, made of nylon, and most are coated with a water repellent polyurethane finish. This can be important when lodging in spike camps or traveling by boat to reach your hunting area. Again, make sure your name and other particulars are on each bag.

One of the areas I have found airlines to be fussy on is the transportation of game meat and antlers. Most outfitters and guides are familiar with what airlines will and will not do and how best to make shipment, some even have special boxes and styrofoam inserts available. When arranging your hunt with your outfitter ask about transporting meat, hides, and horns. I also inquire when making airline reservations whether the carrier has a policy about shipping such material. The last thing you want is to get to the check-in counter after a successful hunt and find your airline will not ship your meat and trophies.

I generally carry a roll or two of duct tape, and when hunting deer, elk, moose, caribou, and other game with pointed headgear, a section of old garden hose. Upon cleaning the head, I cover each point with a section of hose, and then tape it securely. Not only does this protect the points, but many airlines request or demand it to prevent damage to other baggage. Pieces of cardboard taped over the points will also work, particularly on those game heads with "palms" or "prongs," such as moose, caribou, and proghorn. In some cases, carrying these items may not be necessary, but make sure you inquire with your guide or outfitter.

When it comes to transporting meat, it is best shipped frozen, wrapped in plastic bags and cased in boxes. More and more hunting operations across the continent have made arrangements for animals to be butchered, wrapped, and frozen, sometimes even packed for shipment, for their clients. The cost is generally an addition to the price of the hunt, but I have found it is minimal, often less expensive than getting it cut at home, and—versus shipping whole quarters or parts—a whole lot more convenient and less expensive. Ask your outfitter if you need to bring anything for shipment of game, and if so, what.

Blackpowder hunters have a special dilemma when flying as it is illegal to transport blackpowder or Pyrodex aboard commercial carriers. Arrangements have to be made to have propellant waiting for you at the hunting camp or it must be picked up locally or shipped ahead.

In nearly all cases I have found it easier to purchase propellant locally. Just about all commercial flights I have been on terminate in a major city, or a town of good size. From there I usually drive to my final destination or to where I am to meet my outfitter or the outfitter picks me up at the airport. I have time to pick up some propellant, and I have found that blackpowder, and especially Pyrodex, is readily available, even in out-of-the-way places in Canada. It has become part of my routine to ask my outfitter or guide where it can be purchased locally. Looking back, I have purchased so much Pyrodex in various cities and towns over the years, and eventually left the remainder with the guide or outfitter, that I should have stock in the company.

In other cases, I have asked my guide or outfitter to purchase some for me. Most are willing to do so with sufficient advance notice. I simply pay them for it on arrival. In other situations, particularly when traveling somewhere remote, I have had both blackpowder and Pyrodex shipped to an outfitter or guide. According to both UPS and Federal Express, blackpowder and Pyrodex may only be shipped by a licensed dealer. This means your local gun shop or sporting goods store. Establishments I frequent regularly, even many I don't, are willing to make the necessary shipments on request. Shipping and hazardous material costs are extra, but in some cases it is the only way go.

Allow plenty of time for the shipment to arrive. I live in Maine, and if I happen to be hunting out west, a week to ten days is generally ample via regular delivery. This time can be reduced by upgrading delivery, but considering the additional cost involved I would just as soon ship earlier and save money. Delivery services will also provide a general time of arrival, and I make it a rule to call a few days before leaving home to make sure the propellant has arrived. If hunting Alaska or Canada give yourself at least two week, especially when shipping to Canada, considering all packages must go through customs and there may be delays.

Things are much easier when traveling by vehicle, but I hate to drive long distances. Even when hunting in Nova Scotia, Newfoundland, and Quebec in eastern Canada I prefer to fly, and the older I get the more I dislike driving. There is no way I would ever drive across the country. It may be fun when starting out but after the hunt there is that long ride home. Also, unpredictable fall weather can cause problems, and there is always the chance of having truck or car trouble.

I once hunted in Colorado with a bunch of boys from Michigan that drove, figuring they would save money and see part of the country. The weather in the Rockies that year was unseasonably warm, but by mid-week much of the East was getting blanketed by snow, sleet, and high winds. I flew and got home on time. One of the others called me two weeks later and told me it took them nearly nine days to reach home.

When planning to drive any great distance, especially cross-country it is imperative to make sure your vehicle is up for the journey. Get a tune-up, run good tires, map out the best and most direct route unless time is to be taken for sightseeing, carry some tools, and check in from time to time to let someone at home know where you are. It also helps to be a member of AAA or some other automobile service club. If you break down in the middle of nowhere it is nice to know road service is available.

Appendix A

MUZZLELOADING RESOURCES

The following manufacturers and suppliers offer muzzleloading equipment and products.

Thompson/Center Arms
Box 5002, Farmington Rd.
Rochester, NH 03867
603-332-2394
www.tcarms.com

Knight Rifles
P.O.Box 130
21852 Hwy. J46
Centerville, IA 52544
515-856-2626
www.knightrifles.com

White Shooting Systems, Inc.
25 East Highway 40, Box 330-12
Roosevelt, UT 84066
1-800-213-1315
www.shootmti.com

Connecticut Valley Arms (CVA)
5988 Peachtree Corners East
Norcross, GA 30071
770-449-4686
ww.cva.com

Navy Arms Company
689 Bergen Blvd.
Ridgefield, NJ 07657
201-945-2500
www.navyarms.com

Traditions Performance
    Muzzleloaders
P.O.Box 235
Deep River, CT 06417
800-526-9556/860-388-4656
www.traditionsfirearms.com

Lyman
475 Smith Street
Middletown, CT 06457
1-800-22-LYMAN
www.lymanproducts.com

Mowrey Gun Works
P.O.Box 246
Waldron, IN 46182
317-525-6181

Gonic Arms, Inc.
134 Flagg Rd.
Gonic, NH 03829
603-332-8456
www.gonic.com

Euroarms of America
P.O.Box 3277
Winchester, VA 22601
703-662-1863

Remington Arms
870 Remington Dr.
P.O.Box 700
Madison, NC 27025-0700
910-548-8581
www.remington.com

Sturm, Ruger, and Company
Southport, CT 06490
www.ruger-firearms,com

Black Canyon Powder
Legend Products
1555 E. Flamingo Rd.
Las Vegas, NV 89119
702-228-1808

Elephant Blackpowder
7650 U.S. Hwy. 287
Arlington, TX 76017
800-588-8282
www.elephantblackpowder.com

Goex, Inc.
P.O.Box 659
Doyline, LA 71023-0659
318-382-9300
www.goexpowder.comm

Hodgdon Powder Co.
P.O.Box 2932
Shawnee Mission, KS 66201
913-362-9455
www.hodgdon.com
(makers of Pyrodex and related
    products)

Barne's Bullets
P.O.Box 215
American Fork, UT 84003
801-756-4222
www.barnesbullets.com

Buffalo Bullet Co.
12637 Los Nietos Rd., Unit A
Santa Fe Springs, CA 90670
310-944-0322

D.W.R. Custom Bullets
RR 2, #32 Westpoint
Jacksonville, IL 62650
217-245-6403

Hornady Manufacturing Co.
P.O.Box 1848
Grand Island, NE 68802
308-382-1390
www.hornady.com

Speer
c/o Blount, Inc.
P.O.Box 856
Lewiston, ID 83501
208-746-2351
www.blunt.com

Butler Creek Corportaion
290 Arden Dr.
Belgrade, MT 59715
800-423-8327
406-388-7204
www.butletcreek.com

Dixie Gun Works
P.O.Box 130
Union City, TN 38261
901-885-0561
www.dixiegun.com

Michael's of Oregon Co./Uncle
    Mike's
P.O.Box 13010
Portland, OR 97213
503-255-6890
www.unclemikes.com

Mountain State Muzzleloading
    Supplies, Inc.
Rt 2, Box 154-1, Suite 101
Williamstown, WV 26187
304-375-7842
www.logcabinshop.com

Ox-Yoke Originals, Inc.
Blue and Gray Products, Inc.
34 W. Main St.
Milo, ME 04463
800-231-8313
www.oxyoke.com

Penguin Industries,
    Inc/Hoppe's
Airport Industrial Mall
Coatesville, PA 19320
215-384-6000

Rusty Duck/Black Off
Hydra-Tone Chemicals
7785 Foundation Dr., Suite 6
Florence, KY 41042
606-342-5553
www.hydra-tine.com

Green Mountain Rifle Barrel,
    Co.
P.O.Box 2670
Conway, NH 03813
603-447-1095

Cabela's
812-13th Ave.
Sidney, NE 69160
1-800-237-4444
www.cabelas.com

Log Cabin Shop
Box 275
Lodi, OH 44254
330-948-1082
www.logcabinshop.com

The Hawken Shop
P.O.Box 593
Oak Harbor, WA 98277
360-679-4657
Email: greensgunshop@
    dotplanet.com

Ye Olde Blackpowder Shoppe
994 W. Midland Rd.
Auburn, MI 48611
517-662-2271

Golden Age Arms, Co.
115 E. High St.
Box 366
Ashley, OH 43003
740-747-2488

Chem-Pak, Inc.
11 Oates Ave.
Winchester, VA 22601
1-800-336-9828
(blackpowder firearm
    protector/lubricant)

Dynamit-Nobel-RWS, Inc.
81 Ruckman Rd.
Closter, NJ 07624
(percussion caps)
201-767-1995
www.dnrws.com

Williams Gun Sight Company
7389 Lapeer Rd.
Davison, MI 48423
800-530-9028
www.williamsgunsightcompany
    .com

Shooter's Choice
16770 Hilltop Park Place
Chagrin Falls, OH 44023
440-834-8888
www.shooters-choice.com

Ashley Outdoors
2401 Ludelle Street
Fort Worth,TX 76005
888-744-4880
www.ashleyoutdoors.com

L&R Lock Company
1137 Pocalla Rd.
Sumter, SC 29150
803-775-6127
www.lr-rpl.com

Jedediah STARR Trading
    Company
P.O.Box 2007
Farmington Hills, MI 48333
877-857-8277
www.jedediah-starr.com

Rush Creek Roundball
205 W. Franklin St.
Kenton, OH 43326
419-674-4946

Lehigh Valley Lube
http://cap-n-ball.com/lehigh/
719-687-6510

KaDooty Manufacturing
Company
842 South Tamela Drive
Lake Charles, LA 70605
318-477-7502
www.kadooty.com

Leupold & Stevens, Inc.
P.O.Box 688
Beaverton, OR 97075
503-526-5195
www.leupold.com

Steiner Binoculars
97 Foster Rd.
Moorestown, NJ 08057
800-257-7742
www.steiner-binoculars.com

Zeiss Optical
13017 N. Kingston Ave.
Chester, VA 23836
www.zeiss.com

Nikon
1300 Walt Whitman Rd.
Melville, NY 11747
800-247-3464
www.nikonusa.com

Burris Optic Co.
331 E. 8th St.
Greeley, CO 80631
970-356-1670
www.burrisoptic.com

Pentax
35 Iverness Dr. East
Englewood, CO 80112
800-709-2020
www.pentaxsportsoptics.com.

Swift Bullet Company
P.O.Box 27
201 Maine
Quinter, KS 67752
785-754-3959
Fax: 785-754-2359

Nosler Bullets
P.O. Box 671
Bend, OR 97709
800-285-3701
www.nosler.com

Deer Creek Products
P.O. Box 246
Waldron, IN 46182
765-525-6181

Clean Shot Technologies, Inc.
21218 St. Andrews Blvd., #504
Boca Raton, FL 33433
888-419-2073
www.cleanshot.com
(makers of Clean Shot Powder)

Green Mountain Rifle Barrel
Co., Inc.
P.O. Box 2670
Conway, NH 03818
603-447-1095

Blomquist Percussion Works
17406 Tiller Court
Westfield, IN 46074
800-337-1243

TruGlo
P.O. Box 1612
McKinney, TX 75070
972-774-0300/972-774-0323
888-8-TRUGLO
www.truglosights.com

C & D Special Products
309 Sequoya Dr.
Hopkinsville, KY 42240
800-922-6287
(muzzleloading bullets)

Leved Cartridge, Ltd.
P.O. Box 21
Georgetown, TX 78627-0021
512-863-4387
Fax: 512-863-0758
Email: c.kelsey@levedcartridge.
com

Aim-Right Muzzleloader Sights
Rightnour Mfg. Co.
P.O. Box 107
229 Hecla Rd.
Mingoville, PA 16856
814-383-4079
www.rmcsports.com

Muzzleload Magnum Products
518 Buck Hollow Lane
Harrison, AR 72601
870-741-5019
Fax: 870-741-3104

Appendix B

BLACKPOWDER HUNTING ORGANIZATIONS AND MAGAZINES

National Muzzleloading Rifle
  Association-NMLRA
P.O. Box 67
Friendship, IN 47021
812-667-5131
(Publishers of *Muzzle Blasts*
  magazine)
  Longhunter Society (A
  branch of the NMLRA, and
  the official big game record-
  book keeper for blackpowder
  hunting. Publisher of *The
  Longhunter Society Journal.*)

International Blackpowder
  Hunting Association
P.O.Box 1180
Glen Rock, WY 82637
307-436-9817
(Publisher of *Blackpowder
  Hunting* magazine)

Muzzleloader Magazine
Rt. 5, Box 347-M
Texarkana, TX 75501
903-832-4726

Dixie Gun Works Blackpowder
  Annual
Pioneer Press
P.O.Box 684, Gunpowder Lane
Union City, TN 38261
901-885-0374

Blackpowder Times
P.O.Box 842
Mount Vernon, WA 98273

CVA Blackpowder Rifles &
  Hunting Annual
c/o Thickett Publishing
P.O.Box 601
Helena, AL 35080
205-987-6007

Gun Week
P.O.Box 488
Buffalo, NY 14209
716-885-6408
www.saf.com
(Published by the Second
  Amendment Foundation)

Bear Hunting Magazine
7938 University Ave, N.E.
Fridley, MN 55432
763-780-3168

Appendix C

PROFESSIONAL OUTFITTER AND GUIDE ASSOCIATIONS

UNITED STATES

Alaska Professional Hunters
Association
P.O.Box 91932
Anchorage, AK 99509-1932
907-522-3221
Fax: 907-349-9645
www.mochamadness.com/apha

Colorado Outfitters Association
P.O.Box 1949
Rifle, CO 81650
970-876-0543
www.colorado-outfitters.com

New Mexico Council of
Outfitters and Guides
P.O.Box 93186
Albuquerque, NM 87199-3186
505-822-9845
Fax: 505-822-9808
www.nmoutfitters.org

Idaho Outfitters & Guides
Association
P.O.Box 95
Boise, ID 83701
208-342-1919
Fax: 208-338-7830
www.ioga.org

Wyoming Outfitters & Guides
Association
P.O.Box 2284
Cody, WY 82414
307-527-7453
Fax: 307-587-8633
Email: wyog@wtp.net
www.wyoga.org

Professional Recreation
Outfitters of Wyoming
P.O. Box 2697
Cheyenne, WY 82003

Maine Professional Guides
Association
P.O.Box 847
Augusta, ME 04332
207-785-2061
Fax: 207-785-4496
www.midcoast.com/-guides

Montana Outfitters and Guides
Association
P.O.Box 1248
Helena, MT 59624
406-449-3578
Fax: 406-443-2439
Email: moga2initco.net
www.recworld.com

Nevada Outfitters Association
P.O.Box 135
Wells, NV 89835
702-777-3277

New York State Outdoor
Guides Association
P.O.Box 916
Saranac, NY 12983
518-359-7037
Fax: 518-359-7037
Email: foothill2capital.net

Washington Outfitters
Association
709 228th Ave NE, Suite 331
Redmond, WA 98053
425-392-6107
Fax: 425-392-0111

CANADA

Alberta Professional Outfitters
Society
#103, 6030 88 Street
Edmonton, Alberta T6E 6G4
P.O.Box 68167
Edmonton, Alberta T6C 4N6
780-414-0249
Fax: 780-465-6801
Email: info@apos.ab.ca
www.apos.ab.ca

The Professional Outfitters
Association of Alberta
P.O.Box 67012 Meadowlark
Park Post Office
Edmonton, Alberta T5R 5Y3
403-486-3050
Email: poaa2comcept,ab.ca

The Outfitters Association of
British Columbia
P.O.Box 94675
Richmond, BC V6Y 4A4
604-278-2688
Fax: 604-278-3440
Email: GOABC@dowco.com
www.goabc.org

Yukon Outfitters Association
P.O.Box 4548
Whitehorse, Yukon Y1A 2R8
867-668-4118
Fax: 867-668-4118

Manitoba Lodges and Outfitters
Association
23 Sage Crescent
Winnipeg, Manitoba R2Y 0X8
204-889-4840
Email: mloa2mola.com
www.mola.com

New Brunswick Outfitters
Association
P.O.Box 74
Woodstock, New Brunswick
E0J 2B0
800-215-2075

Newfoundland/Labrador
Outfitters Association
107 LeMerchant Rd.
St. John's, Newfoundland A1C
2H1
709-722-2000
Fax: 709-722-8104
Email: n.h.l.2newcom.net
www.gov.nf.ca

Federation of Outfitters
5237 Hamel Blvd., Local 270
Quebec City, PQ G2E 2H2
418-521-3880
Fax: 418-877-6638

Saskatchewan Outfitters
Association
3700 2nd Ave. W.
Prince Albert, Saskatchewan
S6W 1A2
306-763-5434
Email: soa@sa.sypatico.ca

SELECTED BIBLIOGRAPHY

Bashline, Sylvia, *The Bounty of the Earth Cookbook*, ISBN 1-55821-302-3, The Lyons Press

Brakefield, Tom, *Hunting Big Game Trophies*; ISBN 0-87690-214-X; Outdoor Life Books

———, *The Sportsman's Complete Book of Trophy and Meat Care*; ISBN 0-8117-1685-6; Stackpole Books

Clancy, Gary; Nelson, Larry, R. *Whitetail Deer*, ISBN 0-86573-036-9, Cy DeCosse, Inc.

Ehrig, Dave, *Blackpowder Whitetails*, ISBN 0-9662626-0-3, Celtic Moon Publishing

Everything You Need to Know About Muzzleloading Bullets; Hornady Mfg. Co.

Fadala, Sam, *The Complete Blackpowder Handbook*, ISBN 0-87349-175-0, DBI Books

———, *The Gun Digest Blackpowder Handbook*, ISBN 0-87349-177-7, DBI Books

Hangay, George/Dingley, Michael, *Biological Museum Methods-Vol 1*; ISBN 0-12-323301-1; Academic Press

Hodgdon 26th Edition Data Manual; Hodgdon Power Company, Inc.

Johnson, L. W., *Wild Game Cookbook*, ISBN 0-87502-907-8, Specialized Publishing Co.

The Longhunter Society Big Game Record Book; ISBN 0-9606428-2-X; The Longhunter Society

Nesbitt, William H./Wright, Philip, H. *Measuring and Scoring North American Big Game Trophies*; ISBN 0-940864-07-X; Boone & Crockett Club

Ormond, Clyde, *Complete Book of Hunting*; Library of Congress Catalog Card Number 77-169126; Outdoor Life Books

Palmer, Ralph, S., *The Mammal Guide*; Library of Congress Catalog Card Number 53-8002; Doubleday

Rue, Leonard Lee III, *The Deer of North America*, ISBN 1-55821-577-8, The Lyons Press

Strung, Norman, *Deer Hunting*; ISBN 0-397-00984-4, J.B. Lippincott Company

Taylor, J., David, *Game Animals of North America*; ISBN 0-517-65712-0; Discovery Books

Waterman, Charles, F., *The Hunter's World*; Library of Congress Catalog Card Number 76-117666; Random House

INDEX